Hard Travelin'

The Rock and Roll Hall of Fame and Museum® preserves, exhibits, and interprets the living heritage of rock and roll and its related music forms. Through programs, publications, and exhibitions, the museum aims to increase public knowledge and appreciation of the music and its history, to enhance public awareness of rock and roll's vital role in society, and to promote the study of popular music and its culture. The *American Music Masters*™ series annually explores the legacy of an Early Influence inductee of the Rock and Roll Hall of Fame® through a conference, performances, and other programs.

The Woody Guthrie Archives was created in 1995 to catalogue, preserve, and perpetuate the artistic and personal legacy of Woody Guthrie. The core of the collection comes from Woody's wife, Marjorie, who saved thousands of lyrics, songbooks, diaries, essays, manuscripts, letters, artwork, and photographs. The Archives also creates new projects that will continue to bring Woody's unknown, unseen, and unheard works back to the world and to the people from which he drew his inspiration.

For more information contact:

The Rock and Roll Hall of Fame and Museum
1 Key Plaza
Cleveland, Ohio 44114-1022
www.rockhall.com

The Woody Guthrie Archives
250 West 57th Street, Suite 1218
New York, New York 10107

HARD TRAVELIN'

The Life and Legacy of Woody Guthrie

Edited by Robert Santelli and Emily Davidson

WESLEYAN UNIVERSITY PRESS

Published by University Press of New England

Hanover and London

Wesleyan University Press

Published by University Press of New England, Hanover, NH 03755

© 1999 by Rock and Roll Hall of Fame and Museum

Printed in the United States of America   5 4 3 2 1

CIP data appear at the end of the book

Contents

Three   THIS LAND IS YOUR LAND

Illustrations

FIGURES

For Woody

Woody Guthrie, ca. 1943. NORA GUTHRIE COLLECTION. COURTESY OF
WOODY GUTHRIE ARCHIVES.

Preface

I hope that Woody Guthrie—wherever his soul rests—looks down on Cleveland and approves of what the Rock and Roll Hall of Fame and Museum carried out in his name in September 1996. I don't know that he's whooping it up; I suspect the ego of America's greatest folksinger was never so large as any one of his songs. And from what I've read about him, he rarely, if ever, put personal glory over, say, the need to rally workers in song or rail against an unjust Establishment. I wonder how he feels about all the attention paid to him of late: the musical tributes, the academic accolades, the museum exhibits, the media hoopla, this book. He could be quite taken by it all—or genuinely disturbed by the canonizing acclaim.

Woody Guthrie was a folksinger with his finger on the pulse of the common man. During the 1930s and 1940s he wrote reams of simple yet powerful songs that vividly detail the American Experience. From Guthrie came the idea that songs could carry hard-hitting messages of social and political protest. His musical narratives about Depression-era America, including "Pastures of Plenty," "Bound for Glory," "Hard Travelin'," "So Long, It's Been Good to Know You," and his undeniable masterpiece "This Land Is Your Land," are as poignant as any other artistic reflection of the period. Everyone from Pete Seeger and Joan Baez to Bob Dylan and Bruce Springsteen has been profoundly influenced by Guthrie and his music.

Thus Woody Guthrie earned a place in the Rock and Roll Hall of Fame. Inducted in 1988, he joined Jimmie Rodgers, Robert Johnson, Lead Belly,[1] Louis Jordan, and other American music greats in the Early Influence category. Had Guthrie been alive, would he have accepted the award—a symbol of enduring artistic achievement? Would he have worn a tuxedo to the event? (He certainly didn't own one.) Would he have jammed with members of the Beatles and Beach Boys at the induction dinner or sung a song with Bob Dylan? All of these legendary artists were also inducted into the Rock and Roll Hall of Fame that year. But here's an even better question: Would Guthrie have bothered to come at all? Or would he have been out on the road somewhere, or performing for free at a rally for American farmers or an Amnesty International benefit?

The Rock and Roll Hall of Fame and Museum didn't end its tribute to Guthrie with his induction. And, if truth be told, most of what came next can be blamed on me. When the museum's chief curator, Jim Henke, said the institution ought to have an exhibit on the roots of rock and roll, which included folk music, I volunteered to collect artifacts for it. I had always believed that Guthrie's impact on rock and roll was much greater than most historians have acknowledged, and I hoped the exhibit would justify my beliefs.

Thanks in part to the generosity of Woody's daughter Nora and son Arlo, and to Harold Leventhal, the family caretaker, the Rock and Roll Hall of Fame and Museum unveiled a wonderful exhibit on folk music for its grand opening in September 1995. Henke encouraged us to make the exhibit as encompassing as we could. So, in addition to all the Guthrie artifacts on display—Woody's mandolin and fiddle (the only known instruments Woody owned that are still in existence), his song lyrics, journals, drawings, letters, and photographs—the exhibit also included artifacts from Lead Belly and Pete Seeger, since they, too, influenced rock and roll in a significant way and are inductees of the Rock and Roll Hall of Fame.

Still, I thought, it wasn't enough. As head of the museum's Education and Programming Division, it is my job to create programs that complement our exhibits and to develop events that show how and why rock and roll has become one of America's cultural treasures. I thought the best way to accomplish such a mission was to start at the beginning. Along with members of the museum's Education Department—Katie Haggerty, Martha Woodruff, Ruthie Brown, and Emily Davidson—I searched for ways to transform the vast importance of rock and roll's early influences into exciting educational programs.

We chose to begin with Woody Guthrie. In the spring of 1996 I visited with Nora Guthrie and Harold Leventhal in New York and presented to them a plan to celebrate Woody's life and musical legacy in the form of a conference and tribute concert. They embraced the idea and offered to help. At the time Arlo was on tour somewhere in the American heartland, but when he heard about our plans to honor his father, he too offered assistance.

I didn't know it then, but that day in New York we planted the seeds for what the Rock and Roll Hall of Fame and Museum would eventually call the American Music Masters series, an annual event that celebrates Hall of Fame Early Influence inductees. That fall, academics, journalists, music historians, Guthrie family members, fans, and musicians came to Cleveland for Hard Travelin': The Life and Legacy of Woody Guthrie. The weeklong series of events and programs consisted of a photo exhibit and film series at the museum, followed by an academic conference at Case Western Reserve University attended by more than five hundred people.

Arlo gave the keynote address at the conference, which for all its humor and off-the-cuff remarks, added up to a deeply touching and personal portrayal of his father. Afterward, there were panels and seminars: participants included such esteemed Guthrie/folk music scholars as Joe Klein, author of the definitive biography, *Woody Guthrie: A Life* (Knopf, 1980, 1999); Dave Marsh, coauthor with Harold Leventhal of *Pastures of Plenty* (HarperCollins, 1990), an annotated book of Guthrie's writing; Robert Cantwell, author of *When We Were Good* (Harvard University Press, 1996), a history of the 1960s folk revival; and longtime folk music authorities Joe Hickerson from the Library of Congress, Jeff Place from Smithsonian Folkways Records, and Anthony DeCurtis of *Rolling Stone* magazine. The lively discussions heard at Case Western Reserve University that rainy Saturday dealt with everything from Guthrie's music, books, and artwork to his years in the Merchant Marine and his passionate antifascist and procommunist political stance.

The conference ended with a workshop performance of *Woody Guthrie's American Song*, a musical based on Woody's words and melodies. Later that evening Guthrie was celebrated in song at a hootenanny held at the Odeon, a downtown Cleveland rock club. Country Joe McDonald, Jorma Kaukonen, Alejandro Escovedo, Jimmie Dale Gilmore, and others sang Guthrie songs as well as their own to an overflow crowd.

But the big musical event was on Sunday at Severance Hall, home of the internationally renowned Cleveland Orchestra. None of the musicians who came to honor Guthrie that night had ever played this strikingly beautiful, acoustically stunning hall because Severance had rarely hosted anything resembling pop music. As we learned later on, the last time a prominent American folk artist had appeared on Severance's stage was in March 1947, when Lead Belly performed at the hall.

There were some skeptics in Cleveland who thought the likes of Bruce Springsteen, Pete Seeger, Arlo Guthrie, the Indigo Girls, Ani DiFranco, Ramblin' Jack Elliott, David Pirner of Soul Asylum, and Billy Bragg should perform their Guthrie tribute elsewhere in the city. But Severance officials, particularly events manager Richard Worswick, were bent on collaborating with the Rock and Roll Hall of Fame and Museum for such an exciting, first-time-ever event. And so, on 29 September 1996, the artists presented a touching, at times breathtaking, musical tribute to Woody Guthrie.

When it was all over, the Woody Guthrie Archives, which had helped produce Hard Travelin', and the Rock and Roll Hall of Fame and Mu-

seum wondered how we could best share with the rest of the world what
had transpired during the memorable weekend. The music was obviously
heartfelt and well worth commercial release. But the insights and intellectual musings of the conference had their own value as well. Nora and I
looked for ways to get all of it to those who could not be in Cleveland
that September.

It didn't take long to get the ball rolling. One day not long after the
event, Nora received a call from Suzanna Tamminen, the editor-in-chief
at Wesleyan University Press. She was inquiring about the possibilities of
publishing a book of essays from the Guthrie conference. Nora told Suzanna to speak to me about the project, as Nora was already at work on
a major exhibition on her father that the Smithsonian Institution
Traveling Exhibition Service (SITES) planned to open in 1999. By the
time I spoke with Suzanna, the Rock and Roll Hall of Fame and Museum
had already decided that something like Hard Travelin' should occur
every year. We would call the event the American Music Masters series. I
suggested to Suzanna that, as Wesleyan University Press was already
interested in a Woody Guthrie book, perhaps it should sign on for the
bigger American Music Masters series?

Suzanna was intrigued by the idea and said she'd get back to me.
Meanwhile other publishing houses had come forward with inquiries
about the Guthrie conference and the rest of the American Music Masters series. In the end, we picked Wesleyan, in part because it is one of the
foremost academic publishers of popular music studies, but primarily because it was Wesleyan's idea in the first place to create a book from the
conference. Since then, Hard Travelin' has moved into other areas, including a Woody Guthrie public radio special produced by the Rock and
Roll Hall of Fame and Museum, Cleveland public radio station WCPN,
and the SITES, in cooperation with the Woody Guthrie Archives. And a
live album produced by Ani DiFranco and Nora Guthrie featuring tracks
from artists who performed at Severance Hall will be available from
Righteous Babe Records. Read this book, listen to the radio special and
concert disc, visit the Smithsonian's Woody Guthrie exhibition This Land
Is Your Land: The Life and Legacy of Woody Guthrie, and it will be as if
you too had been in Cleveland in 1996 for a little bit of American music
history.

The American Music Masters series moved away from folk music in
1997 and celebrated rock's country roots when it honored Hall of Fame
Early Influence inductee Jimmie Rodgers. In 1998, it was time to turn to
the blues and Robert Johnson, whose impact on rock and roll was like
that of few other artists of any American music genre. Indeed, books
about Rodgers and Johnson are forthcoming from Wesleyan University

Press; their contents also come from the conferences staged at Case West-ern Reserve University and represent some of the most exciting current scholarship in country music and the blues.

It is my intention that the American Music Masters series become a premier event in American popular music and, beginning with this book, that it inspire new research into the roots of rock and roll and the great artists who lent their hands in creating it. With *Hard Travelin': The Life and Legacy of Woody Guthrie*, I think we're on our way.

Robert Santelli
Vice President, Education and Programming,
Rock and Roll Hall of Fame and Museum

NOTE

1. Except in the case of previously published titles, and in accordance with Rock and Roll Hall of Fame and Museum standards and Lead Belly's family's wishes, Lead Belly appears as two words throughout this book.

Editor's Note

The publication of *Hard Travelin': The Life and Legacy of Woody Guthrie* seems timely in a number of respects. As my colleague and coeditor Robert Santelli notes in the preface, there has been a recent resurgence of interest, both in Woody Guthrie and in folk music. This revival has resulted not only in the Rock and Roll Hall of Fame and Museum's American Music Masters series out of which this book grew, but also in numerous other musical tributes and even major museum exhibits. The recent opening of the Woody Guthrie Archives in New York has made accessible a wealth of previously unavailable material including letters, journals, visual artwork, and even more song lyrics than were already known to exist. The Guthrie Archives, which received all profits from the Rock Hall's 1996 celebration, were tapped for many of the drawings and photographs that appear in this book. Finally, it seems important at this time to document the memories and insights of the few remaining people who worked with Woody.

It is with great enthusiasm, then, that we present this collection of ideas and interpretations from the 1996 conference devoted to Woody and his legacy. With this book, we seek to reach not only the few hundred people who came to Cleveland that September weekend, but also the broadest possible audience of those who have been touched by Woody's work. Paralleling the goals of the conference, we aim both to encourage new research and thought among scholars and fans and to introduce Woody Guthrie to a new generation who may know him only as the composer of "This Land Is Your Land." Although this book in no way presents a definitive view of Woody, it does reflect the high quality of thought and dialogue that occurred during the 1996 event. We have included a breadth of opinions on the man, his life, his artistic output, and his ongoing relationship with American culture and music. In addition, readers will notice various writing styles among the essays, ranging from anecdotal to academic. These diverse voices speak of and to the spectrum of people—musicians, political activists, journalists, scholars, and folkies—who have been inspired by Woody's music and myth. Despite the wide array of subjects, however, the essays fall into a few main thematic areas. Accordingly, we have organized the book into three parts, each corresponding to a particular aspect of the multifaceted Woody Guthrie.

Part One focuses on Woody himself, fashioning an intimate and truthful portrait of a complex and conradictory personality. This part opens with a biographical sketch by Mary Katherine Aldin followed by the personal recollections of Woody's close friends and colleagues Harold Leventhal and Pete Seeger. It concludes with the colloquial yet perceptive anecdotes of Woody's son, Arlo Guthrie, who reflects on the lasting meaning of his father's life and work.

Part Two highlights Woody's creative production, including the literary and visual arts as well as his songwriting, performing, and recording legacies. Robert Santelli introduces the subject with a discussion of Woody's impact on rock and roll. Jeff Place then catalogues Woody's recorded output, making clear the enormous impact of the relatively few recordings Woody left to posterity. Craig Werner follows with an exploration of Woody's importance in the American literary tradition. Finally, Ellen Landau's essay, accompanied by previously unpublished illustrations, represents the first time Woody's visual art has been investigated in any but a passing way.

Part Three delves into the social and political issues that remain at the heart of Woody's legend and with which Woody so identified himself. Charles McGovern sets the stage with an examination of the cultural and historical currents that shaped Woody's world. The two essays that follow deal with Woody's radical politics. The first, by David Shumway, explores the ways in which Woody's image has been transmuted from that of a political radical into that of a romanticized "pilgrim." The second, by Ronald Cohen, revisits Woody's relationship with the Communist Party from a 1990 perspective. The final essays, by Robert Cantwell and Dave Marsh, grapple with the thorny issues of race and racism relating to Woody himself and to his status as a cultural icon.

Finally, the book concludes with a comprehensive biblio/discography, compiled by Guy Logsdon, that serves as both a spark to additional scholarly inquiry and a guide to Woody's preferred medium of expression, his music. His songs, of course, are the core of his ongoing artistic and cultural meaning and they should not be obscured by any analysis of his cultural context.

In bringing together these essays, we have tried to show that Woody's life and art remain relevant nearly half a century after his most productive years. Moreover, we have attempted to balance multiple perspectives—from the personal to the philosophical—on the extraordinary talent and body of work that make up Woody Guthrie: who he was and who he has become over the course of time. The book may present more questions than answers regarding that identity; however, if this volume ignites further discourse concerning Woody's life and legacy, we will have fulfilled our purpose.

Emily Davidson
Education Program Manager,
Rock and Roll Hall of Fame and Museum

Acknowledgments

*H*ard Travelin': The Life and Legacy of Woody Guthrie arose out of the productive collaboration of a number of people: Woody's family and friends, musicians, managers, journalists, scholars, fellow Rock and Roll Hall of Fame and Museum staff, faculty and staff at Case Western Reserve University, and people at Severance Hall and the Odeon concert club. We owe them all our heartfelt thanks and sincere appreciation. We hope *Hard Travelin'* lives up to their expectations.

First and foremost, this book could not have been written without the support of the Woody Guthrie Archives. Our appreciation goes to Nora Guthrie and Harold Leventhal, who not only were intimately involved in creating the *Hard Travelin'* program but who also served as sounding boards and provided access to numerous primary source materials. Thanks also to Anna Rotante, George Arevalo, and Amy Danielian for all their assistance.

This book owes its existence to the events that made up the first American Music Masters series in 1996. Its content is primarily inspired by remarks made by panelists at the Case Western Reserve University conference, including Robert Cantwell, Ronald Cohen, Anthony DeCurtis, Peter Glazer, Arlo Guthrie, Fred Hellerman, James Henke, Joe Hickerson, Joe Klein, Guy Logsdon, Jimmy Longhi, Dave Marsh, Charles McGovern, Jeff Place, and Craig Werner, many of whom also contributed essays to the book. Thanks to the additional contributors—Mary Katherine Aldin, Ellen G. Landau, David R. Shumway, and Pete Seeger—who made up the difference. We also acknowledge the assistance of staff and the faculty of the American Studies program at Case Western Reserve University, our partner for the conference, and in particular John Bassett, Atwood Gaines, Sandra Golden, Park Goist, Gladys Haddad, Barbara Klante, and William Marling.

The musical performances held that September weekend were essential to creating the special atmosphere out of which this book grew. We wish to recognize Chris Risner of Belkin Productions and the staff at the Odeon concert club, as well as Richard Worswick, Gary Hanson, and the rest of the Severance Hall staff for being such great partners in this endeavor.

Our sincere appreciation goes as well to all the artists who donated their time and talent to celebrate Woody in song: Dan Bern, Billy Bragg, Ani DiFranco, Joe Ely, Alejandro Escovedo, Ramblin' Jack Elliott, Jimmie Dale Gilmore, Arlo Guthrie, John Wesley Harding, Indigo Girls (Amy Ray and Emily Saliers), Jorma Kaukonen, Jimmy LaFave, Country Joe McDonald, Paul Metsa, Ellis Paul, David Pirner, Tim Robbins, Pete Seeger, Bruce Springsteen, Syd Straw, and the cast of *Woody Guthrie's American Song* (Lisa Asher, Mimi Bessette, David Lutken, Jim Stein, Jeff Waxman, and Neil Woodward). Thanks to Sam Ellis for coordinating the *American Song* performance. Thrill Hill Productions deserves our special gratitude for helping make the Severance Hall concert go off without a hitch. Finally, acoustic performances by RRHFM Musicians Collective members Kevin Richards, Charles Mosbrook, and Jason White were great additions to the weekend.

We thank the staff of the RRHFM Education Department—Ruthie Brown, Katie Haggerty, Santina Protopapa, Lisa Vinciquerra, Deborah Wentz, and Martha Woodruff—for all their support and hard work, both on the production of the initial Hard Travelin' events and on the subsequent book. Thanks go as well to Sally Anderson, Celeste Drehs, Suzan Evans, Ileen Sheppard Gallagher, Andy Golding, James Henke, Erin Hogan, Jon Landau, Ronald Zambetti, and the rest of the RRHFM staff and board members for their support and assistance.

Kenny Barr, John Kircher, and Eileen Rehbein were indispensable sources of support and expertise throughout the Hard Travelin' program. Thanks go to Sarah Lazin, for her advice; to Stephanie Smith at the Center for Folklife and Cultural Heritage, Smithsonian Institution, for her research assistance; to Phyllis Barney and the North American Folk Music and Dance Alliance; to Mark Schwartz and Tim Lachina of Nesnadny & Schwartz for making the American Music Masters design work a labor of love; to the Ohio Lottery Commission for sponsoring the conference; and to Barry Goldenberg for coming in at the last minute to photograph the artwork in this book.

Finally, we owe much to Wesleyan University Press; to Tom Ratko for committing to the American Music Masters book series; and to Suzanna Tamminen, our editor, who came up with the initial idea of creating a book out of the Hard Travelin' conference and whose patience and advice have been much appreciated.

PART one

Ramblin' Round

MARY KATHERINE ALDIN

WAY DOWN YONDER
IN THE INDIAN NATION
Woody Guthrie, An American Troubadour

When young Woodrow Wilson Guthrie was born on 14 July 1912, the world outside his native Okemah, Oklahoma, was far different from what it is today, even though fewer than one hundred years have passed. The year that America's premier folksinger and writer made his debut was the same one in which both New Mexico and Arizona were admitted to the Union; Alfred Adler and Carl Jung each published a treatise on the new science of psychoanalysis; the RMS *Titanic* sank on her maiden voyage, with loss of more than fifteen hundred lives; the Woolworth's department store chain was founded; the Piltdown Man was discovered in Britain; and the First World War was still two years in the future. Okemah, in east central Oklahoma, was then part of Indian Territory, and news of these matters traveled slowly, if at all.

Woody's father, Charles Edward Guthrie, was, in succession, a working cowboy, a district court clerk, and a local politician. Eventually he would have too many business balls in the air at one time, with a great crash as a result. A loyal Democrat, Charley named his second son for then presidential candidate Woodrow Wilson, who would win the election that November. Woody's mother, Nora Belle Sherman, was a housewife who constantly sang to her children; her repertoire, learned from her own mother and grandparents, encompassed folk songs, gruesome murder ballads, and popular tunes of the day. Woody's childhood was full of strange, inexplicable occurrences, including his sister Clara's horrible death from a coal stove explosion (for which Nora, already in the early stages of dementia, may have been responsible). Describing the gradual changes in Nora's behavior that took place during his childhood, Woody once wrote,

Woody Guthrie with his father and mother, Charley and Nora, and older brother George on a porch in Okemah, Oklahoma, 16 May 1926. COURTESY OF WOODY GUTHRIE ARCHIVES.

it was too much of a load on my mother's quieter nerves. She commenced to sing the sadder songs in a loster [*sic*] voice, to gaze out our window and to follow her songs out and up and over and away from it all, away over yonder in the minor keys.[1]

Later, after Woody had left home, his father would be seriously burned in still another unexplained fire. Shortly thereafter, although she was not insane, Nora was committed to a mental institution, where she eventually died. So little was known about Huntington's chorea in those days that her frequent bouts of uncontrollable flailing and twitching and her staggering walk were thought to be symptoms of a mental, rather than physical, disease.

Woody got what formal education he was going to get in Oklahoma, where in high school he worked on the school newspaper. When he was sixteen, he dropped out and moved to Pampa, Texas, where Charley Guthrie had gone after Nora's collapse and his own business failure. Sharing a house with numerous Guthrie relatives, Woody, then seventeen years old, learned to play guitar, harmonica, and a little fiddle ("*very* little," fellow Almanac Singer Lee Hays would thunder in later years) from Charley's brother, Jeff Davis Guthrie. In October 1933 Woody married Mary Jennings, the younger sister of a friend, and the couple would have three children, Will Rogers (always called Bill), Gwendolyn, and Sue. Despite, or perhaps because of, the domestic demands of a wife and family, Woody was soon on the road again, following the restless urge that would become his trademark. Mary coped as best she could on her own with the small blond Guthrie children; Woody sent money back to her when he remembered, and kept moving. He took short trips at first, then longer ones, and soon he was gone for months at a time. Wherever he went he was writing, constantly scratching out cartoons, thought fragments, and verses on whatever was handy: scraps of paper, the backs of envelopes, and notepads.

A major dust storm in 1935 inspired his first song, "Dusty Old Dust,"

Woody Guthrie as a teenager in Pampa, Texas, 1931. COURTESY OF WOODY GUTHRIE ARCHIVES.

Woody Guthrie with Junior Chamber of Commerce Band, Pampa, Texas, 1936. COURTESY OF WOODY GUTHRIE ARCHIVES.

which he set to the tune of Carson Robison's "Ballad of Billy the Kid." This set a pattern of reworking existing melodies with his own original words that would continue throughout his life. He used one Carter Family melody, "Wildwood Flower," for several different songs, including "The Sinking of the Reuben James." Traveling around the country, hitchhiking, working occasionally, bumming rides, and singing or panhandling for change, Woody soaked up influences like a sponge, and spent the mid-1930s developing his repertoire and writing the earliest of what would eventually total more than one thousand songs. In 1937 he drifted out to Los Angeles, where he met up with his cousin Leon "Jack" Guthrie. The two cowrote the cowboy classic "Oklahoma Hills," which Jack would later take to number one on the country charts in July 1945. In 1961 the song would see a revival, with Hank Thompson's version reaching number seven on the charts in May of that year. While in Los Angeles, Woody formed what became a lifelong friendship with the actor Will Geer, who sometimes let Woody sleep in a one-room cabin on his property in rustic Topanga Canyon. In years to come that cabin would become a place of pilgrimage for folk music fans. This unforeseen invasion forced Geer, by then a major television star as "Grandpa" in *The Waltons*, to put up a rather huffy sign in a vain attempt to keep tourists from parading through it.

Woody's "showbiz" career began during this West Coast stay, when he started doing a regular radio program in 1937. He had met a cowgirl singer named Maxine Crissman, who used the stage name Lefty Lou. Woody once described her as ". . . a tall, thin-faced corn-fed Missouri farm girl with a voice rough and husky and I played my southern E chord guitar in back of our voices while we sung as WOODY AND LEFTY LOU and got twenty thousand letters during the almost two years that we sung over the mikes of KFVD."[2] The duo soon became immensely popular, performing a program of songs calculated to appeal in part to the area's large and homesick audience of recent Oklahoma transplants. Lefty Lou and Woody pulled in more mail (more than a thousand letters per month at one point) than any other show on the station. Woody drew curlicued pictures on the borders of the mimeographed newsletters, and eventually the songbooks, that they sent out to their fans. Soon he had made enough money to send for Mary and the children, who arrived by train straight from the shack they'd been living in. Woody, who had evidently forgotten they were coming, showed up to collect them at the train station several hours late.

The *Woody and Lefty Lou* radio show came to an end in 1938. Woody went off on a new tangent, this time ending up, as the result of a chance

Woody Guthrie playing guitar with Mary Jennings Guthrie and their children Sue, Bill, and Gwen; Maxine Crissman (Lefty Lou); and others, 1940. COURTESY OF WOODY GUTHRIE ARCHIVES.

meeting with editor Ed Robbin, writing a daily column for the Los Angeles–based Communist newspaper *People's World*. His contribution was called "Woody Sez," and his homespun philosophizing was often accompanied by one of his own cartoons. He and Robbin became close friends; Woody often slept on Robbin's couch, and Robbin was Woody's agent for a while.[3] Woody's writing style was growing increasingly idiosyncratic. He never had much use for the rules of grammar and punctuation, and capital letters were either overused or missing altogether. Still, the column brought him some attention and a little money once in awhile. Mary was pregnant again, as was Will Geer's wife Herta, and Geer wanted them both to appear in a movie he was making. Eventually, however, Geer returned to New York, and as Woody found less and less to do in Los Angeles, he decided to join him. He dropped Mary and the children off back in Pampa, Texas, on his way east, promising to send for them again as soon as things got better.

Woody's commercial recording career began in 1940 when folklorist Alan Lomax recorded him for the Library of Congress. In April of that same year, RCA Victor recorded Woody's *Dust Bowl Ballads*, which would eventually be released as three books of 78s. During this time he was also a frequent guest on Lomax's radio program. (Pete Seeger, then a recent Harvard dropout trying to learn all he could about folk music, acted as Lomax's unpaid assistant.) Another radio appearance led to more offers and he suddenly found himself enjoying a fair amount of success as a radio performer. CBS was, as he put it, "giving me money so fast I'm using it to sleep under,"[4] and again he sent for Mary and the children. Mary was amazed at the success of the radio show, called *Pipe Smoking Time*, but pleased at the amount of money Woody was making.

Then in 1941 came a major breakthrough. The United States government, at Lomax's suggestion, commissioned Woody to write a series of songs celebrating the Bonneville Power Administration's various hydroelectric projects. Woody piled Mary and the children back into the car and headed west. From these landmark sessions came classics like "Grand Coulee Dam," "Hard Travelin'," and "Roll On Columbia," resulting in a nationwide focus on the Pacific Northwest that was the setting for these triumphant pieces. As Woody himself described it,

I made up 26 songs about the Bonneville Dam, and the thunderous foamy waters of the rapids and cascades, the wild and windward watersprays from the high Sheliloh falls, and the folks living in the little shack house just about a mile from the end of the line. The Department of Interior folks got ahold of me and took me into a clothes closet there at the Bonneville Power Administration house in Portland and melted my songs down onto records.[5]

In July 1941, Guthrie made a series of recordings with Seeger, Lee Hays, and Millard Lampell, who had already recorded together as the Almanac Singers, for the General Label. These recordings later had thematic titles (*Sod Buster Ballads* and *Deep Sea Chanties and Whaling Ballads*) attached to them for handy pigeonholing. Pete Seeger recalled that the sessions were done on the spur of the moment, and Millard Lampell has been quoted as saying that they needed the $250 that General would pay them as session money to buy a used car in which they were all planning to drive to the West Coast the day after the recordings were made.[6] Although Woody had just arrived back in New York from the West Coast, the group did buy the car, and did drive across the country to California in it, a trip that Pete Seeger was to describe as momentous. "We played union halls, rallies, and hoots, anywhere we could," Seeger said later. "We didn't rehearse much, although Mill and Lee certainly tried. But Woody was the kind of fellow who would, as he said, rather rehearse on stage."[7] After Hays and Lampell bailed out to return to New York, Seeger and Guthrie continued their trek through the migrant workers camps of California and down into Mexico. They sang their way back to the East Coast the following year, and all the time Woody was writing. Everything he saw, each new experience, each trip to a different town, became grist to the Guthrie songwriting mill. In addition to the songs that were pouring out of him, he was keeping a journal and writing notes for his autobiography.

During this time things had finally fallen apart for Woody and Mary, with Mary sometimes not knowing where they'd end up next and Woody not seeming to care until Mary had enough. In February 1943, a girl, Cathy Ann Guthrie, was born to Woody and Marjorie Greenblatt, a dancer whose stage name was Marjorie Mazia. A student of the famed dancer Martha Graham, she was a young, intelligent, idealistic woman who was fascinated by the strange little man with the wild hair who never seemed to stop talking. Soon deeply in love, the couple would marry at the end of 1945, after Woody's divorce from Mary was final, and have three more children: Arlo, Nora, and Joady. Also in 1943, Woody and his friends Cisco Houston and Jimmy Longhi joined the Merchant Marine; Longhi, whom Woody described as "an Italian boy with as good an anti-fascist head on him as I have ever seen,"[8] was later to write a book describing this friendship.[9] Guthrie got a fair amount of mileage out of his stint in the service, including a tattoo and enough time in his bunk to write his usual prolific quota of songs as well as some very explicit love letters to Marjorie. Longhi, Houston, and Guthrie survived two torpedo attacks together, episodes that were possibly the inspiration for Guthrie's later song "The Sinking of the Reuben James." Houston, a

strikingly handsome man who was himself a folksinger, was a better guitarist than Woody, and during the years recording for Folkways was often
used as an uncredited second guitarist on Woody's sessions for that label.

Woody seems to have been colorblind, in the political sense. He sang,
slept, ate, worked, and traveled with people of all races, including blues
singers Josh White Sr., Lead Belly, and Sonny Terry and Brownie McGhee.
At a hotel in Baltimore, he once walked out on a concert booking when
he realized that McGhee and Terry would not be allowed to eat in the
hotel's dining room with him. Woody's politics were somewhat left of liberal, and he often feigned a jocular ignorance that made its point, while
fooling nobody: "Left wing, chicken wing, it's all the same to me,"[10] he
once muttered in answer to a question, but his guitar was inscribed with
the words "This machine kills fascists." He was turning out biting songs
of social protest such as "Plane Wreck at Los Gatos (Deportees)," a fact-
based story of the crash of a small plane carrying migrant workers, and
"Pastures of Plenty," in which he pointed out the discrepancies between
the amounts of money made by the dispossessed migrant workers in the
labor camps and the amounts made by those who owned the land they
worked. And, of course, he was the author of America's "other" national
anthem, "This Land Is Your Land." But now he began to notice that
sometimes it was difficult to walk without stumbling; sometimes, unwilling to think about how his mother had died, he drank too much, which
covered the stumbling, or at least made it seem as if he were only drunk.

In 1943 Woody's autobiography *Bound for Glory* was published, and
his visibility increased immediately.[11] In 1944 he began a lengthy series of
recordings that would eventually be issued on the independent New York
City–based label Folkways Records. Folkways was owned by Moses
Asch, son of the widely read novelist Sholem Asch, and young Moe, as
everyone called him, was famous for his lack of attention to paperwork
details. He never kept proper logs of the countless recording sessions he
produced, and his failure to pay regular royalties was legendary. Still,
Moe could always be counted on for small loans from time to time, and it
is thanks to his effort that the bulk of Woody Guthrie's recordings was
made and preserved.[12] Another project Woody undertook in 1945 was
the composition of a series of songs, commissioned by Asch, focusing on
the trial and subsequent executions of two Italian immigrants, Nicola
Sacco and Bartolomeo Vanzetti. In a Massachusetts case that was one of
the most sensational of the 1920s, the two were tried and found guilty of
robbery and murder, and were executed in 1927. Fifty years later, they
were posthumously pardoned by Governor Michael Dukakis.

Woody's children were a constant source of inspiration, and he wrote
and recorded several albums' worth of songs especially for them. Count-

ing songs, play songs, game songs, and humorous ditties with easily learned choruses, such as "Take Me For a Ride In the Car Car," have helped parents and teachers all over the country entertain and inform several succeeding generations. Not far from a child himself in many ways, he loved his own children dearly. The death of his four-year-old daughter Cathy Ann by fire in 1947 conjured up long-forgotten memories of his sister's death the same way, making him withdraw into an ever-deepening depression. Although no one knew it yet, the onset of Huntington's disease was already at work in his system; constant movement was becoming more urgent even as it became more difficult, and Marjorie saw less and less of him as his travels took him away for longer periods at a time.

His performances, however, seemed to have a life of their own. His vocal limitations were more than made up for by the brilliance of the songs, and his dry, irreverent delivery and the rambling, droll stories he told between songs left his audiences in stitches. As his physical condition deteriorated, the stories became longer, their points more obscure. Songs were sometimes started but not finished, as the words eluded him. Although he was drinking heavily by this time, it is difficult for us to know today how much of his erratic behavior on- and offstage was due to the alcohol he was consuming, and how much to the genetic disaster that was consuming him.

In January 1952 Woody made his final commercial recordings, for the Decca label, and shortly thereafter he was diagnosed with Huntington's chorea. Although he would make a few later recordings for Folkways, by that time the disease had progressed to the point where the material was not deemed appropriate for release. He made one final, desperate flight back to California, where he stayed at Will Geer's place in Topanga Canyon. There he met the young woman who would become his third wife, twenty-year-old Anneke Van Kirk Marshall. When she became pregnant, Woody got a hasty divorce from Marjorie in Juarez and married Anneke. But by then the Huntington's disease was so far advanced that the inexperienced, gently raised Anneke couldn't cope with the strange, twitching, jerking, dirty, wild-eyed man she had married. Shortly after she gave birth to their daughter, Lorina Lynn, there was another accidental fire, this one involving Woody and a can of gasoline, and his arm was severely burned from wrist to elbow. Anneke admitted that she was unable to cope, and a short time later Woody went back to New York, and to Marjorie, for the last time.

He was to spend most of the remaining fifteen years of his life in hospitals, trapped in a body he could no longer control. His speech grew more and more slurred and his spastic movements became entirely unmanageable. He was visited from time to time by young singers like

Ramblin' Jack Elliott and Bob Dylan, both of whom idolized and imitated him. Dylan commemorated these visits in the poignant "Song to Woody," which appeared on his eponymous debut album in 1962. But as the disease progressed toward its inevitable conclusion, Woody's friends found it harder and harder to communicate with the shell that was left, and finally out of respect for his privacy the family asked all but a few trusted friends to stay away.

Some of Woody's children seemed to have inherited the streak of tragedy that had pervaded his family for generations. Of his three children by Mary Jennings Guthrie, Sue and Gwen both died of Huntington's disease, and Bill was killed in a car accident that may have been suicide. Anneke put Lorina Lynn up for adoption, and at the age of nineteen Lorina, too, was killed in a car accident. However, except for tiny Cathy Ann, Woody's other children by Marjorie are currently in good health. Arlo is himself a successful singer and actor. Joady continues his father's rambling ways. Nora, assisted by Woody's longtime friend Harold Leventhal, manages and administers her father's publishing and estate. The work begun by Marjorie Guthrie to find a cure for Huntington's disease continues as well. In October 1997 the Guthrie family was honored by the Huntington's Disease Society of America, the group Marjorie founded in 1967, for their ongoing contributions to researching the still-incurable illness.

Since his death on 3 October 1967, Woody Guthrie's renown has only increased. Guthrie and his songs continue to inspire other writers, from Bob Dylan and Jack Elliott to Bruce Springsteen. Guthrie songs like "This Land Is Your Land" are sung in classrooms and around campfires by children all over, and subsequent generations of folksingers continue to perform his songs in nightclubs and concert halls around the world. In 1976 his life was the subject of a full-length movie, *Bound for Glory*. Joe Klein's biography, *Woody Guthrie: A Life*, was published in 1980. In 1988 Columbia Records released *A Vision Shared: A Tribute To Woody Guthrie and Leadbelly*, a project on which artists like Springsteen, Dylan, Pete Seeger, Taj Mahal, Brian Wilson, Little Richard, Emmylou Harris, U2, and other stars performed Woody's and Lead Belly's songs; the album won a Grammy Award for Best Traditional Folk Recording. Most recently, in 1998 he was honored by the U.S. Post Office with a commemorative postage stamp as part of the Post Office's American Singers series. In a recording career that spanned only twelve short years, Woody Guthrie became the primary influence on the entire folk music boom of the fifties, as well as on the protest-song movement of the sixties. His timeless music is testament to his creative spirit, and his legacy will live on as long as his songs are being sung.

NOTES

1. Woody Guthrie, ed., *American Folksong* (New York: Moses Asch Oak Publications, 1961), 2.

2. Ibid., 4.

3. Ed Robbin, *Woody Guthrie and Me: An Intimate Reminiscence* (Berkeley: Lancaster-Miller Publishers, 1979).

4. Woody Guthrie in a letter to Alan Lomax, quoted in Joe Klein, *Woody Guthrie: A Life* (New York: Knopf, 1980), 167.

5. Woody Guthrie, *Roll On, Columbia: The Columbia River Collection* (songbook) (Bethlehem, Pa.: Sing Out Corporation, 1991), 86.

6. This material was reissued by MCA Records in 1996 on a CD entitled *The Almanac Singers, Their Complete General Recordings* (see biblio/discography).

7. Interview with the author, February 1993.

8. Guthrie, *American Folksong*, 6.

9. Jim Longhi, *Woody, Cisco and Me: Seamen Three in the Merchant Marine* (Champaign-Urbana: University of Illinois Press, 1997).

10. Klein, *Woody Guthrie*, 122.

11. Woody Guthie, *Bound for Glory* (1943; New York: Plume, 1983).

12. Today the entire Folkways catalogue, acquired from the Asch estate, is owned by the Smithsonian Institution, and is under the direction of Jeff Place and Guthrie scholar Guy Logsdon. Smithsonian-Folkways records has reissued several CDs of these historic recordings (see biblio/discography).

HAROLD LEVENTHAL WITH ROBERT SANTELLI

REMEMBERING WOODY

I first came to know Woody Guthrie in late 1949 when I became the manager of the folk group the Weavers, following their appearance at the Village Vanguard in New York's Greenwich Village. Two years earlier, I had established a friendship with a banjo player named Pete Seeger, who was in the group. I went to a few hootenannies in New York where he and musicians such as Lead Belly, Sonny Terry, Brownie McGhee, and others would perform. At the time, folk music was new to me. My background was on the pop side of music, particularly, the music publishing business. Prior to the Second World War, I had worked as a song-plugger for the great American composer Irving Berlin and then for the Regent Music Company, the publishing house set up by jazz bandleader Benny Goodman. I was part of the Tin Pan Alley scene and very much involved in big band jazz or swing music.

I was born in upstate New York, but raised in New York City. Sometime around the time I turned nineteen, I got my job with Berlin. I started as what they called a counter boy: I would be stationed at the reception desk, and when people came in for sheet music, I'd get it for them. Eventually I was promoted to junior song-plugger, and I was usually given the bands that didn't quite make it. Back then, plugging songs and working with radio to make sure certain songs and bands got played over the air was an important part of the music business. After a couple of years with Berlin, I began working for Benny Goodman's music company. But in 1943 I was drafted, which put a hold on my music business career. I was stationed in India for a little over two years. I was trained to be a pigeoneer, that is, to fly pigeons that delivered military messages. The concept went all the way back to the Civil War, but in India pigeons didn't last half an hour in the air before the vultures got them. Later I was transferred to pole line construction in the Signal Corps. Although the work was rough, I traveled around India and met amazing people, including Mahatma Gandhi and Jawahalal Nehru, who would eventually become India's first prime minister. I lived in Calcutta for a year and immersed

myself in the political and cultural matters of India just before her independence from England. It was a very powerful time for me.

When I returned home from the war, I went back to the music industry.
All throughout the prewar years and those after the war, I was also very
much interested in left-leaning political issues. What I learned during my
early introduction to folk music was that this kind of music, more than
any other kind, could embrace political ideas, and that there were many
people writing folk songs who had the same left-wing ideals about America's future that I did. With the end of the Swing Era after World War II, I
followed a path right into folk music and have been with it ever since.

Pete Seeger and Lee Hays, another member of the Weavers, were close
friends of Woody Guthrie and had performed with him in an earlier folk
group, the Almanac Singers. Woody would always seem to be around
when the Weavers rehearsed at Pete's house in Greenwich Village. I knew
his name because I used to read his column in the *Daily Worker*. Woody
wasn't much of a talker; my earliest recollection of him is sitting off by
himself scribbling notes or lyrics on a piece of paper.

In 1950 the Weavers began to record for Decca Records. Some of the
songs the group recorded were Woody's, including "So Long, It's Been
Good to Know You," which became a big hit for the group later that
year. Woody was at the recording studio in New York City when the
Weavers recorded his song. He stretched out on the floor and wrote new
verses for the song on paper bags. The royalties he received from "So
Long" amounted to the first substantial income that Woody had ever
earned. At the time, Woody was still married to his second wife, Marjorie, who used some of the royalty money to open up a dance studio on
Coney Island.

When Woody was in New York and not drifting out on the road, he
would follow the Weavers wherever they performed. One evening the
Weavers were headliners at a trendy East Side nightclub, the Blue Angel.
Just before the show started, the club's doorman came looking for me.
"Hey, there's this guy looking to get in, says he's a friend of the Weavers
and he's expected. Trouble is, he looks kind of beat and unkempt." I
knew it was Woody. I brought him down through the cellar and up to the
kitchen where I borrowed a jacket and bow tie, put a white dishtowel
over his arm and had him masquerade as a waiter while watching the
Weavers perform.

Afterward Woody sought me out and told me he wanted to stay for
the late show, but that he was tired and wanted a place to rest until the
next set started. Pete had parked his car just outside the club. I got his car
keys and brought Woody to the car. He jumped into the back seat to take
a nap. I told him to be back in the club in an hour. "Of course," Woody

Woody Guthrie with members of the Weavers Jean Ritchie,
Fred Hellerman, and Pete Seeger in WNYC studio, New York,
New York, 1949. COURTESY OF WOODY GUTHRIE ARCHIVES.

replied. I brought the keys back to Pete, and then went home, not staying for the late show.

The next morning I got a desperate call from Marjorie. "Where is Woody?" she asked. "He didn't come home last night." I immediately phoned Pete upstate in Beacon, New York. Sure enough, Woody was there. He had fallen asleep in the car and never made it back into the Blue Angel for the Weavers' late set. Pete didn't notice that Woody was sleeping in the back seat of his car and drove home with Woody in it. When Pete got home, he discovered Woody still asleep. Pete let him spend the rest of the night in the car where he seemed to be quite comfortable.

During this period my wife Natalie and I ran Folkways Theater, one of the first New York Off-Broadway theaters. The actor Will Geer often performed there. It was a place where politically blacklisted actors could work. Woody would come around, always wanting to be part of the program and always seeming to find a role for himself. He never really asked if he could perform or take a role in whatever was happening on-stage, he simply interjected and got up onstage.

One rainy night in 1953 he appeared at the theater very wet, holding a little baby. By this time he had separated from Marjorie and married a woman called Anneke Marshall, with whom he had recently had this baby. He put the baby on the chair and was all set to join in onstage. But something was wrong. Physically, he couldn't handle his guitar; he seemed drunk. Most of the actors and musicians there that night were annoyed by his behavior. No one knew that Woody was suffering from the onset of Huntington's disease.

Time passed and Woody somehow wound up in Topanga Canyon, just outside of Los Angeles. By this time Marjorie, even though they weren't living together any more, asked me to handle matters for Woody and to seek the proper protection of his literary and song rights. This new situation brought me in closer contact with Woody. Woody was delighted that he now knew where to go to get "a few dollars advance."

One day I got a call from a Topanga Canyon real estate agent who informed me that Woody Guthrie was buying property. "Buying property?" I asked, incredulously. "Yes," the agent replied. "He's buying a piece of land next to his friend, Will Geer." The "land" Woody had his eyes on was nothing more than a very steep hill, impossible for building any kind of structure. I stepped in and eventually convinced Woody that the land he wanted was worthless and the deal was nixed.

It was obvious to all of us close to Woody that his health was deteriorating. Huntington's disease had begun to take its toll on him. Marjorie was very concerned; she still cared for Woody and had three children by him—Joady, Nora, and Arlo. "We have to organize something to take care of Woody," she said. A meeting was set at the Brooklyn Heights home of composer and songwriter Earl Robinson. Pete Seeger, folklorist Alan Lomax, Lou Gordon, Marjorie, Lee Hays, and I formed the Guthrie Children's Fund. I was authorized to get legal papers from Woody in which he would turn over to this fund whatever he had. At that point he had very little; royalties had come in from the couple of songs of his that the Weavers had recorded, but there wasn't much else as far as income was concerned. We set up papers that Woody signed that stated his three children with Marjorie would be entitled to any future income. At the time I wasn't familiar with his first marriage to Mary, with whom he also had three children. But in late 1954 I was given the responsibility to look after things: to watch over his songs, to copyright them, and find a publishing home for them.

At this time Woody had begun to go for voluntary treatment at Brooklyn State Hospital, but wouldn't stay long. He could come and go as he pleased. Not long after these treatments began, Woody decided to visit me at my apartment on Central Park West in Manhattan. I wasn't in, so he sat at my door practically the whole day until I returned. He wanted ten dollars. He came into my place, sat on the couch, and lit a cigarette, which fell onto the couch and burned a hole in it. Woody seemed oblivious to it all.

One day shortly after this incident, Woody took a bus ride to Philadelphia to visit some old friends. When the bus stopped for a break in New Jersey, Woody got off the bus, but didn't get back on. Instead he began to hitchhike to Philadelphia. That afternoon I got a phone call. "Are you Mr. Leventhal?" "Yes," I answered. "Mr. Leventhal, I am an officer of the New Jersey State Police and we picked up a Mr. Woody Guthrie. He told us to phone you." I asked if he was charged with anything, and the officer answered that Woody had been charged with vagrancy. The officer added that Woody was wandering on the road, was unkempt, and had no money on him. Right after this, Woody was committed to Greystone Park State Hospital, a dilapidated mental institution in Morris Plains, New Jersey, less than an hour outside New York.

Woody's health had deteriorated, as had the political climate in the New York City folk community at the time. McCarthyism had arrived in America and every left-leaning citizen, especially folksingers and those who were part of the folk scene, were at serious risk. Those of us who were part of the Left had the FBI watching us. Many times the FBI came to my house demanding an interview with me. They'd follow me to the subway; they'd call on the telephone. I got scared, but I didn't give in. I knew that once you opened your mouth to them, they had you. At the same time I was being harassed, the Weavers were called before the House Un-American Activities Committee in Washington, D.C. These were rough times because nobody on the pop side of the music community came to our defense. Nobody. The Weavers were the only musical entity that was officially blacklisted. In a sense, so was Woody, but his days of fighting the system with song were, for the most part, over. At first we were all still able to sing at union meetings and for whatever remained of the Old Left in the early 1950s. But the government even cracked down on the unions, leaving folksingers with practically nowhere to perform. I survived because my needs were minimal. I was doing promotion and publicity work. People in the music industry would tell me, "Well, if you drop the Weavers, we can get other clients for you." I scoffed at them. They didn't understand what it was all about.

Woody's bad health only made worse his other personal problems. He had a very limited sense of self-discipline. He routinely put himself first over his family, for instance. That was something that bothered people close to him, but many artists I've known suffered from the same problem. Woody, like some other creative people in the music and theater worlds, found it difficult, even impossible, to commit to family or friends. Fortunately, Woody had good people around him who understood his problems. Pete was a very good friend to Woody; he admired Woody and learned a lot from him. Woody's wife Marjorie was a very efficient person and very devoted to Woody. She tolerated things from Woody that many other wives would not have. Even after their divorce she remained concerned about him in a very loving way. She knew that Woody was someone special, which is why she saved whatever she could that Woody created: letters, songs, lyrics, drawings, poems, short stories, journals, diaries. Thanks to Marjorie there is a Woody Guthrie Archives today. More than 60 percent of what we have in the archives came from her.

And finally, there was Cisco Houston, a wonderful human being and folksinger, very talented, very political, and very much a close friend of Woody's. Woody would pay attention to Cisco. When I first met Cisco he was working in a mine out in Colorado. I gave him money to come east. He would play around New York and collaborate on songs with Lee Hays. I got him an assignment from the State Department to tour India with bluesmen Sonny Terry and Brownie McGhee. I remember getting a call from the people who organized the tour; they wanted to know if Cisco was an alcoholic, of all things. I told them Cisco drank, but that he wasn't an alcoholic. Cisco did the tour in 1960 and six months after he returned to the States he was dead from cancer. Cisco could have been a big folk star had he lived. He loved Woody and watched him to make sure that he didn't stray too far or travel down the wrong path too often.

Woody had personal faults, but there was never any doubt as to his integrity and resolve when it came to political principles. Money or making it big never mattered to Woody Guthrie. He wasn't one who would say, "Hey, are any of my songs on the *Billboard* charts?" or "How come I'm not rich or famous?" A lot of people have asked me, "Well, if Woody were alive today, where would he stand?" Right there next to Pete Seeger is my answer.

As the 1950s gave way to the 1960s, Woody's health worsened. He was confined to the hospital and visitation was limited. But sometimes on weekends we'd send a car out to the hospital and bring Woody home. He'd sit in a corner, but he'd still be in the room with friends and family. He couldn't talk, but I still wanted him to be part of the scene. There was also a couple in New Jersey, Bob and Sidsel Gleason, who made sure Woody was doing okay at the hospital. They'd come and pick Woody up and bring him home. When Bob Dylan became aware they were doing

Woody Guthrie with his personal manager Harold Leventhal, Arlo Guthrie, and Marjorie Guthrie with Guthrie's Interior Department Award, 1966. Last photo of Woody ever taken. Photograph by John Cohen. COURTESY OF WOODY GUTHRIE ARCHIVES.

this, he'd go over to their house and entertain Woody by playing him his songs. Unfortunately, Woody was rarely aware of what was going on.

The last time I saw Woody was at a visit to the hospital. I sat on the cot with him, talked to him, and took him outside. There really wasn't much I could say, though, other than "How you doing, Woody?" and "How are you getting along?" For me it was a very depressing experience because I had to accept that for Woody Guthrie, the end was near. It came in October 1967. I got a telephone call at six in the morning. When you get a phone call that early in the day, it usually means trouble or bad news. It was Marjorie. "I just heard from the hospital. Woody passed away," is what she said. She seemed to feel relieved, as I think all of us who were close to Woody did.

Marjorie asked me to make the funeral arrangements. I called a left-wing funeral home in New York that we knew and the people there told me that they needed official authorization from a family member over twenty-one to get funeral proceedings moving. Marjorie couldn't do it; her divorce from Woody made it impossible. I called one of Woody's relatives in California. I asked her to send a telegram to the funeral home authorizing the funeral parlor to retrieve the body from the hospital, which she did. Then I got on the phone, and the first call I made was to Pete who was on tour in Japan at the time. The second call went to Mary, his first wife, asking her to call her children. Then Will Geer and everyone else who knew and loved Woody were called. By eleven that morning it was announced on the radio that Woody Guthrie had died. Later that afternoon I got a call from Bob Dylan. He had heard about Woody's death and told me that if there should be any kind of memorial, to count him in. After that, it hit me. Woody was gone.

We did celebrate Woody's life and music at a memorial in January 1968, a couple of months after his death. Dylan was there, as was everyone else who was invited to perform. It was a very emotional event. People cried throughout the evening. Yes, Woody had passed away, but one thing was certain: we would never forget him. What he taught songwriters was that they needed to create songs that were meaningful to common people. That's what Woody did. He expressed in song the soul of America. Above all else, that's what made him great.

HOBO'S LULLABY

I dropped out of Harvard College in the spring of 1938. That fall I went to New York City to try to get a job with a newspaper. No success. My politics were left-wing, and it wasn't too long before I was making acquaintances with other left-wingers. Having plenty of time on my hands, I briefly joined a little art group, which led me to something called Stage for Action where the actor Will Geer was teaching some classes. Remember Grandpa Walton? That was Will Geer. Will became interested in me, a Yankee banjo picker trying to learn country songs.

A year later Will was working in Hollywood. He wrote me, "Pete, I've met a great ballad singer named Woody Guthrie. You got to meet him. I'm trying to persuade him to go to New York." Not long after, Will mailed me a copy of Woody's mimeographed songbook *On a Slow Train to California*, which was a takeoff on a book of jokes back then called *On a Slow Train Through Arkansas*. They used to sell it on railroad trains and in stations to people who got bored with traveling. Woody's little book of songs and jokes cost 25 cents.

At the time Woody had a job with a radio station that paid him a dollar a day. Between songs Woody would say, "Folks, if you want the words to these songs I'm a-singin', remember, I've got a little book out." On a page in the front of the book Woody wrote something like: "This book has an iron-clad copyright, number 586704235791038. Anybody caught singing one of these songs . . . will be a good friend of mine, because that's why I wrote 'em."

I met Woody in March 1940 when he came east. In February Woody had written "This Land Is Your Land" as he hitchhiked across the nation. Some of his other well-known songs—"So Long, It's Been Good to Know You," "Pretty Boy Floyd," "Do Re Mi"—he had already written a few years before. Woody came to New York because Will Geer, who by this time was in New York playing the lead in the Broadway play *Tobacco Road*, had written Woody that he'd help find work for him. Will got the use of the theater for a midnight benefit concert for California farmworkers. In addition to Will, the evening also featured Burl Ives, Lead Belly, Josh White, Earl Robinson, Aunt Molly Jackson, and the Golden Gate Quartet, among others.

I was allowed to sing one song on the program because my friend folk-lorist Alan Lomax insisted on it. I wasn't entirely welcome; it was a full program and there were a lot of dependable performers already part of it. But Alan said, "If you're asking me to be on it, you've got to have this young fella, Pete." So the director gave me one song to sing. I remember walking out to the front of the stage and singing, very amateurishly, the outlaw ballad "John Hardy." I got a smattering of polite applause.

Woody was the star of the show. This midnight concert was a benefit for California agricultural workers, and there was Woody, a genuine Okie with a cowboy hat shoved back on his head. He'd tell a joke and sing a song, and then he'd tell another joke. I remember him saying something like this: "You know, Oklahoma is a very rich state. You want oil in Oklahoma, just go down a hole and get it. If you want coal, why, we've got coal in Oklahoma. Jus' go down a hole and get it. You want lead, we've got lead mines. Go down a hole and get you some lead. If you want food, clothes, groceries, just go in a hole . . . and stay there [*laughter*]." And then he'd go right into "Do Re Mi." He must have been onstage for twenty minutes, more than any other member of the cast. Backstage, he was still singing, so I got to accompany him with my banjo. We got well acquainted that night.

A couple of days later I was with Woody again in Washington, D.C., where he had come to record some songs for Alan Lomax. We were making music all day long, then we'd go in the evening and play some little party that Alan arranged. Alan was full of energy. He planned on bringing about a folk revival all by himself if he had to. And he was sure he knew how to do it.

My first impression of Woody was that he was a very honest person with a wonderful sense of humor. I didn't realize then quite how hard he made it for his first wife, Mary. She tried to be a good wife, but Woody was always running off. In New York, he landed a job for $200 a week, the equivalent of $3,000 or $4,000 now. All Woody had to do was sing one song for the Model Tobacco radio show once a week. But he quit after a couple of weeks. He didn't want to sing the songs Model Tobacco wanted him to sing. Woody wanted to sing the songs *he* felt were the right ones to perform. Mary probably said, "We've bought a car. How are you going to pay for it now? We've got bills to pay. Couldn't you keep a job long enough so we can get out of debt?"

But Alan Lomax had said to Woody: "You are a great ballad-maker. Do not let anything in this world stop you from being that. You're the

Woody Guthrie on guitar; Pete Seeger on banjo, ca. 1940. COURTESY OF
THE WOODY GUTHRIE ARCHIVES.

same kind of person who wrote the great ballads of the past, whether
they were the musical tales of Robin Hood or Jesse James. Don't let anything or anyone stop you from what you're already doing." And Woody
didn't. He took Alan's advice. And why not? Alan was a very persuasive
individual. He had the authority of the Library of Congress behind him,
and he had the vast folk music collections of his father John as well as the
experience of collecting thousands of American folk songs himself. Alan
was able to reach people where they were. He was able to stay a good
friend with Lead Belly, for instance, even when Lead Belly never wanted
to see old John, Alan's father, again. Lead Belly got along well with Alan.
It was the same with Woody.

As for me, well, I was a very naive, puritanical New Englander. It's a
wonder Woody put up with me. But I was a pretty good banjo picker
who also happened to have a good ear. I could find the right notes to

accompany him anytime. I didn't try anything too fancy. Woody didn't like a lot of fancy chords, so I stuck to the chords he wanted.

One evening down in Washington, Woody asked me if there were some mountains around. I told him "Sure. Down in Virginia they got the Blue Ridge." He asked me how far that might be from Washington, D.C. I told him a few hours' drive. He says, "I've got a couple of hours. Why don't we drive down." It was ten o'clock at night. When we were about ten miles beyond Washington out in the Virginia countryside we saw an old woman walking down the road with a big sack of things on her back—groceries or laundry. We slowed down and asked her if we could give her a lift.

"Why sure. Thank you, boys." As she climbed in the back seat she asked, "And where you boys headed at this hour of the night?"

"We're goin' to see the mountains," Woody answered. The old woman looked at us, thought hard for a moment, then said, "Boys, let me out here."

"But you won't get another lift this late."

"I said, let me out here." We let her out.

Woody had faults, but he was also an extraordinarily thoughtful and original talent. He had the genius of simplicity. When I first heard "This Land Is Your Land" I didn't perceive how great it was. I thought to myself, "That song is just *too* simple." I actually believed it was one of Woody's lesser efforts. Shows you how wrong you can be. It took me a while to perceive his genius. In the beginning I just thought he was a real good ballad-maker, and I was learning a lot from him. Occasionally, I'd teach him a song. I don't think he knew the ballad "John Henry" until I sang it to him. I learned it (the way I play it now) from a record in the Library of Congress. I don't think he knew all the Uncle Dave Macon songs that I knew. I loved Uncle Dave, and I listened to every one of his records that I could get hold of.

I didn't think of myself as a songwriter. I was trying to learn songs, not write them. I did, however, write one song with Woody. We were riding down Route 66 and Woody was making up verses. He was fiddling around for a tune. I said, "How would this be?" Woody listened. "Hey, that's pretty good." That's how my tune fit his words for "66 Highway Blues." That's the nearest thing to songwriting I went in for back then.

People often wonder who were Woody's biggest musical influences. The Carter Family and Jimmie Rodgers had probably the biggest impact on him, outside of the music he got from his mother and father. Later on, of course, he heard many other things by many other artists. But he still knew what he liked, and he stuck with what he liked. I remember that he was not approving of my being so experimental, so eclectic. In 1941,

*Almanac Singers Woody Guthrie, Millard Lampell, Bess Hawes, Pete Seeger, Arthur Stern,
and Sis Cunningham perform in 1941.* COURTESY OF WOODY GUTHRIE ARCHIVES.

after we had started the Almanac Singers, I made up a song about a
woman in Harlem organizing domestic workers. Dora Jones was her
name. I put a West Indian–type melody to it. When Woody heard it he
said, "That's not our kind of music. Those people really know how to
make that music, let them make it." Woody didn't stop to think that his
kind of music wasn't always my kind of music. I knew as much about
Bach and Beethoven as I knew about his Oklahoma music.

On the other hand, Woody didn't mind borrowing a good melody if he
needed one. He once took the melody from a calypso song, "It's Love,
Love Alone That Caused King Edward to Leave the Throne." He liked
that melody and used it for his ballad about Matthew Kimes, the outlaw
who kept breaking out of jail. Woody wasn't always consistent with his
views on music. In fact, when talking about Woody Guthrie, you find
contradictions and inconsistencies are the rule rather than the exception.

The days Woody and I spent as members of the Almanac Singers have
never left my mind. The group started indirectly because of a book project Woody and I had worked on in Spring 1940. Alan Lomax had a pile
of protest songs that he had accumulated and hoped to put into his
father's books on American folk music—except that his conservative
father John Lomax had no intention of including them. "Those are not
the kind of songs I want in my collection." Now Alan suggested to us,
"Why don't you two work all this into a book?" We took him up on the
idea and in April and May 1940 we put together the book published

twenty-five years later as *Hard Hitting Songs for Hard-Hit People* (which the University of Nebraska will reissue in the year 2000). In 1940 no publisher was interested in our project.

Later that year, I went on the road west and south. Woody had taught me how to ride freights and sing in bars. In December 1940 I arrived back east and was going through Boston to visit my old stomping grounds in New England. I found out that none other than Woody Guthrie was singing that night at a left-wing fund-raising dinner in a Boston hotel. I met up with him and tagged along, not to go onstage but to get a free meal. Well, Woody got up on the stage and started telling stories, one story after another. The woman in charge of the event finally asked me to get Woody to do some singing instead of storytelling. "He's been onstage for twenty minutes and hasn't sung one song." I walked onstage and whispered to Woody to sing a song, since there was no more time for his tales. He looked at me, said okay and moved right into "The Ballad of Jesse James."

Woody left to go out west shortly after that. He probably hitchhiked there. While in Texas, he persuaded Mary, his wife, to go with him back to California. This was around the time the government was looking for a ballad-maker who could write songs to help sell the Bonneville Dam Project to the people of the Pacific Northwest. Alan Lomax suggested that Woody Guthrie was their man. Mary and Woody went to Oregon and were there for all of one month while he wrote twenty-six songs. Then he was off again.

After my brief trip to New England that December, I returned to New York City and I heard that there was a man named Lee Hays trying to get a book of union songs published, a project that sounded similar to the book Woody and I had put together. It seemed sensible for us not to duplicate each other's books. I looked up Lee Hays and found he had a roommate, Millard Lampell. We all became friends. One night when Lee and I went to sing at a fund-raiser, Mill tagged along. He joined us in singing that night and it sounded fairly good. Pretty soon the three of us were singing all around New York City ("the subway circuit") and living together in a loft on Twelfth Street and Fourth Avenue (the East Village now). We began throwing Sunday afternoon rent parties to raise a little money, have a little fun, do a little singing. We didn't know the word "hootenanny" yet, but we would get a keg of beer and sing all afternoon. During this time Woody was back west, but somehow I'd find ways to get letters through to him. One of those letters told him how much fun Lee, Millard, and I were having singing together and that maybe he should join us. The next thing I knew Woody abandoned Mary again, hitchhiked across country and arrived in New York at our door about 23 June 1941.

Hitler had just invaded the Soviet Union. Woody had this wry grin on his face. "Well," he said, "Guess we won't be singing any more peace songs, will we?" Within two days of Woody's arrival we did indeed quit singing peace songs. In their place we sang union songs. The Almanac Singers had a new member.

Lee and Millard had been the main songwriters in the Almanac Singers. We stayed in New York just long enough to earn some money to make two albums, *Sod Buster Ballads* and *Deep Sea Chanties*. In all, we made $250. With the money we bought an old limousine with bulletproof glass from some Mafia people Millard's brother-in-law had known. We wanted to take to the road: our destination was California.

The old limo used one quart of oil every seven miles or so. It was a gas hog *and* an oil hog. But we could sleep in it. Two people could stretch out in the back and get some sleep while two sat up front.

It was a great trip. Millard, Lee, Woody, and me—we made up song after song. We made up songs passing through Pittsburgh, Chicago, Milwaukee, and Denver. We'd sing a fund-raising party here, a union meeting there. We stayed with a left-wing dentist in Pittsburgh. In Chicago we slept on the floor of the apartment of Studs Terkel and his wife Ida. In Milwaukee Woody got drunk and goosed the wife of a prominent union organizer. In Denver we stayed with a left-wing Chicano family that was determined to get Chicanos into the unions. No one really knew who the Almanacs were except for union members and lefty organizers. But our two records had been widely publicized in the *Daily Worker*, so Communists all across the country knew about us.

Lee's health wasn't too good, and our trip across the country didn't do anything to improve it. He had to push himself to keep up with us. I always had far more energy than anybody should have. I kept going day and night. Mill and Woody had their share of energy too. But Lee just couldn't stay with us, so after we made it to the West Coast, he took a bus back east. He bid us farewell and told us he'd find a place for everyone to live back in New York—we'd call it Almanac House. Sure enough, when we returned to New York that September, Lee and a part-time Almanac Singer named Pete Hawes had rented a place next to the firehouse on Tenth Street, just west of Greenwich Avenue.

But meanwhile Mill, Woody, and I went to Los Angeles for a month. Mostly we sang for unions. We were in the Labor Day Parade in Los Angeles and just about everyone who marched was singing "Union Maid": "Oh, you can't scare me, I'm sticking to the union!" Until then, I didn't realize what a good song it was. Woody's verses weren't all that great, but the chorus: it had meaning and a rhythm that couldn't be denied.

(In the spring of 1941 Mill, Lee, and I had recorded an album of union songs, since our record of peace songs had sold rather well—in lefty circles at least. While we were in the recording studio one song didn't work. Someone said, "Pete, what other union song can you all do?" I sang the chorus of "Union Maid."

"Great! What're the verses?" I could only remember two. Mill Lampell said, "Give me twenty minutes." And that's really all he took. He went into another room and came back with a third verse to go along with the two I could remember. Minutes later we were recording the song.)

When we left southern California for points north, Millard decided he'd go back east as Lee had done earlier. He was a writer, he decided, not a singer. He told us he had ideas for plays and novels and he headed back to New York. Woody and I figured we could still carry on as the Almanac Singers, even if we were just half-strength. We drove up the northern California coast. I saw the redwoods for the first time. We continued to push north, into Portland, Oregon, and finally to Seattle, Washington.

While in Seattle we picked up a couple of temporary Almanacs to join in on choruses. We stayed with Ivar Haglund and taught Ivar the old song "Acres of Clams" (after World War II he started a famous seafood restaurant and gave it that name). And it was in Seattle that Woody and I came across the term "hootenanny." We liked the sound of the word. I inquired as to its origins and was told "hootenanny" came from Indiana, that it was an old country word for "party." Not a planned party, just a good party.

Woody and I took the word "hootenanny" back to New York with us and used it for our rent parties. A few years later ABC television got hold of the term and put a registered trademark on it. I remembered too late that people had said to me, "Don't you think you ought to copyright that word?" I said, "Well, it's an old word. Who's got a right to it?" But I was wrong. In a world of private property, anything that is not nailed down can be taken and claimed.

When we left Seattle and turned east, the Almanac Singers were just two in number again. We went over the Rocky Mountains and stopped to sing for copper miners in Butte, Montana. Then we went on to Duluth, Minnesota, and stayed at the home of Hank and Irene Paull. She wrote for the lumberworkers' paper under the name of Calamity Jane. Hank Paull, a labor lawyer, arrived home late and called upstairs, "Irene, who are these two guys sleeping on the floor in the living room?" It was Woody and me.

When Woody and I left Duluth, we headed straight for New York. Lee Hays and Pete Hawes had rented a place that had a basement and three stories. That's where Woody wrote new verses for "Deep Ellum Blues"

("I went into the toilet, and I pulled the toilet chain, and the polar bears and icebergs come sliding down the drain / Hey, pretty mama, I've got them Arctic Circle blues / Hey, pretty mama, I can't raise no heat on you"). Woody wrote those lyrics for Sis Cunningham and her husband Gordon Friesen, who joined the Almanac Singers soon after we got back from the West Coast.

I didn't realize Lee was not happy with the situation. He kept saying, "I'm sorry, I don't feel well." He wouldn't sing any more. The others kept saying to me, "Pete, you have to ask Lee to leave the Almanacs. He's just malingering."

I suppose some people can get along with one or two others, but getting along with five or six becomes harder. It happened with the Almanac Singers and four years later with People's Songs. Lee and I started People's Songs, but a few months after its inception, the board of directors said, "Pete, you have to ask Lee to leave. He doesn't know how to work in an organization." I talked to Lee just before he died. I told him, "I now realize that I should have listened to you. Things were going wrong and you were right. But I was just pushing ahead." Lee just said, "Well, it's a long time ago." He had forgiven me and he had put it in the past. But I know now he was dreadfully hurt at the time.

When Lee left the Almanacs, he moved to Philadelphia and lived with Walter Lowenfels. Walter, who in Paris had shared a poetry prize with e. e. cummings, was a sophisticated avant-garde poet. He knew how to satirize the left wing, just like Woody did. Once at a Communist Party function, Walter was called upon to recite a poem. He got up from his chair and this is what came out of his mouth: "My mama and my papa / both come from Omaha. / Oh mama, oh papa, / Omaha." And he sat down. Everyone looked at him: that's a progressive poem?

When he became a Communist Walter worked on the *Daily Worker* and the *Sunday Worker* as did Woody. But Woody referred to the latter publication a little bit differently than Walter did. Woody used to say he wrote a column for a little paper called the *Sabbath Employee*.

Woody considered himself a Communist. Was he a member of the Party? Not really. The Party turned him down. He was always traveling here and there. He wasn't the kind of guy you'd give a party assignment to. He was a valued fellow traveler. Somebody I met in Brooklyn claimed to have been in the Communist Party group that turned him down. On the other hand, Sis Cunningham, who was a much more disciplined person than either me or Woody, was in a Greenwich Village branch of the Party. She got Woody in. She probably said, "I'll see that Woody acts responsibly." And so, Woody was briefly in the Communist Party. But what did being a Communist mean? It meant that you were in favor of all the working people in the world getting together so that there never again would need to be war. Woody went along with that. Even so, he wasn't a pacifist. "I don't want a war, but if somebody is going to lynch me just for my politics, I'm going to fight back," is what Woody used to say.

I didn't see Woody much during World War II, with me in the army and him serving in the Merchant Marine. We did write to each other, though. And just as soon as the war ended, we got together again. Lee Hays and I started People's Songs in January 1946 in my mother-in-law's living room on McDougal Street in the Village. Lee was the executive secretary and I was the president. I knew little about organization and even less about schedules and budgets. Woody kept in touch, but he was busy raising a new family. Arlo, Nora, Joady (and Cathy, who died in a fire) were all Woody's and Marjorie's kids. I'd run into Woody at hootenannies, but he seemed distant. He'd say, "I've got to go recharge my batteries," and he'd be off, hitchhiking somewhere. Eventually he'd show up again and act as if he'd never left.

Around 1947 Marjorie and Woody came to our house one day with a proposition: "How about starting up the Almanac Singers again?" I looked at Woody and said, "Woody, I don't think it'll work. You're raising a family. I'm raising a family. And the Almanacs were like a family. I don't think I could be a member of two families at once." So I turned him down. I'm sorry I did. I might have been able to help him more. I don't know.

Marge thought Woody was drinking too much, but of course what she was witnessing were attacks of Huntington's disease. She divorced him about 1950. Woody went out west to see Will Geer. When he returned to New York in 1951, he had with him a pregnant new wife. The child didn't live very long; she died as a teenager. It may have been Huntington's disease that killed her, although of that I'm not certain. I went and saw the girl once when she was twelve. She was living with foster parents. They asked me if I thought they should let her know more about her father. "She knows his songs and she likes them." I told them that maybe she was a little bit too young to hear the story of Woody Guthrie. "Why don't you wait a few years?" I suggested. A few years later she was dead. Woody never knew her; he was permanently hospitalized in 1956.

I always liked being in a singing group, which is why I helped start the Weavers in late 1948. Woody was amused by the Weavers. He really didn't approve of us; we got a little too fancy for his tastes. But he came down to the little nightclub we played in, in order to hear us. He was quite pleased when we had a hit with his "So Long, It's Been Good to

Know You." Woody even accompanied us to the recording session with Decca Records when we cut the song. A Decca executive had said, "The Dust Bowl is history. Why don't you just sing a good song about saying good-bye?" So Woody sprawled out on the floor of Gordon Jenkins's hotel room and wrote brand-new verses for his song. There was no mention of dust storms. It wasn't as good as the original version, but it was good enough for the Weavers to take it to the top of the *Hit Parade* in early fall of 1950.

My guess is that if Woody had stayed healthy, over the years he would have made up maybe twenty versions of "So Long" because of its great chorus. He might have had a Dust Bowl version, a Joe McCarthy version, a civil rights version, a Vietnam version. He might even have had a Ronald Reagan or a Bill Clinton version. Who knows?

The Weavers toured out west in 1951 and Woody went off hitchhiking again. But Huntington's was beginning to take its toll on him. In 1952 he was admitted into New Jersey's Greystone Park Hospital. When Lee Hays and Fred Hellerman went to see him at Greystone (Woody referred to the place as "Gravestone"), they asked him if they were treating him all right. Woody answered, "Oh yeah, the food's fine. Everything's okay. Besides, this is the freest place in America. I can jump up on the table and shout 'I'm a Communist!' and they'll say, 'Oh, he's crazy.' You try doing that anywhere else in America." A couple of years later he really couldn't say much, couldn't sing, couldn't play the guitar. He'd shake my hand and I'd sing him a few tunes.

The last couple of times in the 1960s that I saw Woody he was pretty far gone. Once, when I went to the hospital to visit him, Marjorie had two huge sheets of paper that she put on his bed. One said "Yes" in great big letters, and the other said "No." Those sheets of paper must have been two feet high and two feet wide. They were that big because Woody couldn't focus his eyes anymore. Marjorie said, "Woody, Pete's come to visit you. Do you recognize Pete?" His hand flailed around through the air and landed—whump!—on the "Yes" paper. That's how he communicated with the world, since he couldn't control his tongue or anything else on his body, for that matter. The disease had practically overwhelmed Woody. It was a sad thing to witness.

About eight months before he died in 1967, I visited him once more, this time with Sonny Terry and Brownie McGhee. Woody was in a wheelchair. He couldn't walk anymore, so the hospital attendant wheeled him out onto a porch where it was warm. Sonny, Brownie, and I played some music for Woody. We did "Rock Island Line," with Sonny blowing his harp, sending beautiful notes into the air. Woody must have liked what he heard because you could see how much he wanted to be a part of our little group. He tried to get his arms going, but they were just flailing around like a windmill. It got to the point where it looked as though he might hurt himself, so the attendant said, "You better quit playing that loud tune. He's tryin' to join you and he can't." So we stopped "Rock Island Line" and played some quiet blues instead. We played and sang until it was time to say goodbye.

I saw Woody Guthrie alive just one more time. I was with his son Arlo and together we played for Woody one of his favorite songs, "Hobo's Lullaby." It was the only song we could have sung that made any sense. Shortly thereafter, Woody Guthrie, himself a weary hobo, left this hard world.

ARLO GUTHRIE

GOING BACK TO CONEY ISLAND

Hi! I never had this job before. I didn't even know what a keynote was. Some of you may know that Studs Terkel was going to be doing this keynote address and couldn't make it. So they tried to find somebody who could talk for a time and not say too much and that ended up being me. But they were worried about that to begin with so they decided to show a film so that I wouldn't have to think for too long, and at this time in the morning, that's probably appropriate. Not only that, they went beyond the call, actually showing different films and I was thankful for that time also. I gained another fifteen minutes right there. So here we are.

It's hard to tell what to say at an event like this. And the thing that occurred to me, aside from having some of my own memories, which I will share with you in a moment, was how timely this whole thing seems to be. I don't know how long we could go and not have the people who are here still be here. This is one of those moments when you begin to realize that time is going by and there are people with valuable things to say. If my dad's life really pointed to any one particular thing, it was that it wasn't his own as much as it was shared by lots of people who felt similarly, but not all exactly the same, about some things, at some time. Some of those people are still here. I don't know if these people actually have even seen each other for quite some time. But to gather them in one spot and sit down and go over the next few days with some of their thoughts and some of their ideas, I think will help some of the younger people here to understand what Woody Guthrie was all about.

I remember, from when I was a kid, the time when my dad brought home a baby carriage that had been thrown out in Coney Island. It was a rare find, because in those days, nobody threw away anything that had any value. And he came home with it and turned it into a sort of "kidmobile" and put me and my brother and my sister in it. I was generally in the

This essay is excerpted from remarks made during Arlo Guthrie's keynote address for the Hard Travelin' conference, 28 September 1996, Case Western Reserve University, Cleveland, Ohio.

bow. And we would go the ten blocks or so to Nathan's for breakfast (which explains me to a lot of people without having to say anything else). I remember passing all of the amusements and the rides that were, at the time, a part of Coney Island. Some of them are still there. And occasionally when we'd have some money or something, you know, we'd go on the kid things like the merry-go-round. I don't have a lot of the memories that some folks have of my dad in the ways that people would have with people their own age. But I do remember some things in particular: going up and down the road meeting people. And actually running into them, as it were. And growing up in a crazy neighborhood, filled with wonderful people who shared in common the fact that nobody had much. And none of us knew that because nobody had anything more—or less—than anybody else anyway. And I remember later on, going to the hospital every week when we were growing up. As I read the things people write about me or things that people write about my father, it seems as if we had this sort of gulf that was driven in by the things that had happened to us in life. But the truth is, me and my brother and my sister, we had our life with our dad. It may not have been the kind of life you see on TV, but every week when we were kids, we would go and hang out for a day, at different hospitals, you know, and my dad would come down and play with us, and chase us up trees and around bushes, and that's a lot more than some truckers get to hang out with their kids. So we didn't feel too deprived.

I remember later on, in the fifties, when the folk boom, as they called it, was getting under way. Every weekend we'd bring him home from one of these hospitals out in Howard Beach there, in Queens, where we were at the time. And we'd have a stack of records that had come in that week from around the world, where people had recorded his songs in all of these different languages that we never heard of, couldn't read, or understand, but he'd sit there, you know, eating hot dogs, and we'd play that stack of records over and over again. And I always thought that was one of the things he enjoyed; he had some idea, I think, of how many of his songs had moved people around the world enough to sing them. I mean, even the stupid ones, you know the Disneyland-sounding songs. You know, I think he still got a kick out of them. At least he didn't show any particular interest in any one more than another one. Actually, he showed more interest in the hot dogs than in the records we were playing. As a matter of fact, later on in life I remember going down to Disney World one time—it must have been when my kids were young—and I remember seeing Mickey Mouse coming down the main drag there, singing "This Land Is Your Land," and it wasn't just Mickey either, it was everybody, you know. Goofy and Donald and . . . I always wondered what my dad

Woody Guthrie with his children Arlo, Nora, and Joady on a bench in Coney Island, 1950. COURTESY OF WOODY GUTHRIE ARCHIVES.

would have thought about that. I know at the very least, it would have been an occasion for a drink. At least to ponder properly the situation, you know.

I think these are the kinds of things that in some way we share with parents or good friends, even if they're no longer around. I mean, here we are still laughing at this stuff, and the truth is, it's still going on. And I get a kick out of that. That's one of the joys of my life, seeing how these ideas and these songs and these words get moved on from generation to generation. Now I'm old enough to actually say that. I remember, of course, when I was growing up I understood this, but I understood it only in the sense that I remember my Bar Mitzvah very well: it was in a loft in Greenwich Village. And as soon as people found out my dad was there, I don't think anybody said a word to me. They were all sort of hovering around him. And I wasn't complaining about that; I was thankful for that! And I still am.

But I understood that some of these things that happen to you and to your family you make a part of your own life. And some of the things we saw, I think my dad made a part of his life. He exists today in a lot of people who are here, not just me. And he exists in ways that mean different things to different times. I think one of the wonderful things about my dad that I learned from him—not from him personally, but from his work—was his propensity toward wanting to be himself. I didn't just learn it; I also appreciated it. I began to realize some of the sacrifices that a person has to make when you're dealing with things like being free: free in every moment to pursue and to be who you are. There's a price that has to be paid for those things. It's not easy. You're not born with that. Things have to happen to you. You may have to lose things. I don't know how to say it, except that my grandfather's claim to fame was that he had lost a farm a day for thirty days during the Wall Street crisis back years ago. In some way, it's those kind of events that inspire you to become less dependent on things like farms. This freedom that you have just doesn't spring up from nowhere; it comes from life's experiences, which are not always easy to deal with. As a kid you may not understand them, but as I get older and I share some of those same things as everybody who gets older begins to share, at some point or another I began to realize the price that people pay for freedoms that they enjoy. And they are all the more precious when you realize what that's all about.

You know, I also wanted to say a couple of things about going back to Coney Island a few years ago. I was actually doing a show there. I had been back a few times to go to Nathan's, but it was sort of a genetic thing, like salmon going back, you know, and I didn't even eat: I was a vegetarian at the time actually, and still had to just sit there and watch it and smell it. But I went back. Most of the rides were gone. Of course the house where we grew up was bulldozed years ago, and there wasn't much left of anything. But I was standing there, and actually there was a bunch of very ancient-looking people—must have been in their nineties or so— coming over saying, "I was your babysitter." And I'd say, "Who are you?" And they'd say, "I don't know." But they remembered me and I thought that was good enough. I'm kind of like that too. And I walked off by myself, and the merry-go-round started up, you know, and it started playing "This Land Is Your Land." And I thought of all the things that would have impressed my dad the most about his musical contribution, it probably would have been something like that. Not the legions of young singer-songwriters pasting pictures of him on their guitars so much, or singing his songs even in their own ways, although I think that might have pleased him to some extent—at least in the sense of being sort of amused at the way the universe unfolds. But to see your work come back in your own place that you love, where you don't expect it, just to show up one day. Those are the kind of simple pleasures I wish in some ways he could have enjoyed. But if he didn't that's okay, I have shared them with you and with my kids and my grandkids at this point, and I think that carries on some of the feelings of what it means to be a human being.

The other thing that I was going to mention was that you have to have a sense of humor about these things. At least we did, about not just his life, even about his death, you know. He died in October of 1967, about thirty years ago now, and the joke in our family was that he had heard the record I'd had a chance to have made and I don't know if it's just a coincidence or not, but that was the joke, of course. He heard it and left. So I have found it amusing from time to time to think about that. It means that there's hope for me and my kids, I guess.

You know, one of the stories that he used to tell—this is a short story, but I'll tell you anyway—it's one of those ones that I have actually heard my mom also tell. She inherited it from him and I guess I got stuck with it. But it's one of my favorite tales that we tell from time to time. And I think it sort of speaks to some of the issues that surround the hopes we have for each other, that I'm sure he had and that got passed along. I'm not in the industry part of the music business, but I've been making music now for quite some time. Actually, maybe I am involved in the industry part. I don't have the same sort of seriousness about it that other people do, but I enjoy doing what I do, but only because it's really all that I know how to do, and so you make the best of it. But everywhere that we get to go, I've been privileged to meet people who come up to me and talk, not just about my dad, but about my mom too. Little women come up and say, " I danced in your mom's dance school." Or some kid comes along and says. "You know, I just discovered your dad last week and I want to play the guitar." And people ask me, as if I knew something, and of course, I pretend that I do. I don't have any qualms about it. I think one of the graces you get when you get older is that you get to look like you know something, even if it's not founded on any truth. So I talk to them about it all. I'm glad to see some of the ideas and the songs and the stories get passed along from time to time.

And in more and more places too, there is the kind of belief that you can make your own music, and maybe not change the world, but just change the moment. Sometimes you can just change one little moment from one situation to another by inspiration of a song, or a couple of words, or just having fun or playing, and moment by moment, the world seems to change on its own. You don't necessarily have to consider the big thing: you just have to worry about that one moment and that's what I get out of listening to some of these old records that these guys made together. You know, with Cisco (Houston) and Sonny (Terry), and all . . . I mean, you listen to them and what you really get—what I get out of it— is this fathomless joy that just seems to spread around. It's nice to see that it's still doing that.

You know, when I was a kid, nobody thought you could make a living singing folk songs. I mean, my kids believe that because they actually see it. But, in my world, that was ridiculous. I mean, folk songs were what you did when you got home from doing the real stuff. So there may be some inclination to ascribe some Woody Guthrie something or another to the fact of going out and singing songs and trying to change the world, but in fact, when I was a kid growing up nobody in their right mind thought that this was something you could actually make a living at. But there are more and more people playing it anyway, whether they're making a living or not. There are more guitars being sold and manufactured, more people singing songs and writing them, and thinking of things to say, and dreams to write about, than ever before. It's more and more and more and more everywhere you go, and not just in this country, but in every country in the world that I have ever been to. More and more people feeling like the music belongs to them. And I think these are some of the philosophical and political beliefs that my dad and others—you know, Pete Seeger, and those sort of folks—shared back then with each other and still share with some of us today. The fact that these songs don't belong to any particular person—even though thank God for copyrights, at least in our case. Put me and my sister and my brother through school and it's still helping out occasionally. We just want to say thank you to everybody who bought the records.

At any rate, what I was saying is that more and more wherever you go, it seems like people have taken up the belief—have come to believe somehow or other—that writing songs and singing them and sitting around is more a part of who we are than anybody ever thought. I've noted that it's only in the last fifty years or so that people have let TVs and radios do their singing for them, you know. We've been sitting around as human beings for a couple hundred million years or whatever—I don't know how long we've been here—but we've been sitting around campfires singing songs, and before that, just regular fires, and singing these kinds of songs and making up stories and passing on who we are from one generation to the next. And it's nice to see that continuing. And it's nice to see that it doesn't belong to any particular group of people, or any one person, but sort of just belongs to everybody.

Which brings me to this story I was waiting to tell you here. It's the story of two rabbits: the Mama Rabbit and the Papa Rabbit out in the woods one day. And I heard my mom tell this story one time, when she was done doing her Huntington's disease work, and she was looking for something to do, and she came to me and said, "Arlo, I want to go on the road with you, I think." And I said, "Mom! You're out of your mind! What do you mean—out on the road with me?" She says, "Well, yeah. I've done what I wanted to do here, and I'm looking for something to do." I said, "Mom, you don't understand. This is rock and roll, I mean, you know—people smoking dope out there, you know, guys looking for chicks, I mean, you know, I mean—you know what I mean. It's rock and roll out there." And it didn't scare her. And she said, "Well, that's all right. I just won't say nothing." And, of course I knew my mom, so I knew she was lying. And she would have had a lot to say, just by the look in her eye and stuff like that. Anyway, I heard her tell this story the last time at a thing where they were dedicating some wing of a hospital or something to her. And I was very thankful doctors had inspired her to make these speeches and keep her busy enough so that she forgot about going on the road with me, at least for a while.

But I think the story holds up. So here's these two rabbits, Mama Rabbit and Papa Rabbit, out in the woods one day, munching on things like rabbits like to do. And the wind kicked up a little bit. And on the wind came the sound of dogs off in the distance. But the wind was swirling around, so the rabbits couldn't tell where the sound of the dogs was coming from. So they just went back to munching on things, but now they were nervous. Now they were paying attention. And after a while, the wind died down and the rabbits could tell that the sound of the dogs was coming clearly through those trees on the hill and so they stood up and they looked. And there through the trees on the hill was this bunch of dogs jumping up and down. And by some cosmic coincidence, when the two rabbits stood up to look at the dogs, the dogs jumped up and saw the two rabbits down below. And the dogs got happy. And their faces started smiling and their feet started running, their tails were going, their eyes were smiling, happy, barking, yelping, running dogs. And when the rabbits saw the dogs coming, they bolted and they ran this way and that way. 'Round the trees and over the rocks and through the shrubs. But no matter where they went, and no matter how quick they were, the dogs kept getting closer and closer, until finally the dogs were just about on top of them and the rabbits started getting tired. And just as the dogs were on them, the rabbits ducked into the hollow of a log. And in the next instant, the dogs were all over the log and they were making a big racket because they couldn't get in. And deep in the hollow of the log, above all the noise outside, the Mama Rabbit looked at the Papa Rabbit and said, "You know, Pop, I don't believe we're going to get out of this alive." And the Papa Rabbit just smiled and said, "Well, that's all right. We'll just stay here until we outnumber them."

You know, I think my dad took that story to heart, frankly. He didn't have a bunch of wives for no reason. He didn't have a bunch of kids for nothing else to do. And he didn't feel like singing these songs because there was nothing good on TV. I mean he, in some way, began to understand, that sometimes when you get enough of us, things change. And there's more and more of us around the world today who have some idea of what it means to be "more of them." And I hope that some of the people here will take the occasion to listen to some of those who, in another thirty years from now, are not going to be here. And I may be one of them—you never know. But we are at that point in time, when we're taking a real life and making it into something that people are going to remember whether it's real or not. I have never been an opponent to myths, and in my dad's case, you don't actually have to mythologize a whole lot. Frankly, he was wild enough to be actually living it. That's the only regret that I have ever had dealing with things with my dad, is that sometimes people who've written about him or had occasion to talk about him didn't have the thing inside to be able to share with him the thing he tried to express the most, which was this fabulous, wonderful gift of just being in the moment. Being right there and not worrying about what the future was going to be so much, or what the past had been. But just grasping it, and munching it fully and completely, as if it was the only moment that was ever going to be. He did that. I try to do that in my own way. Not just because he did it, but because it seems that if he could get away with it, somebody else could. And I have tried not to make the price so dear, in some ways. But I think that is for each one of us as individuals to decide: how we want to share with each other what we have left. What we think is worthy of passing on, editing as we go. Leaving some of the things off we don't think are so important, even if they're true. And making up stuff if it seems like we need to do that.

I've done pretty well here, considering. I wasn't actually referring to content, just to the time. At any rate, I hope you never have to be a keynote speaker in your life. Thank you very much.

PART two

Pastures of Plenty

ROBERT SANTELLI

BEYOND FOLK
Woody Guthrie's Impact on Rock and Roll

If there is one year that best sums up the impact Woody Guthrie has had on rock and roll, it must be 1988. In January of that year, Guthrie was inducted into the Rock and Roll Hall of Fame as an Early Influence, a special category that pays tribute to rock's predecessors and chief influencers. Held at the Waldorf-Astoria Hotel in New York, the induction ceremony was the third of the Rock and Roll Hall of Fame Foundation's annual ritual honoring artists whose lifeworks have left their marks on the ever-evolving music form.

It was a powerful and memorable event. The artists inducted included the Beatles, the Beach Boys, the Supremes, the Drifters, and Bob Dylan, while Berry Gordy Jr. went into the Hall in the Non-performer category. Inducted with Guthrie in the Early Influence category were fellow folk great Lead Belly (Huddie Ledbetter) and electric guitar pioneer Les Paul, rounding out a Rock and Roll Hall of Fame class that still stands with the best of them.

There was another Guthrie–rock and roll connection in 1988. A number of country, folk, and rock artists joined together that year and recorded an album called *A Vision Shared: A Tribute to Woody Guthrie and Leadbelly* (Columbia). Their intention was to raise money so that the Smithsonian Institution, at the time one of the few major repositories of American folk music and folk music–related artifacts, could purchase the vast Folkways Record catalogue begun nearly a half century earlier by the late Moe Asch.

A Vision Shared says nearly as much about the Guthrie-rock connection as his induction into the Rock and Roll Hall of Fame. The album includes interpretations of Guthrie's and Lead Belly's music by a wide assortment of contemporary artists, many of whom, it seems on the surface, have little or no musical link to either Guthrie or Lead Belly.

It was obvious why Woody's son Arlo, or Pete Seeger (himself a future

Rock and Roll Hall of Fame inductee) would contribute to the album. The inclusion of Bob Dylan and Bruce Springsteen is hardly a surprise; both are direct musical descendents of Guthrie. But John Mellencamp, Willie Nelson, Emmylou Harris, and U2? What do they have to do with Woody Guthrie? Or, better, what does Woody Guthrie have to do with them? How could such a diverse group of rockers and country artists be so moved by Woody Guthrie, or be so personally influenced by his music, that they would feel compelled to be part of the project? (Interpreting Lead Belly on *A Vision Shared* are the Beach Boys' Brian Wilson, early rock and roll legend Little Richard, and bluesman Taj Mahal, along with Sweet Honey in the Rock, Fishbone, and Doc Watson.) It is quite a cast, quite an album and quite a display of roots-bearing evidence that has surely turned more than one rock or country fan back to the original music of Guthrie and Lead Belly. In fact, in 1989 a follow-up album titled *Folkways: The Original Vision* was released by Smithsonian-Folkways Records. It contains Guthrie's and Lead Belly's original versions of the songs interpreted on *A Vision Shared*, as well as other selections.

Listening to these works side by side was, and still is, a concise lesson in American music history. What we learned was this: Woody Guthrie's influence (and Lead Belly's too) was greater than most rock fans and pop music observers probably had imagined. Folkies had always been moved by Guthrie's wonderfully accessible melodies and witty lyrics, but here for the first time is proof, absolute proof, that his reach in rock was both long and lasting.

A Vision Shared reminds us that Woody Guthrie politicized rock and roll. Mostly through Bob Dylan, Guthrie gave rock and roll its conscience and its urge to use popular song as a means of protest, be it political or social. Without Guthrie's influence, rock and roll might well have remained apathetic in such areas, content to focus on the many ways to encapsulate teen angst and sexual restlessness in a two-minute song.

Guthrie also opened up to rock songwriters new avenues of lyrical expression. He inspired rock artists to include the song-story and first-person narrative, common communication strategies in folk music, in their writing arsenals. Woody Guthrie made rock and roll artists rethink their ideas about the songwriting process. After absorbing elements of Guthrie's common-man view of America, rock's songwriting vision has never been the same. "Like Walt Whitman, Guthrie saw himself as the voice of the inarticulate and powerless poor," wrote Jerome Rodnitzky, "or from the Marxist historical viewpoint, as an edge of the historical wave."[1]

Actually, if the order of Early Influence induction into the Rock and Roll Hall of Fame has anything to do with the importance of the artist to rock and roll, then Woody Guthrie was two years late in being honored. The first class of the Rock and Roll Hall of Fame included as Early Influence inductees Robert Johnson, Jimmie Rodgers, and Jimmy Yancey. No one could argue with either Johnson's or Rodgers' inclusion in the maiden class. But Yancey's selection remains the oddest of all Early Influence choices. A prewar Chicago boogie-woogie pianist, who, along with Albert Ammons, Pine Top Smith, Meade Lux Lewis, and Pete Johnson helped define boogie-woogie as a blues-jazz hybrid, Yancey was, nonetheless, dwarfed by Johnson and Rodgers, whose impact on rock and roll has been sweeping. A better selection than Yancey would have been Guthrie, whose influence on rock and roll rivals that of Johnson and Rodgers.

Despite such impact, Woody Guthrie's influence on rock and roll came after the music had established itself as part of America's pop music landscape. If Elvis Presley or Chuck Berry, two of the principal architects of rock and roll in the early 1950s, had heard any of Woody Guthrie's music, it most likely would have been by an artist interpreting Guthrie. With McCarthyism running rampant in America during the time of rock and roll's earliest shouts and stomps, Guthrie's recordings were rarely, if ever, played on radio. Elvis Presley biographer Peter Guralnick says, however, that Presley's record collection numbered hundreds of albums and included works by Dylan, Ian & Sylvia, Odetta, and Peter, Paul and Mary—all major folk artists in the early 1960s.[2] It is possible that any of them could have covered a Guthrie tune on an album in Presley's collection and that Presley had listened to it and was moved by it. It is more probable, considering the song's popularity in the 1960s, that somewhere he had heard a version of Guthrie's masterpiece, "This Land Is Your Land." But, as Presley was not a songwriter, was politically right of center, and was more attuned to Southern country and sacred artists than to the intellectualized slant of the New York urban folk crowd Guthrie ran with, it's safe to assume that Guthrie had little or no effect on Presley.

Listening to Chuck Berry's rock and roll, particularly the lyrics, we might suppose that he stood a better chance of being influenced by Guthrie. Here too, however, there is scant evidence to suggest it. Guthrie, for instance, is never once mentioned in Berry's autobiography. Still, of all the 1950s rock and roll songwriters, Berry was among the very few who, like Guthrie, wrote lyrics detailing the American Experience. Of two Berry songs in which America is the central theme, neither "Back in the U.S.A." nor "Promised Land" is controversial in a political sense. Despite being black, Berry merely reproduced the standard 1950s view of white middle-class America in his lyrics, celebrating freedom, opportunity, and materialism. In the latter song Berry, according to Timothy Scheurer, "mines the mythology of cars and mobility to reaffirm the notions of opportunity in the promised land. His is a youthful vision of the country, one that completely eschews the heavy overtones of theocratic ideals or the efficacy of the individual."[3]

Though Little Richard, another first-generation rock and roll artist, is represented on *A Vision Shared*, his introduction to Guthrie came much later. During an educational program at the Rock and Roll Hall of Fame and Museum in 1997, Little Richard remarked that he "wasn't much aware of white music in the 1950s except for Elvis, Pat Boone, and whatever might have been on the radio."[4] Guthrie, of course, could do little to promote himself or his music, even if the political climate in America had been warmer to folk music. By 1954, the year Elvis Presley made his first records for Sam Phillips and Sun Records and effectively changed the course of American popular music, Guthrie was already besieged by Huntington's chorea, the disease that would ultimately kill him in 1967. "Woody had no idea who Elvis Presley was, even in 1956, when Elvis's name was all over the place," said Harold Leventhal, his close friend and caretaker of the Guthrie family. "He didn't listen to the radio or watch television. From a musical point of view, it didn't really matter. Things were bad in the early 1950s for folksingers. There weren't a lot of places to play and no real chances to make records."[5]

That is not to say that American folk music disappeared during the decade. Robert Cantwell writes that many folksingers in the 1950s resided in Greenwich Village and "many found an audience there."[6] In 1956, Leventhal, Pete Seeger, and Lou Gordon produced a benefit folk concert to raise music for the Guthrie Children's Trust Fund. According to Cantwell, "the concert was a kind of reunion, bringing the old left-wing community, the Almanac Singers and the People's Songs cohort, together with younger aficionados who had come under that generation's influence at school and camp."[7]

Cantwell correctly believes that the concert was "the beginning of Woody Guthrie's canonization."[8] With the popularity of American folk music largely diminished in the early part of the decade, the roots of what would become a full-on revival in the 1960s began to emerge after the 1956 Guthrie Trust Fund concert. Guthrie's recognition even began to spread beyond the United States. Leventhal recalled attending a private party in England in the early 1960s, at which he met the Beatles' Paul McCartney. "We talked and I mentioned my connection to Woody," continued Leventhal. "Paul surprised me when he said, 'I love Woody Guthrie and really admire the kind of songs he writes.'"[9]

With Guthrie's mental and physical health in steady decline, it would take a disciple of the folksinger, particularly someone fresh on the scene, with charisma, vision, and media attractiveness, not only to carry Guthrie's presence into the early 1960s folk revival, but also to carry it into rock and roll. That person was Bob Dylan. "I first heard Woody Guthrie over at a house party," wrote Dylan in the liner notes to *A Vision Shared*. "He had a sound . . . and he had something that needed to be said. And that was highly unusual to my ears. Usually you would have one or the other, you know, but he always had something to say."[10] Dylan recollected that "there was a time when I did nothing but his songs" and that "I was completely taken over by him. By his spirit, or whatever. You could listen to his songs and actually learn how to live, or how to feel. He was like a guide."[11]

Dylan sang Woody Guthrie songs. He also dressed like him, regularly visited him in the hospital, read his books, talked like him, wrote songs like him ("Song to Woody," found on Dylan's eponymous debut album, is one of the more touching compositions in his early song catalogue), and exuded the same homespun innocence that made Guthrie so irresistible, with or without guitar in hand. Dylan was, in short, a Woody Guthrie clone in the early 1960s. And although he was still very much a traditional folksinger at this point in his career, he would soon transform himself into a rock artist, carrying Guthrie's spirit and influence in his soon-to-be-electrified music.

Despite all but abandoning his Guthrie-esque folk music roots by 1966, Dylan would never completely shed his Guthrie connection. He was the artist who singlehandedly introduced the works of Woody Guthrie to rock. From Dylan flowed Guthrie's social and political consciousness and his penchant for writing topical songs. Dylan was the eldest son of "Woody's Children,"'a term occasionally used to describe the many young folkies (Tom Paxton, Phil Ochs, Joan Baez, and others) in the early 1960s who had been greatly influenced by Guthrie. Many of these artists, most prominently, Dylan, began to attract a following with rock fans who preferred songs that carried social and political significance rather than the pop pap rampant in pre-Beatles' 1960s rock and roll.

By the end of the decade Woody's influence could be felt in many corners of rock music and culture. A new hybrid, folk-rock, had been born in 1965. The *New Rolling Stone Encyclopedia of Rock & Roll* describes folk-rock this way: "The idea was to set the folk songs of the hootenanny era, especially those of Bob Dylan and his many disciples (and to a degree the work of their predecessors, such as Woody Guthrie), to a rock & roll beat."[12]

Folk-rock made groups such as the Byrds and duos such as Simon and Garfunkel major trendsetters in the mid-1960s. Even though their songlists were light on Guthrie material, many of the folk songs they interpreted, including Dylan's, possessed social and political commentary that could be traced back to Guthrie. When the Byrds did interpret Guthrie, they did it well; their version of Guthrie's "Pretty Boy Floyd," which appeared on their *Sweetheart of the Rodeo* album, was a high-water mark for the group in the late 1960s, matching the critical acclaim garnered by their interpretations of Dylan's "Chimes of Freedom" and "The Times They Are a-Changin'" a few years earlier.

Other 1960s rock artists, including Country Joe and the Fish, Ry Cooder, Jay and the Americans, and Jesse Colin Young also recorded Guthrie songs, introducing them to audiences not old enough to have remembered versions of the songs recorded earlier in the 1960s by folk groups such as the Kingston Trio, the Chad Mitchell Trio, and the Brothers Four.

Rodnitzky points out that Guthrie might even have influenced 1960s hippie fashion, speech, and daily outlook. "The wild long hair, the faded denims, the careless and outlandish combination of clothes, and the profanity were all natural to Woody long before they became modish symbols for studied counter culturalists. In short, Guthrie was an original alienated man and a natural enemy of bourgeois society."[13]

Guthrie's music and influence turned up in other places as well. Wayne Hampton recalls that United Airlines and the Ford Motor Company used "This Land Is Your Land," which by now had become something of an alternative national anthem, in commercials.[14] In his quest for the presidency, the liberal senator George McGovern used the song as a campaign rallying cry in 1972.

Also, there can be no doubt that Barry McGuire's number-one hit, "Eve of Destruction," which remained at the top of the charts for ten weeks in 1965, evolved from Guthrie's political protest songs, as did the Beatles' "Revolution" which was a hit as the B side for "Hey Jude." Add to this list the Jefferson Airplane's "Volunteers," from the album by the same name, and the Rolling Stones' "Street Fighting Man" from *Beggar's Banquet* as further proof of Guthrie's influence on rock and roll in the late 1960s.

The Woody Guthrie influence on the Beatles was most felt on John Lennon, although, as already pointed out, Paul McCartney knew and admired Guthrie's music. Hampton calls Lennon, Guthrie, and Dylan (along with union leader Joe Hill), the important figures in the rise of protest music within the realm of pop. Hampton sees Lennon as "a working class hero" and a true musical offspring of Guthrie. Rock had now become the most effective means of impacting politics and culture, and Lennon was one of the music's main leaders.

Like Guthrie, Lennon often used humor and satire to make his political points. In the song "Freeda People" (*Mind Games*, 1973), Lennon sings, "We don't want no Big Brother scene" because "a million heads are better than one." Hampton quotes Lennon's "Declaration of Newtopia," which he and Yoko Ono proclaimed in 1973: "We announce the birth of a conceptual country, Newtopia. . . . Newtopia has no land, no boundaries, no passports, only people."[15]

In 1971 Lennon and Ono had moved to Greenwich Village, had become friends with Yippie leaders Jerry Rubin and Abbie Hoffman, and had performed at a benefit show at the Apollo Theater for prisoners at Attica State Prison and another one in Michigan for rock radical John Sinclair, who had been convicted of possession of a small amount of marijuana and sentenced to ten years in prison. The following year Lennon and Ono cohosted the *Mike Douglas Show*, sending forth from television land for one week political diatribes and songs to millions of viewers.

By 1980, however, after personal and artistic turmoil, Lennon had largely abandoned his radicalism, just as Dylan had done a decade and a half earlier. Other rock artists now had taken up the Cause. Other than Lennon, the most important Guthrie-sque artist in the 1970s wasn't American or even English, but Jamaican.

Bob Marley might never have heard a Woody Guthrie recording, but surely he was familiar with the work of Dylan. In his biography of Marley, Stephen Davis points out that as early as 1963, the year Dylan's Guthrie-inspired folk-protest music began reaching beyond America, Marley and his cohorts, the Wailers, were hearing the message. "In the States Bob Dylan was riding the crest of protest music, applying angry new lyrics and a civil rights consciousness to the old tunes and ballads of the folk-song movement," writes Davis. "Bob Marley, Bunny Livingston, and Peter Tosh may have been enchanted by the Impressions and the Drifters, but they were hearing these other impolite sounds too, and these definitely had an effect on them."[16]

By the mid-1970s, the greatest reggae artist of all time was writing songs filled with revolutionary fervor and stinging criticisms of a Jamaican society both corrupt and utterly careless in its handling of the poor and unemployed, particularly in the island's capital city of Kingston, birthplace of reggae and its religious complement, Rastafarianism. Coming out of the ghetto himself, Marley emerged as a Jamaican Dylan, though his "chinka-chinka" reggae "riddims" and deep-seated bass sounds made his music much more confrontational than Dylan's softer early 1960s folk style. Another Marley biographer, Roger Steffens, views the Jamaican in the loftiest of terms. He has called Marley "a hero figure, in the classic mythological sense," with an "icon-like status more akin to that of the rebel myth of Che Guevara than to that of a pop star."[17] By the time of his death in 1981, Marley had become a cultural/political/musical spokesman for the Third World; his rebel reggae had assumed a broad universality, much like Dylan's and Guthrie's best political protest songs.

At the very least, Marley carried the spirit of Woody Guthrie in his music. With songs such as "Them Belly Full (But We Hungry)," "Concrete Jungle," "Rebel Music (3 O'Clock Roadblock)," "I Shot the Sheriff," and "Get Up, Stand Up" (cowritten with Peter Tosh), the stirring anthem for people politically or economically oppressed the world over, Marley's main concern were those who had been bruised or beaten by the System.

Marley's songs were more incendiary than Guthrie's. There was no homespun comfort or rounded edges in them. His lyrics relied less on wit and satire and more on a straight-ahead, attacking word-power that shot straight for its targets: racism, poverty, prejudice. Guthrie might not have understood nor have approved of the Rastafarian link to Marley's sociopolitical songs, but he would have agreed that Marley was fighting the good fight with an unstoppable weapon: music.

Bruce Springsteen began his recording career in 1973, the same year that American rock fans were first being introduced to Marley's reggae. But it would be later—ironically, right around the time of Marley's death in 1981—that Springsteen discovered the music of Woody Guthrie. Despite his late introduction to Guthrie, it is Springsteen who most authentically has carried out the Guthrie influence in modern rock and roll. He has acted as the musical conduit for those younger songwriters seeking a Guthrie-esque style in which music becomes a potent sociopolitical force.

Springsteen's introduction to American folk music occurred in the early 1960s. Growing up on the New Jersey Shore, Springsteen often accompanied a cousin to the beach where local folkies strummed guitars and sang songs made popular by Peter, Paul and Mary, the Kingston Trio, and Pete Seeger. Oddly, Springsteen doesn't recall Dylan's early, Guthrie-inspired political protest songs, which were appearing during this time on albums such as *The Freewheelin' Bob Dylan* (1963), *The Times They Are a-Changin'* (1964), and *Another Side of Bob Dylan* (1964). "I didn't become familiar with Dylan's early work until much later on," Springsteen recalled in a 1998 interview. "The way I knew Bob Dylan first was as a rock artist. I had heard albums like *Blonde on Blonde* and pored through his electric stuff. This is how I first created a relationship with his music."[18]

Interestingly, it was through Springsteen's exploration of country music in the early 1980s, particularly the work of Hank Williams, that led him to Dylan's early recordings and ultimately to Guthrie. Moved by what he heard from Guthrie, Springsteen embarked on a musical study of his recordings and how folk music impacted culture and politics. Springsteen read Joe Klein's *Woody Guthrie: A Life*, absorbed Guthrie's *Dust Bowl Ballads*, and studied the manner in which Guthrie was able to say so much with so few words and with such simple melodies. Springsteen, though, was most impressed with how Guthrie's songs so connected with people. "I was tremendously moved with his sense of community," Springsteen continued. "He worked his way into the souls of people and examined what they were thinking and feeling about themselves and the world around them. And he did this better than anyone I had ever heard before."[19]

The first indication of Guthrie's influence on Springsteen occurs on *Nebraska*, arguably his best album, although strains of Hank Williams, Jimmie Rodgers, Robert Johnson, and Bob Dylan also run through the work. Released in 1982, *Nebraska* is a folk album, rough-cut and raw, that largely examines the underbelly of America in the starkest of terms. Springsteen biographer Dave Marsh described the songs on *Nebraska* as having "the quality of stillness associated with the great Library of Congress folk recordings of the 1930s and 1940s."[20] In his *Rolling Stone* review of the album, Steve Pond commented that Springsteen was now "telling simple stories in the language of a deferential common man."[21]

Many of the songs on *Nebraska* reflect a sociopolitical desperation with roots firmly embedded in the conservative "me-ism" that had begun to run wild in Ronald Reagan's America. Springsteen also seemed to dwell on a "meanness" in America. In the album's title song, the main character commits a series of murders, and when confronted with the brutality of his crime, he utters a simple explanation for them: "Well, sir, I guess there's just a meanness in this world." Guthrie, too, wrote of a mean world: "1913 Massacre," for instance, is an account of a vigilante attack on miners during Christmas in which scores of young children are killed. But rarely were Guthrie's song-stories so blunt and unforgiving, as are many of Springsteen's songs on *Nebraska*.

Although Springsteen didn't celebrate his Guthrie influence on record again until 1995 with the release of *The Ghost of Tom Joad*, in concert he included songs from *Nebraska*, set amid his full-blown rockers, that kept the link intact. In the mid-1990s, however, Springsteen embraced his Guthrie influence more than ever before, both in the recording studio and on the concert stage. *The Ghost of Tom Joad* lays it out bare. After viewing the John Ford–produced film of John Steinbeck's literary masterpiece, *The Grapes of Wrath*, Springsteen wrote his cinematic, multiversed paean to the main character, Tom Joad. While "The Ghost of Tom Joad" is one of Springsteen's more powerful songs of his post-*Nebraska* period, it succeeds in part because of the tribute it also pays to Guthrie's song, "Tom

Finale of Hard Travelin' concert at Severance Hall, Cleveland, Ohio, 29 September 1996. From left: Indigo Girls (Amy Ray, Emily Saliers), Nora Guthrie, Country Joe McDonald (in rear), Ani DiFranco, John Wesley Harding, Joe Ely (in rear), Ramblin' Jack Elliott, Arlo Guthrie, Jimmie LaFave (in rear), Bruce Springsteen, Billy Bragg (in rear), Tim Robbins, Jimmie Dale Gilmore (in rear), Syd Straw, Paul Metsa, David Pirner (in rear), and others.
PHOTOGRAPH BY ROGER MASTROIANNI. COLLECTION OF ROCK AND ROLL HALL OF FAME AND MUSEUM.

Joad," which Guthrie recorded in 1940 and which first appeared on *Dust Bowl Ballads*. There's a Guthrie-like flow to the song and a commitment to detail that mark many of Guthrie's gems and that Springsteen deeply admired about Guthrie's writing style. Springsteen also included in the song parts of Tom Joad's poignant end-of-film monologue: "Wherever there's a cop beatin' a guy / Wherever there's a fight against the blood and hatred in the air / Look for me Mom, I'll be there." Rarely has an artist so magnificently celebrated his influences, while at the same time creating a unique voice able to speak of issues still so chillingly relevant in America.

Using primarily a Southwest setting, Springsteen tackled in *The Ghost of Tom Joad* themes of homelessness, unemployment, and the shattered lives of migrant workers, ex-cons, and witnesses to the continuing decay of the American Dream. Onstage, the songs took on added vitality and meaning, and Springsteen's *Ghost of Tom Joad* tour, though hushed and void of the anthemic rockers that made him the greatest performer rock has ever known, managed to bring Woody Guthrie back to life again.

Today, Guthrie lives on in the work of other rock and folk-rock artists, perhaps most appreciably in that of Billy Bragg. In 1998 he and the group, Wilco, released *Mermaid Avenue*, an album featuring the music of Bragg and newly discovered lyrics of Guthrie that for years lay nestled among his journals, diaries, short stories, and letters in the New York–based Woody Guthrie Archives. The album not only celebrates Guthrie's influence on Bragg, an English social and political protest singer of considerable talent, but also offers the chance for yet another generation of rock artists to embark on an exploration of Guthrie's music, and, most important, for the results to show up in contemporary rock music in new forms and in new sounds.

Both Bragg and Springsteen performed at the Rock and Roll Hall of Fame and Museum's first American Music Masters program in 1996, which honored Guthrie and his influence on rock and roll. Called *Hard Travelin': The Life and Legacy of Woody Guthrie*, the pair of concerts held in Cleveland that September complemented the conference from which most of the essays in this book arose. Other performers that weekend included Ani DiFranco, who will produce a live album of the final show at Severance Hall called *Hard Travelin'*, the Indigo Girls, David Pirner of the rock group Soul Asylum, Pete Seeger, Arlo Guthrie, Jimmie Dale Gilmore, Ramblin' Jack Elliott, Country Joe McDonald, and others. Those concerts exemplified better than any words on paper Guthrie's ongoing connection to rock and roll.

"Woody wouldn't have been much of a rock and roller had he lived to take part in all that has happened to American music since his passing," his son Arlo remarked in a conversation after the *Hard Travelin'* events. "But I suspect he would have gone on along for the ride."[22]

NOTES

1. Jerome L. Rodnitzky, *Minstrels of the Dawn: The Folk-Protest Singer as a Cultural Hero* (Chicago: Nelson-Hall, 1976), 51.

2. Interview with Peter Guralnick, October 1998.

3. Timothy E. Scheurer, *Born in the U.S.A.: The Myth of America in Popular Music from Colonial Times to the Present* (Jackson: University Press of Mississippi, 1991), 169.

4. Little Richard, Hall of Fame Series, September 1997, Rock and Roll Hall of Fame and Museum, Cleveland, Ohio.

5. Interview with Harold Leventhal, April 1997.

6. Robert Cantwell, *When We Were Good: The Folk Revival* (Cambridge, Mass.: Harvard University Press, 1996), 290.

7. Ibid., 290.

8. Ibid., 292.

9. Leventhal interview.

10. Various artists, *A Vision Shared: A Tribute to Woody Guthrie and Leadbelly* (CK 44034, Columbia, 1988), liner notes (Dylan's remarks transcribed from a BBC radio interview).

11. Ibid.

12. Patricia Romanowski and Holly George-Warren, *The New Rolling Stone Encyclopedia of Rock & Roll* (New York: Fireside, 1995), 343.

13. Rodnitzky, *Minstrels of the Dawn*, 61.

14. Wayne Hampton, *Guerilla Minstrels: John Lennon, Joe Hill, Woody Guthrie, and Bob Dylan* (Knoxville: University of Tennessee Press, 1986), 141.

15. Ibid., 22.

16. Stephen Davis, *Bob Marley* (London: Granada, 1984), 60.

17. Rita Marley, exec. ed., *Bob Marley: Songs of Freedom* by Adrian Boot and Chris Salewicz (New York: Viking Studio Books, 1995), 12.

18. Interview with Bruce Springsteen, October 1998.

19. Ibid.

20. Dave Marsh, *Glory Days: Bruce Springsteen in the 1980s* (New York: Pantheon, 1987), 112.

21. Editors of *Rolling Stone*, *Bruce Springsteen: The Rolling Stone Files* (New York: Hyperion, 1996), 132.

22. Interview with Arlo Guthrie, 1996.

JEFF PLACE

WOODY GUTHRIE'S RECORDED LEGACY

The recordings of Woody Guthrie have proved to be some of the most influential of the twentieth century. What is interesting about Guthrie's career is that almost all of his important recordings were done in a seven-year period from 1940 to 1947. Also, the vast majority of Guthrie's recordings come from a handful of key recording sessions. Nonetheless, to say that Woody was prolific is a rather major understatement. He frequently would write out or type a dozen songs a day. Although literally thousands of these printed song lyrics are now located in various archival collections, more stray songs still turn up from time to time, casually left behind at someone's house or in an office somewhere.

The first recording date of Guthrie's career took place on 21 March 1940 for Alan and Elizabeth Lomax at the Library of Congress. Alan Lomax and his father, John, had been in charge of the Library of Congress Archive of Folk Song since the 1930s and were famous for their field recordings. Among the important folk artists that the Lomaxes had discovered in their travels were Louisiana songster Huddie Ledbetter (a.k.a. Lead Belly) and Mississippi bluesman McKinley Morganfield (a.k.a. Muddy Waters). Alan Lomax had seen Woody performing at the Forrest Theater in New York on 3 March as part of Will Geer's "Grapes of Wrath Evening." That evening Woody appeared with Aunt Molly Jackson, Geer, Lead Belly, Alan and Bess Lomax, and others. Geer, an activist and actor whom Woody met in California, encouraged Woody to come to New York. When Alan Lomax encountered Woody he had finally found the great populist frontier ballad writer for whom he had been looking and who he suspected must exist.[1]

Lomax saw to it that Woody came down from New York to Washington, D.C., to make the recordings. The sessions took place in the Radio Broadcasting Division of the Department of the Interior. Woody recorded sixty-six songs and monologues between 21 and 27 March. He returned to record seven more songs in January of the following year. What is interesting about the Library of Congress sessions, as opposed to his later commercial sessions in New York, is that Woody turned on the professional "Okie" act for Lomax, peppering his introductions with "folksy" language and mannerisms. Other than these recordings, very little of Woody speaking has been released commercially, but if one listens to his delivery during union radio programs you hear a very different Guthrie, certainly a more straightforward one. Jac Holzman of Elektra Records released most of these Library of Congress songs as a three-record box set in 1964 during a time when Woody began to take on a founding father status for the urban folk song revival movement. The collection was reissued in 1988 by Rounder Records.

At the same time that Alan Lomax was arranging sessions for Woody at the Library of Congress, he convinced Victor Records to record Woody. Woody's first commercial recordings were done for Victor in Camden, New Jersey, on 26 April 1940. Victor was curious about the marketability of folk music.[2] This session resulted in his famous Dust Bowl collection, probably the best-known set of recordings of his entire career. They appeared as two separate 78 albums with three records in each. On the cover was a black-and-white photograph of a house bearing the brunt of a dust storm. Victor suggested that Woody include a song about Tom Joad so as to connect the collection to the popular Dust Bowl novel, John Steinbeck's *Grapes of Wrath*. Pete Seeger recalled:

I remember the night he wrote the song "Tom Joad." He says, "Pete, do you know where I can get a typewriter." I said, "Well I'm staying with someone who has one." He says, "Well I gotta write a ballad. I don't usually write ballads to order but Victor wants me to do a whole album of Dust Bowl songs and they say they want one about Tom Joad, the character in the movie *The Grapes of Wrath*." I said "Have you read the book?" He said "No, but I went and saw the movie, great movie." . . . My friend said, "Sure, you can use my typewriter." Woody had a half-gallon jug of wine with him. He sat down and started typing away and stood up every few minutes to test out a verse on his guitar and then sat down and typed some more. About one o'clock me and my friend got so sleepy we couldn't stay awake. . . . In the morning we woke up and there was Woody curled up under the table, half-gallon of wine was almost empty and the completed ballad was sitting near the typewriter. It's still one of his masterpieces.[3]

Although he told Pete that he didn't usually write "ballads to order," Guthrie frequently wrote songs to fit a particular need. Pete Seeger pointed out that "many of the songs he wrote were for occasions that happened and he made them up and didn't expect them to last. I remember in

1944, there was a young lady that came over from Russia, she was a sniper and gotten some kind of medal for shooting down the most Nazis. So Woody took over an old tune and put new words to it for her. They had a big dinner party. The original tune was 'Roll on the Ground.'"[4] Years later, Woody's song "Miss Pavalchencko" is still known. Woody rarely played what would be known today as a paid concert. He tended to play rallies and hootenannies and he would write songs for each event. One such song was "Union Maid," written for Bob and Ina Wood, local union organizers in Oklahoma.

Woody came to New York with an amazing memory for traditional folk and country music songs, many of which he picked up from his mother, radio programs, and his travels. During his radio shows of the 1930s, he performed many of these songs and published them in songbooks that he sold on the air. This body of material became the source for many of the melodies that he adopted for his own creations. For instance, the melody of "John Hardy" was used for "Tom Joad." One of the groups that influenced Woody the most in this regard was the Carter Family, a family singing group from Maces Springs, Virginia. The Carters started recording in 1927 and continued to record into the 1940s (their children have continued to record as the Carter Family). The Carters' songs could frequently be heard on border radio stations in the Southwest. Woody used adaptations of Carter melodies for many of his songs. Their "Wildwood Flower" was used for "The Sinking of the Reuben James." If you listen to the beginning melody of the Carter hymn, "When This World's on Fire" you can hear the melody that became "This Land is Your Land" in Maybelle Carter's guitar lead.

Guthrie's use of well-known melodies for his own lyrics was fairly standard practice among topical songwriters of his day and is still frequent today. When one looks back at union songbooks from the early part of the century one frequently sees "To the tune of . . ." in the upper righthand corner. If you put the new lyrics to a well-known melody, everyone can quickly learn and use the new song without much practice.

In May 1941, Woody found himself in Oregon as a newly hired temporary employee of the federal government. The Bonneville Power Administration wanted Woody to write a number of songs to celebrate and promote hydroelectric power. The intention was to use his songs as part of a soundtrack to a film, but in actuality only three of the twenty-six songs he wrote as part of his employ were used in that capacity. Many of the others were recorded and some of them like "Grand Coulee Dam" and "Pastures of Plenty" are considered among his best-known and loved songs. They were recorded on acetate discs in the basement studio of the BPA[5] and the originals were lost or destroyed. Up until 1948, master recordings were done directly to disc as tape technology was not developed until after World War II. These discs were either aluminum, acetate on aluminum, or acetate on glass. They can be either quite brittle or frequently lose the shellac (acetate) layer over time. For this reason some of Guthrie's 1940s recordings no longer exist as almost all of his sessions took place before the invention and use of tape. In the case of the original BPA recordings, one theory is that they were destroyed in 1953 by an incoming Republican administration suspicious of Guthrie's politics.[6] In 1987, Bill Murlin, an employee of the Bonneville Power Administration, located copies of the originals of these discs among former employees of the BPA. From these acetates the 1987 Rounder Records' collection *Columbia River Collection* was created.

Among the people that Woody knew, lived with, and musically collaborated with during the 1940s were Pete Seeger, Millard Lampell, Lee Hays, and Bess Hawes. This group of individuals as well as ever-changing additional members made up the Almanac Singers. Frequently different groups of Almanacs would spread themselves around various political rallies to maximize effect. Many songs were written at the Almanac House in New York, including the collaborative composition of "The Sinking of the Reuben James."[7] The Almanacs recorded for both the independent Keynote and General labels in 1941. The Keynote Recordings included *The Strange Death of John Doe*, an antiwar album that later came back to haunt the group during the House Un-American Activities hearings in the 1950s. Of the Almanac Singers' recordings for Keynote, only the record "Song for Bridges" backed with "Babe O'Mine" includes Woody. The General recordings were more standard folk songs. General released both *Deep Sea Chanties and Whaling Ballads* and *Sod Buster Ballads*. Both collections included Woody as part of the group. The General recordings were reissued by MCA records on compact disc in 1996.

During the early 1940s, Guthrie was also part of a number of radio programs in New York. Some transcription discs of these programs have survived to the present day and can be found in the Library of Congress and Smithsonian Institution collections. Many of these shows were performed on the publicly owned radio station WNYC. They included shows like *Back Where I Came From* and the *Ballad Gazette*. On the latter, Guthrie would pick a topic like outlaws or whaling ships and fill fifteen minutes with songs, both his own and traditional folk songs, about the topic of the day. With each topic as a case study, it is apparent just how many of these songs he actually knew and could perform when called upon.

Other than the sessions just mentioned, almost every other recording Woody Guthrie made was done for one man. Moses Asch (1905–86) was a New York City recording engineer who started a local record company to supply his neighborhood with Jewish music recordings, a market that had not been served by others. His first venture into folk music was to record Lead Belly singing children's songs in 1941. Asch recalled that "I heard about Woody from Pete [Seeger] and Alan Lomax. It was more Woody heard about me than I heard about him." Woody came into Asch's studio, plopped on the floor and engaged Asch in conversation. Asch remembered,

So he sits there on the floor, and he says, "Asch?" and I say "Yes." He says, "I've heard about you" and I said, "I've heard about you, too." And we got into a conversation—a conversation dealing with the philosophy of life. Because I wasn't interested in a guy just because Alan had recorded him for the Library of Congress; I was interested in someone who would express something. We were a very small record company and I wanted to make sure whatever went into a record meant something for future purposes. People should be able to listen to a contemporary of the period expressing his views. You began to realize after talking to him for a while, that this was a very serious person and a very articulate person. The simplicity of his speech was so deep you start to remind yourself of Walt Whitman.[8]

Woody first recorded for Asch in 1944 and recorded for him up until 1954. Their relationship was beneficial to both. Asch considered himself "the pen with which the artists themselves wrote."[9] His attitude gave Guthrie an outlet to record the songs exactly as he wished. Although Asch took an inactive role in Guthrie's recordings, the two men's relationship ran deeper than just producer and artist. For instance, when Woody needed money, Asch would supply it on an as-needed basis. Woody would also listen to other Asch recordings and review them for the producer. Said Asch, "He wrote me the most important critiques of my records I ever had. He would spend a whole page or two of typed observations of the contents whether it was Greek or Indonesian or African or American folk."[10]

Much of the material Asch recorded has been issued over the years on a myriad of record labels. Many of these recordings are simply unauthorized bootlegs of Asch material but some come from two sets of events. The first occurred when Moses Asch went into a partnership with Herbert Harris, who ran the Union Record Shop in New York, in the early 1940s. Harris also owned Stinson Records. During World War II, there was a shortage of blank acetate discs because of military use of shellac. Asch had a small recording studio and his own company, Asch Records, and many of the most important recording artists in New York were ready to record for him. In addition to Guthrie, Asch recorded Lead

Belly, Pete Seeger, Josh White, Sonny (Terry) and Brownie (McGhee), Richard Dyer-Bennet, Burl Ives, Coleman Hawkins, James P. Johnson, Mary Lou Williams, Langston Hughes, Les Paul, and others. Asch's problem was that he had no discs. Harris had discs but no artists. The relationship between Asch and Harris lasted until it became no longer necessary. Some of the original discs went to Stinson, some stayed with Asch. To make things even more confusing, some of the metal pressing plates at the plant and other acetates were lost in the bankruptcies of Asch Records and its successor, Disc Records. Moe Asch personally retained many of the discs and continued to release them over the years in various combinations.

The second set of circumstances that resulted in numerous Guthrie recordings involved Woody's relationship with Cisco Houston (1916–61) who met Woody through actor Will Geer in California. Houston and Geer had been listening to Woody on a local radio station and decided to pay him a visit. Cisco would prove to be Woody's most important friend and musical partner. Cisco's voice, without the edge that Woody's had, was smooth—perhaps too smooth for folk music—and for this reason he never received the respect he deserved. He had wanted to be a motion picture actor and hoped his movie-star looks would be his ticket. Unfortunately, poor eyesight made it impossible for him to read the scripts. Houston also recorded independently for Asch and was a frequent presence in Asch's studio. His steady guitar work frequently kept Woody's erratic playing in time and he appears with Woody on many of the recordings he made. His harmonies can also be heard on many of the Guthrie recordings. Asch remembered, "It became much easier after Cisco got in, because Cisco was so good at the guitar and so good at adapting himself to others. Woody could do whatever he wanted to do without having to worry what the next guy was doing. Cisco covered it up."[11]

Profoundly influenced by World War II and the events happening in the rest of the world, Cisco, Woody, their friend Jim Longhi, and their guitars joined the Merchant Marine and served two tours of duty wanting to do their parts. Woody was always proud to say that they had been torpedoed twice and it was on break from the Merchant Marine in April 1944 that Woody and Cisco, perhaps feeling especially mortal, visited Asch and unloaded into his microphones as many songs as they could record. They recorded more than 160 songs during a six-week period in Asch's studio. This mother lode is the bulk of Guthrie's recorded legacy. It includes dozens of traditional folk and country songs as well as many of Woody's own songs. It was in one of the late April sessions that Guthrie first recorded "This Land is Your Land." Woody first wrote the song in 1940 as a reaction to the song "God Bless America." His version was

Woody Guthrie and Cisco Houston playing guitars and singing during FDR Bandwagon stint, 1944. COURTESY OF WOODY GUTHRIE ARCHIVES.

originally called "God Blessed America for You and Me" and contained two additional verses that are not found in later versions. One of them is a protest against the ownership of private property. It was thought for years that Woody had never recorded this version of the song, but the April 1944 recording does include the "private property" verse. These sessions frequently also included North Carolinian harmonica player Sonny Terry as well as occasional help from Lead Belly or Pete Seeger. Much of the surviving material recorded at these sessions was issued by Smithsonian Folkways in 1997–98 as the *Asch Recordings*. In addition, Woody and Cisco recorded a number of anti-Hitler, antifascist songs that were never issued by Asch as the war ended before Asch was able to get the planned record out.[12]

During his ownership of Asch Records, Moses Asch released Woody Guthrie recordings as part of his *Blues* (Asch 550) recording and his Folksay series (Asch 432). In addition he had two album collections of Woody's material, *Woody Guthrie* (Asch 432) and *Documentary #1: Struggle* (Asch 360).

Besides his work with Asch, in 1944 Woody also appeared as a member of the cast of an Alan Lomax radio play *The Martins and the Coys*.

The show used the model of the famous Kentucky Hatfield and McCoy feuds to portray two feuding families who instead turned their anger to fighting the Nazis. The play had included many of the artists from the New York folk song movement and it featured many of Woody's original songs including "You Fascists Bound to Lose." The show had been broadcast over the BBC as Lomax was unable to find an American station to broadcast it. It was recorded by the BBC and copies of the recording remained with Lomax.

In 1945, Asch Records went out of business and Asch followed it with Disc Records, a collaboration between himself and jazz impresario Norman Granz. Granz later went on to found Verve Records taking with him the jazz titles. The Disc release *Jazz at the Philharmonic* proved to be both hugely successful and, ironically, the label's undoing. Disc simply did not have the cash flow to handle demand for the record and the subsequent demand for lucrative artist contracts that success bred. The label went out of business in 1947. Asch and Granz later briefly joined forces again in the 1960s with the short lived Verve/Folkways label.

The most important Guthrie recordings on Disc before its demise were his children's songs. During this time Woody and his second wife Marjorie Greenblatt (stage name Mazia) were living in the Coney Island neighborhood of New York City. Woody made up songs to sing to his daughter Cathy, to whom he referred lovingly as Miss Stackabones. He claimed that Cathy helped him with songs like "Car Song (Riding in the Car)" and "Clean-o." Many of these are still loved by children today. In 1947, Disc Records released *Songs to Grow On: Nursery Days* (Disc 605), with *Songs to Grow On: Work Songs for Nursery Days* (Disc 601) issued a year later. Owing to their importance, Guthrie's children's recordings were among the very first Asch issued whenever a new format came along. Moses Asch also had a children's label called Cub Records that issued *Songs to Grow On* material in 1948 with packaging more consistent with the children's market.

In April 1947, Woody was again asked to come out to Spokane, Washington, to sing songs in support of the Bonneville Power Administration. Woody wrote Asch on 22 April that the BPA wanted Asch to put together an album of the BPA Songs.[13] Upon his return, Asch got him to record fresh versions of his Columbia River songs and some of his Dust Bowl ballads.[14] These were issued as *Ballads from the Dust Bowl* (Disc 610).

On 1 May 1948, Asch, along with Marian Distler, started what was to become his most famous record label, Folkways Records and Service Corporation. He would go on to issue more than 2,100 albums over the next thirty-eight years, the equivalent of about one a week. During the history of Folkways he continued to issue Guthrie material from the remaining masters he had from the 1940s.[15] The Folkways label and Moses Asch's collection of recordings and papers came to the Smithsonian Institution in 1987 with the stipulation that all recordings remain in print. His work has been continued as Smithsonian Folkways Recordings, which was founded in 1988.

Also in 1948, Victor discontinued *Dust Bowl Ballads*. On 26 July 1948, they wrote Woody as Woodward W. Guthrie (not Woodrow), "It is not our intention to release these records again for public sale for the time being. It is entirely conceivable that some time in the future when we feel that the market is in better shape we might release one or both of the albums once more."[16] Woody and Moses Asch used this letter as a justification to re-release the recording on Folkways, which they did later in the year (Folkways FP 11/5212).

Although Woody frequently had ideas for recordings, sometimes Asch suggested a topic. For instance, Asch commissioned Woody to write a set of songs commemorating the twentieth anniversary of the deaths of labor martyrs Nicola Sacco and Bartolomeo Vanzetti. Woody came down with a rare case of writer's block when it came to this recording. Never one to be loose with his money, Asch felt this project was important enough to sponsor a monthlong field trip for Woody and Cisco to Boston to retrace the steps of both men. Guthrie still hesitated and wrote Asch, "I think the best thing we can do is postpone the recorded songs based on the frame-up of Sacco and Vanzetti. To delay the most important dozen songs I have ever worked on is more of a pain to me than it could ever be to you, but I feel like the trip to Boston and its outskirts was a bit hurried and hasty."[17] Woody finally wrote the songs in the days before the session in January 1947. Listening to these songs, one can hear some hesitation in the voices of both Woody and Cisco, as if they are still reading from the printed lyrics. The record was not released until 1960 on Asch's Folkways label (#5485, reissued as Smithsonian Folkways 40060).

Instead of doing the Sacco record, Woody suggested doing a recording based on other labor martyrs.[18] Also in the letters to Moses Asch, which can be found in the Asch Collection at the Smithsonian, Guthrie suggested many other projects, sometimes designing the graphics as well. On 12 February 1945, Guthrie wrote and suggested a number of projects. On his list were an album of fiddle tunes, an album of pioneer songs, a cowboy songs record, and one of sea songs. Guthrie wrote, "I really have high hopes for this sea album, especially since I've been listening a lot to General's album of *Deep Sea Chanties and Whaling Ballads*. We could do a lot better this time around with the same idea." In June 1946, Woody wrote Asch and stated, "First, by my way of thinking we have not touched the bulk of my best things. No, not even with the several jillion masters we made together with Sonny, Cisco and others."[19] According to Asch, "We would sit together and plan projects. Like authors he would be interested in ideas from others. He planned at least forty different albums."[20] Another record suggested by Woody was a followup to *Documentary One: Struggle*, a record called *Documentary Law and Order*. "The way these lynchings, hangings, tarrings, featherings, and blindings have been taking place all over our good nation, I have been working up an idea of an album of records, another issue of our *Documentary Struggle* album."[21] Of the songs Woody suggested, including a song he strongly promoted called "The Blinding of Isaac Woodward," none of them seem to have been actually recorded. The only one that is still known is "You Fascists Bound to Lose." Woody also suggested an album of songs he had written about World War II heroes.[22] The typed lyrics for many of these projects are part of the Smithsonian Asch Collection.

Guthrie's marriage to Marjorie introduced Woody to his wife's Jewish heritage. Her mother, Aliza Waitzman Greenblatt, wrote poetry in Yiddish and was known in the Jewish community.[23] Woody made an effort to learn as much as he could about the Jewish faith. He recorded a five-minute telling of the Hanukkah story of his own composition. He also wrote a number of children's Hanukkah songs for Asch. Asch, who was also Jewish, wanted to release a record of Hanukkah songs. Woody's creations consisted of switching a few words here and there of old American folk songs to the Hanukkah theme. "How Many Biscuits Can You Eat?" became "How Many Latkes Can You Eat, It's Hanukkah."

Another offbeat recording project was Woody's interpretation of the *Rubaiyat* of Omar Khayyám into 1940s terms. He recorded it with Cisco Houston and it consisted of a dozen or more sides of segments. No record exists of the proper order and it is quite hard to follow. The entire *Rubaiyat* remains unreleased.

Starting in 1951, Woody recorded a number of songs for his publisher, the Richmond Organization. The publisher lent Woody a tape recorder and he recorded many of his compositions for documentation. In a letter to Howard Richmond, Woody stated, "This is the best way to show you, and even other artists, just how I aim for my music and notes to go."[24] These recordings, now in the Woody Guthrie Archives in New York, have never been released commercially but they constitute an amazing collection of his more obscure songs.

Woody did record two songs for Decca Records (which released the Weavers' recordings). The session was on 7 January 1952 and consisted of "This Land is Your Land" and "Kissin' On (Gave Her Kisses)."

Woody was somewhat ambivalent about the Decca sessions. He wrote Asch reflecting on his Disc recordings, "To see my songs grow joine [sic] up hands and spirits and fighting plans with you long shelf of ethnical recordings, makes me a good bit prouder than anything I am ever apt or liable to cut very deep for Mr. Deccyyye [sic]."[25] However, the effects of Huntington's disease, which had begun to consume him, are apparent in his voice and the sides were never released.

Moses Asch was unaware of the history of Huntington's disease in Woody's family and its presence in Woody. As Woody's behavior became more unstable, Asch assumed it was alcohol, and Woody recorded less and less for him. One last session on 18 January 1954 included Sonny Terry, Ramblin' Jack Elliott, Brownie McGhee, and Alonzo Scales. The disease is apparent in Woody's voice, a situation not helped by the drinking going on in the studio. At the end, Woody sadly spent fifteen minutes trying to remember the words to "The Sinking of the Reuben James." Asch finally cut the tape and excused them for the day (from Smithsonian reel FW-093). It would be Woody's last recording session.

Woody did not record again after 1954, but his influence on future musicians cannot be overstated. The image of the troubadour with harmonica rack and guitar that Woody put forth became especially iconic with the imitation of Bob Dylan. In the years since, many artists have recorded his songs and there have been numerous recorded tributes to him. Bob Dylan's first album includes his "Song to Woody," including lyrics put to the tune of Guthrie's song "1913 Massacre." In 1996, the British singer Billy Bragg commenced a project to put music to some of Woody's lyrics that had not been recorded, resulting in *Mermaid Avenue*, an album featuring Bragg and the roots-based contemporary rockers Wilco, in 1998.

It is intriguing to contemplate Woody's impact: he rarely played an organized paid engagement and sold very few records during his active career. In the late twentieth-century world of videos and large concert tours, for someone to have as much influence as he did is exhilarating. Various archives and collections have been busy at work preserving and cataloging Woody's recorded legacy. With these efforts, Woody's music will be accessible to all in the next century and will continue to be influential as his legend grows.

NOTES

This essay would not have been possible without the lifelong dedication and research of Guy Logsdon of Tulsa, Oklahoma, who uncovered much of this information. Also, The Smithsonian Center for Folklife and Cultural Heritage in Washington, D.C., houses many research sources, including the Moses and Frances Asch Collection. The archive is open by appointment and can be reached at (202) 287-3180 or by e-mail at cfpcs.jeff@ic.si.edu or by Internet at www.si.edu/folkways.

1. Joe Klein, *Woody Guthrie: A Life* (New York: Knopf, 1980), 143.

2. Ibid., 158.

3. Pete Seeger, from taped interview in a London hotel room, 1 March 1964; Smithsonian reel FW-1252.

4. From Folkways LP 31002.

5. See the biblio/discography, this volume.

6. Timothy Egan, "40s Songs by Guthrie for Project are Found," *New York Times*, 4 August 1991.

7. Guy Logsdon, liner notes to Smithsonian Folkways CD 40021.

8. Moses Asch, "Interview conducted by Guy Logsdon, New York," 8 July 1974 (from interviewer's transcript).

9. Moses Asch to Israel Young, *Sing Out!* 26, no. 1 (1977).

10. Asch, "Interview."

11. Ibid.

12. See *That's Why We're Marching: World War II and the American Folk Song Movement* (Smithsonian Folkways 40021).

13. Letter to Asch, Smithsonian Asch Collection.

14. Guy Logsdon, liner notes to Smithsonian Folkways 40100.

15. See the biblio/discography for titles.

16. Letter to Guthrie from J. L. Hallstrom, RCA Victor, Smithsonian Asch Collection.

17. Letter to Asch, 4 November 1946, Smithsonian Asch Collection.

18. Letter to Asch, 2 January 1946, Smithsonian Asch Collection.

19. Letter to Asch, 21 June 1946, Smithsonian Asch Collection.

20. Asch, "Interview."

21. Undated letter to Asch, Smithsonian Asch Collection.

22. Letter to Asch, 22 June 1947, after midnight, Smithsonian Asch Collection.

23. Klein, *Woody Guthrie*, 224.

24. Letter to Richmond, 4 January 1951, letter courtesy of Guy Logsdon.

25. Letter to Asch, 8 November 1951, Smithsonian Asch Collection.

CRAIG WERNER

DEMOCRATIC VISIONS, DEMOCRATIC VOICES
Woody as Writer

When Walt Whitman titled his epic of American democracy "Song of Myself," he invoked an image that remains central to our populist literary tradition: the writer as singer. For Whitman and Vachel Lindsay, for Carl Sandburg and Langston Hughes, the ideal of America could not be separated from the ideal of a truly American voice, a voice they heard more clearly in the songs of the American people than in our novels and poems. As one of the few American writers who was a singer first and a writer second, Woody Guthrie occupies a special place in the tradition that flows from Whitman through Jack London and Theodore Dreiser to Sandburg, Hughes, the young John Dos Passos, and John Steinbeck, who was probably the most powerful of Woody's literary inspirations. Like Whitman, Woody conceived of language as an expression of "the average, the bodily, the concrete, the democratic, the popular."[1] Like Steinbeck, he viewed writing as political struggle, not as Wordsworth's romantic expression of "emotion recollect'd in tranquility." Woody believed that, whatever their failings, the people he'd grown up with in Oklahoma and the hoboes he met on the road had a more clear and trustworthy understanding of America than the intellectuals who professed to define literary excellence. Casting his lot with the dispossessed, Woody sought to forge a writing style that rang with the communal energy of "This Land Is Your Land," "Hard Travelin'," or "Goin' Down the Road Feelin' Bad."

Woody Guthrie's importance in the American literary tradition cannot be separated from the sound of his voice. He shared Whitman's belief that the American voice must be truly American, not a pale imitation of an English or classical model. That voice, Whitman and Woody agreed, must not resonate with the rhythms of Shakespeare and Chaucer, but roll with the strong cadences and "varied carols" of the American people: the riverboat pilots on the Mississippi; the women sweeping the dooryards of Kentucky and Kansas; the sons and daughters of slaves gathering in the Baptist churches and juke joints of Alabama and Mississippi; the Cherokee and the Chippewa and the Cheyenne; the carpenters and blacksmiths in Whitman's Brooklyn, Sandburg's Chicago, and Hughes's Harlem.

At its best, Woody's writing is at once intensely personal and broadly democratic. Paradoxically, his work sounds less democratic when Woody attempted to imitate the voices he heard around him. His representations of the spoken language of Mexicans and blacks too often descend into near minstrelsy. He's at his best when he sounds most like himself, most like the singer who welcomed the actual sounds of those voices into his own consciousness. In Woody's voice, you can hear echoes of everything he ever heard; his songs reach easily across lines of race and class and region. Democracy sings in each of us individually, Woody intimates, as long as we understand that who we are—what we sound like—is shaped by and at best responds to everyone we hear.

Woody's connection with the populist tradition was conscious and intense. He read and admired Whitman's poetry. At times he experimented with Whitmanesque verse forms. The unpublished poem "Voice" reads like an extension of Whitman's catalogues in "Song of Myself" or "A Song for Occupations":

> Oh but I have not even heard this voice, these voices
> On the stages, screens, radios, records, juke boxes,
> In magazines nor not in newspapers, seldom in courtrooms
> And more seldom when students and policemen study the faces
> Behind the voices
> And I thought as I saw a drunken streetwalking man mutter
> And spit and curse into the wind out of the café's plate glass,
> That maybe, if I looked close enough, I might hear
> Some more of my voice.[2]

Even as he made use of Whitman's stylistic innovations—the lengthy lines, the accumulation of concrete detail—Woody maintained a certain suspicion of Old Walt who by the 1930s had become part of the "official" literary tradition. If Whitman played a central role in Mike Gold's attempts to construct a radical literary tradition for the readers of the *Daily Worker*, he was also a favorite of Fourth of July orators who sought to make the Whitman of "O Captain, My Captain" safe for sentimental jingoism.

For Woody, the problem stemmed not from Whitman's attitude, but from the sound of his voice, which remained literary despite his thirst for something more immediate. In a 1947 notebook passage, Woody turned his attention to three of the writers most frequently celebrated as linchpins of the radical tradition. Woody begins by raising a fundamental issue: "I ask me this question and if I didn't answer it I couldn't go on. Does Whitman, Sandburg, or [Russian poet Alexandr] Pushkin, either one, actually talk in the lingo, brogue, and ways of talking through of the kinds and breeds of the working people I've met and dealt with?" The answer, sadly, is no. Woody credits Whitman with making "glorious the works, labors, hopes, dreams and feeling of my people" but emphasizes his failure to speak "in the sorts of words my people think, talk, dance and sing."[3]

The final words are crucial. Woody's people "dance and sing" more readily than they read and write. Never confusing their orality with simplicity or stupidity, Woody's voice grew as he sang for them while they danced and sang along with him. His reputation, quite rightly, rests primarily on his songwriting. It would be possible to make an argument for his place in American literature based on the "literary" qualities of "This Land Is Your Land," "Pastures of Plenty," and "Plane Wreck at Los Gatos (Deportees)." But there's no real point to confusing songs and literature; lyrics almost always work better when they're sung than when they're read on the page. Conversely, most literary works benefit from the reader's ability to return to lines, savor images, and grapple with complexities that are lost even during the most effective public readings. The distinction was even clearer in Woody's time than in our era when, as Walter Ong points out in *The Presence of the Word*, technological developments have blurred the difference between oral and written forms.[4] The effectiveness of dense literary lyrics like Bob Dylan's "Desolation Row" or "Just Like Tom Thumb's Blues" depends largely on the recordings that allow audiences to return to the same performance again and again. In contrast, Woody and poetic blues lyricists like Robert Johnson knew that their songs had to communicate clearly to an audience that was unlikely to pore over symbolism, pursue allusions, or ponder dense metaphors.

This doesn't mean musical performance is inherently less complex than literature. The complexity, however, derives more from the context of performance and the shared energies of the group than from the text itself. The comparison between Steinbeck's *Grapes of Wrath* and Woody's "Tom Joad" helps illuminate the difference. In his novel, Steinbeck juxtaposes the immediately accessible story of the Joad family with far-reaching meditations on the mythic energies of the American landscape. Woody's adaptation of Steinbeck in the song "Tom Joad" functions both to spread the word and to expose the novel to an audience with relatively little access to the type of education needed to interpret Steinbeck's subtleties. The song doesn't do the same thing as the novel; rather, the oral and written voices complement one another. And at every stage, Woody's primary point is to expand the democratic vision expressed in both forms.

Not that Woody saw his songwriting as entirely separate from his literary endeavors. He filled his notebooks with songs and fragments of lyrics, many of which he never recorded. The powerful antilynching song "Slipknot" certainly compares favorably with the blues poetry of Hughes or Richard Wright. The repetition of the first line marks the piece as a song lyric, but the final stanza loses little of its power on the page:

> I don't know who makes the law of that slipknot.
> I don't know who makes the law of that slipknot.
> But the bones of many a men are a whistling in the wind.
> Just because they tie their laws with a slipknot.[5]

If Woody's importance in American culture generally rests on his music, his place in the populist literary tradition rests largely on his ability to infuse his writing with the communal energy that powers his best songs. His 1943 autobiography *Bound for Glory* stands alongside Steinbeck's *Of Mice and Men* and *The Grapes of Wrath* as one of the best books on life during the Great Depression. Although clearly less effective than *Bound for Glory*, Woody's posthumously published novel *Seeds of Man* contains scenes that suggest he could have developed into a significant proletarian writer had he devoted more of his energy to fiction.

The real power of Woody's literary voice, however, emerges most clearly in the montage of unpublished writing assembled by Dave Marsh and Harold Leventhal and published under the title *Pastures of Plenty: A Self-Portrait*. As the anthology demonstrates, Woody's restless imagination made use of practically every type of writing imaginable: letters, lyrics, aphorisms, notebooks, poetry, fragments of essays, scenes from never-completed works of fiction. Woody wrote constantly. He analyzed political events, engaged in erotic flights of fantasy, and constantly reflected on how his personal experience illuminated his dreams and fears for America. Woody's newspaper column, "Woody Sez," carries on the satirical tradition of newspaper humorists from Mark Twain through Langston Hughes, who created a similarly "simpleminded" protagonist for his column in black America's leading newspaper, the *Chicago Defender*. The following passage from "Woody Sez" gives a representative sense of how Guthrie's everyday voice cuts through the layers of political rhetoric: "I never stopped to think of it before, but you know—a policeman will jest

Woody Guthrie signing a copy of his autobiography, Bound For Glory, 1943. COURTESY OF WOODY GUTHRIE ARCHIVES.

stand there an let a banker rob a farmer, or a finance man rob a workin man. But if a farmer robs a banker—you wood have a hold dern army of cops out a shooting at him. Robbery is a chapter of etiquette."[6]

Woody shared both hopes and fears with Whitman. As he entered the last stage of his career, Whitman composed a manifesto titled "Democratic Vistas" that remains a touchstone of populist aesthetics. Questioning the relative optimism of his own earlier work, Whitman defines the role of the American writer as that of a "physician diagnosing some deep disease."[7] Gazing out on a literary scene defined by irony and a "scornful superciliousness," Whitman calls on America's writers to create "a new founded literature, not merely to copy and reflect existing surfaces, or pander to what is called taste—not only to amuse, pass away time, celebrate the beautiful, the refined, the past, or exhibit technical, rhythmic or grammatical dexterity—but a literature underlying life."[8] The key to such a literature lies in forging a voice, at once individual and communal, capable of encompassing "our own combination, continuation, and points of view."[9] Failing to do so, Whitman warned, would be fatal to the democratic ideal:

not having which native, first-class formulation, she will flounder about, and her other, however imposing, eminent greatness, prove merely a passing gleam; but truly having which, she will understand herself, live nobly, nobly contribute, emanate, and, swinging, poised safely on herself, illumin'd and illuming, become a full-form'd world . . . the main thing being the average, the bodily, the concrete, the democratic, the popular, on which all the superstructures of the future are to permanently rest.[10]

If Whitman sets out the theory of the populist artist, Woody Guthrie provides a case study in its application. His primary contribution involves the way his literary voice incorporates the energies that powered his music. Writing on the connections between West African and African-American culture, Ed Pavlic has developed an approach that helps illuminate the connection between music and literary texts. Pavlic focuses on the intersection of what he calls "horizontal" and "vertical" processes. Horizontal processes are those that take place between people in the social world: conversations, dances, performances where the audience and artist directly interact. Vertical processes are those that take place primarily in the consciousness of the individual artist, often located in seclusion from the social world. In African-American culture, "call and response" provides the point of connection between the two. A musical performance begins with the artist "calling" to the audience by singing a line or playing a riff. Although the call is shaped by the leader—who frequently crafts it while separated from the community—the material of the initial call usually comes from a body of images familiar to most members of the community.

Those images have survived in large part because they express something about the shared experience of the group that has been passed down through many previous performances. That Woody almost always used familiar melodies for his lyrics reflects his understanding of this dimension of call and response. Once the call has been issued, the audience is free to respond in any way it sees fit: through shouts of "amen," shifts in body posture, repetitions of the riff, or rhythmic variation. The response doesn't always have to be affirmative. Other voices, each drawing on its own vertical process, can agree, argue, redirect the dialogue, raise new questions. Any response that gains attention and elicits a response of its own becomes a new call. Usually the individual who issued the first call responds to the response and remains the focal point of the ongoing dialogue. But it doesn't have to be that way. The position of leadership can pass from individual to individual, community to community.[11]

Woody's description of the blues speaks to the heart of the horizontal process: "And you're going to hear lots of other people singing your blues right along with you. The blues is the voice of the finger that points to your world and shows you what's wrong, shows you how to get together and fix it."[12] At its best, the call and response dynamic provides communities lacking access to the networks of official culture a way of comparing their experience and analyzing its meaning. In musical terms, call and response relies on the immediacy of physical presence. The energy of the performance passes through horizontal space, gathering energy as additional voices enter the conversation. The effectiveness of a horizontal process is never the result of individual genius in any isolated romantic sense. It is truly a group process and, as such, is difficult to discuss in aesthetic terms that place a primary value on concepts such as "originality" and "individual genius."

One of the most stirring episodes in Woody's life reflects his profound understanding of how little those concepts had to do with his sense of the democratic American voice. Recounting his experiences as Woody's shipmate in the Merchant Marine during World War II, Jimmy Longhi tells a story about his friend's confrontation with segregation in the military. Midway through a particularly perilous Atlantic crossing, their ship came under heavy attack. Jimmy, Woody, and Cisco Houston ventured below decks to sing for the troops, hoping to take their minds off the depth charges exploding all around them. During a pause in their performance, Woody heard the sound of a "glorious Negro chorus."[13]

Seeking the source of the sound, Woody discovered fifty black soldiers crowded into a toilet room. Longhi describes entering the room to encounter an energetic call and response between the group and its commanding officer Daniel Rutledge. Reaching deep into the shared images of the gospel tradition, Rutledge sang out his sermon on the coming "Judgment Day" and the soldiers responded with cries of "Free! Free!"[14]

Accepting Rutledge's invitation to sing for the troops, Woody surprised them by singing "John Henry," initiating an exchange of songs. When Woody offered to let Rutledge play his guitar, the black officer noticed Woody's slogan—this machine kills fascists—and improvised a sermon on the connection between the war against Hitler and the struggle against American racism. Rutledge called out "An' we know that after we win this war, when the king of slavery is dead, when the king of slavery is dead, things is gonna *change* for the people of Israel!"[15] When the men responded "Change! Change!" Rutledge held Woody's guitar "above his head like a weapon" and hammered home the main point of the movement that returning black veterans would help define and carry through: "An' the walls will come tumblin' down!"[16]

The most immediate wall, Longhi recalls, was the one separating the black and white troops on Woody's ship. Hearing the commotion in the toilet, a white officer arrived to summon Woody back to the white soldiers waiting for him to resume his performance. Woody refused to return unless the black soldiers could come with him. Refusing to accept the officer's insistence that segregation was a policy he didn't support but was powerless to change, Woody insisted on seeing higher and higher-ranking officers until he found himself face to face with the ship's commander. Determining that the commander was a fan of Benny Goodman's swing band, Woody pointed out that Goodman's group included black musicians Teddy Wilson and Lionel Hampton. Although many of the clubs Goodman played in banned integrated "dance bands," Goodman circumvented the Jim Crow laws by defining Wilson and Hampton as "concert performers." When the commander acquiesced, Woody and Rutledge proudly led the black troops back to the "white" area of the ship where Woody's "no dancing" pledge lasted about as long as it did in the clubs where Goodman played.

However stirring such moments were—and Woody worked hard to duplicate them whenever he sang—his experience with publishing made it clear that the literary world had little understanding of or interest in horizontal processes. Even at a time when the success of *The Grapes of Wrath* and Richard Wright's *Native Son* demonstrated the commercial potential of radical writing, the response to a project put together by Woody, Pete Seeger, and Alan Lomax provided strong evidence that the literary elite was at best indifferent to the sound of America's horizontal voice. During 1941, Woody, Seeger, and Lomax joined on a project designed to increase awareness of the songs that America was actually singing. Relying on Lomax to collect the songs of working people throughout the country, Woody and Seeger contributed their musical knowledge to a manuscript titled *Hard Hitting Songs of Hard-Hit People*. It was intended both as a record of the American voice and an inspiration for those willing to join in the song. Steinbeck, then at the peak of his popularity, agreed to write an introduction. But no commercial house was interested in publishing the work. By the time it was finally published in 1964, it was more of a historical curiosity than a contribution to a living political struggle.

If the literary world resisted or ignored horizontal communal processes, it was more open to individual reflections about those processes, especially those grounded in what Pavlic calls "vertical" processes. Vertical processes are usually conceived in terms of psychological rather than social space. The artist—usually a writer, composer, or painter working in relative isolation—contemplates the complexity of his or her own experience, reaching down into the infinite depths of the self rather than out into the social world. At times, the process of introspection can result in significant social insights. But it can just as easily slip into solipsistic denial of the external world. At the time Woody began to write, approaches to modernist literature that emphasized vertical exploration at the expense of social engagement dominated discussions of American literature in academia and most mass-market literary periodicals. By the 1950s, the emergence of a particularly nihilistic strain of existentialism in intellectual life—along with the rise of McCarthyism in American politics—had created a literary context in which any nonironic treatment of horizontal dynamics was viewed as a mark of profound naïveté.

Like Steinbeck and Hughes, Woody refused the premise. Recall that his criticism of populist literature rested on the fact that even Whitman and Sandburg spoke with the voices of poets rather than those of the common people. In his own writing, Woody reflected on the problem posed by trying to write the singing voice. Especially in *Bound for Glory*, he attempted to forge a style that displayed both the personal exploration and the horizontal awareness that made him who he was. When Woody does portray inward-looking psychological processes, they are almost always associated with destructive energies. The clearest case concerns Woody's mother, who retreated deeper and deeper into a vertical space, interacting only distantly with the social world, including her family. Shortly before she is institutionalized, she is reduced to "staring at a lump of melted glass crystals" left over from the fire that killed Woody's sister Clara. As Woody observes with sadness: "She concentrated on her worries until it got the best of her."[17]

Rather than retreating into his own private world, the young Woody determined to find a voice capable of connecting with the people around him. "I got a little braver," he writes, "and made up songs telling what I thought was wrong and how to make it right, songs that said what everybody in that country was thinking. And this has held me ever since."[18] Shortly after the publication of *Bound for Glory*, Woody published an essay in the *New York Times* in which he elaborated on his belief that "singing and working and fighting are so close together you can't hardly tell where one quits and the other one begins."[19] Woody observes that music speaks with a collective voice: "Music has got to say what we're all trying to say."[20] Emphasizing the immediacy of horizontal processes, he challenges composers to move beyond the comfortable stance of their vertical processes: "People need music to march by and to fight with, and if you composers don't dish it out right on the split second, you'll find folks passing you up and making up their own and playing and singing it."[21] Woody concludes the article with a humorous reflection on the limitations of his own writing: "And rather than me to keep on scribbling here, it would be a whole lot better if we both always keep our eye peeled and our ear cocked to what all of us are trying to say."[22]

Repeatedly, Woody emphasizes that the spirit of the music is revolutionary. The sound, as much as the lyrics, communicates a shared determination to overthrow the institutions that refuse to hear the people's voice. In his essay on the blues, Woody describes Blind Sonny Terry's music as a call to arms: "Here is a spirit, a spirit not only of the hard hit, poll tax, sharecropper South, but a spirit that seems to bust loose out of the landlord's very hands, and a spirit that tramples old Jim Crow into the dirt of the earth."[23] Woody calls on the audience that listens to his records in the privacy of their own homes to connect their vertical meditations with the horizontal energies that shaped the music: "Let your mind roam and let your thoughts ramble just like I've done here. Listen for a spirit, and a big broad, world wide feeling."[24]

Bound for Glory opens with a scene that emphasizes music's ability to transcend social divisions. The first paragraph emphasizes the shared burdens imposed on common people of all colors by the economic system that forces them out onto the rails. Writing in a voice that balances the personal "I"—the nearly obsessive focus of almost all autobiographical writing—and the communal "we," Woody describes

men of all colors bouncing along in the boxcar. We stood up. We laid down. We piled around on each other. We used each other for pillows. I could smell the sour and bitter sweat soaking through my own khaki shirt and britches, and the work clothes, overhauls and saggy, dirty suits of the other guys. My mouth was full of some kind of gray mineral dust that was about an inch deep all over the floor. We looked like a gang of lost corpses heading back to the boneyard.[25]

The passage establishes Woody's basic theme of solidarity through images of song. Sharing their horizontal space on a train "headed sixty miles an hour in a big cloud of poison dust due straight to nowhere,"[26] the riders—Woody specifically identifies them as black, white, Mexican, and Indian—raise their voices in a song so deeply embedded in the American consciousness that no one knows or cares whether its origins are "black" or "white": "This train is bound for glory, / This train!"[27]

Immediately, however, Woody underscores the difficulties of maintaining the sense of democratic connection. One white rider aims a racial slur at a black companion, calling him "Stepinfetchit."[28] Attempting to resist the divisive forces that can explode into forms of violence that serve the interests of the oppressors, Woody reminds his fellow riders that all of them are subject to attack by the railroad police. Despite Woody's efforts, the scene disintegrates rapidly into something akin to the Battle Royal scene in Ralph Ellison's *Invisible Man* in which ten black boys are blind-folded and placed in a boxing ring where they flail away at one another for the entertainment of a circle of "respectable" white citizens. Woody describes the fight that breaks out in the boxcar as a doomed and futile struggle. The men, he suggests, are venting their frustration not against the economic system that denies them work and subsidizes the police who brutalize them but against what they experience as the intractable powers of the universe:

Men fighting against men. Color against color. Kin against kin. Race pushing against race. And all of us battling against the wind and the rain and that bright crackling lightning that booms and zooms, that bathes his eyes in the white sky, wrestles a river to a standstill, and spends the night drunk in a whorehouse.[29]

Beneath the chaos, however, Woody hears a different type of energy in the natural world: "The cloudbursts got madder and splashed through all of the lakes, laughing and singing, and then a wail in the wind would get a low start and cry in the timber like the cry for freedom of a conquered people."[30]

As much as any white writer of his era, Woody understood the central-ity of race to the social struggle. As *Bound for Glory*'s opening scene indi-cates, he knew that racial divisions could drive people apart. He never makes the romantic mistake of confusing social connection with peace, harmony, and oneness with nature. He knows that the poverty of dispos-sessed communities frequently sets them against one another. His experi-ence growing up in a part of the country where blacks, whites, and In-dians interacted made it clear that race often provided the spark that set violence off. Nonetheless, he saw and expressed the powerful democratic possibilities hidden in the diversity. His descriptions frequently sound a note of Whitmanesque celebration: "The town was alive, booming with the mixed voices of Negro farmers, the broke-down, hungry, dirt farm-ers, and the talking of the Indians that sometimes took on a high note, when some buck pointed away out yonder with his hand, and made a big curving motion, so that you could tell that he was talking about the whole country, the whole thing, the whole problem and, probably, the whole people."[31] Woody knew that a truly American voice—the encom-passing voice of the Indian contemplating the vast landscape that had been stolen from his people—could not leave anyone out.

Music is crucial in attaining an inclusive voice and vision. Near the end of *Bound for Glory*, Woody provides a stirring description of how he and Cisco Houston used music to defuse a jingoistic mob bent on attack-ing a Japanese-American grocery shortly after Pearl Harbor. As the group defending the grocery sing the resistance anthem "We Shall Not Be

Moved," the attackers are exposed as the cowards they are: "Our singing hit the mob of rioters like a cyclone tearing into a haystack. They stopped—fell back on their heels like you had poked them in the teeth with a ball bat. Fumbled for words."[32]

In contrast, even the most politically conscious "literary" voices fail to reach many of the common people Woody encounters on his journeys in *Bound for Glory*. When he settles briefly into the camp on the "jungle hill" near Redding, California, he hears a radical speech delivered by a young man whose "voice had the sound of books in it when he talked."[33] Although Woody sympathizes with the young man's socialist message, he juxtaposes it with the much deeper impact of the music that brings the camp families together once the sun goes down. Woody joins two Okie girls singing "It Takes a Worried Man to Sing a Worried Song," "Columbus Stockade," and "I Ain't A-Gonna Be Treated This A-Way." The music, Woody reflects, "done something a lot better, something that's harder to do, something you need ten times more. It cleared your head up, that's what it done, caused you to fall back and let your draggy bones rest and your muscles go limber like a cat's."[34] Beyond that, music provides a way of engaging immediate political concerns and connecting with people who may have little interest in bookish social theory: "you'll find a train load of things you can set down and make up a song about. You'll hear people singing your words around over the country, and you'll sing their songs everywhere you travel or everywhere you live; and these are the only kind of songs my head or my memory or my guitar has got any room for."[35]

When Woody goes to New York City to audition for a job at a club "where the shrimps are boiled in Standard Oil,"[36] he confronts the highbrow culture's attempt to reduce the voice of the people to rustic stereotype. One of the club's staff members suggests that Woody sing his song riding in a "hay wagon piled high with singing field hands." Suggesting that Woody wear a "darling clown suit," she provides an extremely bookish analysis of why Woody's music isn't really authentic: "your work is a bit, so to say, incomplete, that is, as far as the cultural traditions represented and the exchange and interrelationships and overlappings of these same cultural patterns are concerned, especially here in America, where we have, well, such a mixing bowl of culture, such a stew-pot of shades and colors. But, nevertheless, I think the clown costume will represent a large portion of the humorous spirit of all of them."[37] After Woody makes his escape from the clutches of the entertainment industry, he walks down along the waterfront and begins singing. "Folks joined in like one voice in the dark," Woody recounts, "And I knew that I was glad to be loose from that sentimental and dreamy trash, and gladder to be edging on my way along here singing with the people." In contrast to the "humorous spirit" invoked by the woman at the Rainbow Room, Woody hears the singing as "something with fight and guts and belly laughs and power and dynamite to it."[38]

At its best, Woody's writing captures much of the power and dynamite he associated with music. His descriptions of the dispossessed common people well up from sources where the differences between blacks, whites, Mexicans, Indians, and Japanese-Americans signify little. Many of his most stirring passages incorporate images and cadences from music and folk expressions. Describing the two young boys with whom he rides in the opening chapter, Woody writes:

I'd seen a thousand kids just like them. They seem to come from homes somewhere that they've run away from. They seem to come to take the place of the old stiffs that slip on a wet board, miss a ladder, fall out a door, or just dry up and shrivel away riding the mean freights; the old souls that groan somewhere in the darkest corner of a boxcar, moan about a twisted life half lived and nine tenths wasted, cry as their souls hit the highball for heaven, die and pass out of this world like the echo of a foggy whistle.[39]

The voice is Woody's, but it's also the voice of the blues and the loneliest moments of the Mexican-American *corridos* (ballads). It's the voice Woody was reaching for in "The Word I Want to Say," the selection Marsh and Leventhal chose to conclude *Pastures of Plenty*. "It's not a secret word or a magic word," Woody wrote. "I've said this one word in every tongue and language and unto every color of face, lips, ear and hair. To the brown, to the red, to the yellow, to the black skin and to the blankskin." Reiterating the vision that makes him central to our populist literary tradition, he celebrates the "free word that no jail can hold, no cell can keep, no chain drag down." The word that "keeps democracy alive," it is the touchstone of the American voice, "the word I want to say."[40]

NOTES

1. Walt Whitman, "Democratic Vistas," in *Poetry and Prose* (New York: Library of America, 1982), 994.

2. Woody Guthrie, *Pastures of Plenty: A Self-Portrait*, ed. Dave Marsh and Harold Leventhal (New York: HarperCollins, 1990), xxvi.

3. Ibid., 180.

4. Walter Ong, *The Presence of the Word: Some Prolegomena for Cultural and Religious History* (1967; Minneapolis: University of Minnesota Press, 1981).

5. Guthrie, *Pastures*, 37.

6. Joe Klein, *Woody Guthrie: A Life* (New York: Knopf, 1980), 126.

7. Whitman, "Democratic Vistas," 937.
8. Ibid.
9. Ibid., 940.
10. Ibid., 994.
11. Ed Pavlic, "Crossroads and Consciousness: Horizontal and Vertical Processes in African-American Culture," Ph.D. diss., Indiana University, 1998.
12. Guthrie, *Pastures*, 206.
13. Jimmy Longhi, *Woody, Cisco, & Me: Seamen Three in the Merchant Marine* (Champaign/Urbana: University of Illinois Press, 1997), 230.
14. Ibid., 231.
15. Ibid., 233.
16. Ibid., 233.
17. Woody Guthrie, *Bound for Glory* (1943; New York: Plume, 1983), 136.
18. Ibid., 178.
19. Guthrie, *Pastures*, 115.
20. Ibid.
21. Ibid., 117.
22. Ibid.
23. Ibid., 211.
24. Ibid., 212–13.
25. Guthrie, *Bound for Glory*, 19.
26. Ibid., 26.
27. Ibid., 19.
28. Ibid., 23.
29. Ibid., 35.
30. Ibid.
31. Ibid, 107.
32. Ibid., 268.
33. Ibid, 251.
34. Ibid., 253.
35. Ibid., 254.
36. Ibid., 293.
37. Ibid., 294.
38. Ibid., 299.
39. Ibid., 31.
40. Guthrie, *Pastures*, 248.

ELLEN G. LANDAU

CLASSIC IN ITS OWN LITTLE WAY
The Art of Woody Guthrie

My brain feels like a loft where I chop and paint and dance and sing up a hundred pictures to work on at the same time.[1]—WOODY GUTHRIE, 21 April 1945

A real good artist / not afraid of / his paint.—WOODY GUTHRIE, 8 August 1947

In his introduction to *Woody Sez*, a compendium of some of the best columns Woody Guthrie wrote in the late 1930s and early 1940s for the Los Angeles Communist newspaper *People's World*, Guy Logsdon remarks that Guthrie was a man of many talents: "folk poet, folksinger and author, country boy in a big city, family man who wandered, individualist with a world vision."[2] Logsdon's list details the key elements that comprise the mighty Guthrie myth, except that one important (admittedly little-known) ingredient is missing: Woody Guthrie also had a powerful visual imagination. There is no way to measure his actual output, but in the neighborhood of six hundred drawings in pencil, ink, watercolor, and gouache remained in his estate after his death, only a small portion of which directly illustrate his lyrics.[3] Clearly, expressing himself in pictures was an independent creative activity for Woody Guthrie, albeit one that provided an important corollary to his extraordinary career as a writer of songs, poetry, and prose.

Guthrie's artistic aptitude, according to his biographer Joe Klein, was recognized early, around 1924 or 1925, by Blanche Giles, a seventh-grade friend in Okemah, Oklahoma. Presumably using Giles as a source, Klein describes the adolescent Woody's budding talent:

He was fine at caricatures, but best of all were his stick figures: the little men with the pointy knees and elbows who always seemed to be racing off somewhere . . .

and always looked more than a bit like Woody himself. He would draw little lined faces on them, and top hats that he could shade just right to make them look shiny, and he did it all with astonishing speed.

"You're going to be a great cartoonist someday," Blanche would whisper.

"Naw, they'll never let me," he'd reply.

"Yes, you will [Blanche replied]. You'll be famous someday."[4]

Guthrie's father Charley, a strong believer in self-education, was willing to indulge his son's budding talent, ordering him a correspondence course in cartooning by the time he was seventeen. According to Klein, after Woody joined his dad in 1929 in Pampa, Texas, he plastered the walls of Charley's roominghouse with cartoons of the local farm girls and oil-field boys who paid to sleep in shifts on rows of cots. In a curious prefiguring of his subsequent obsession with women dancing—a fascination that would have a strong impact on his personal life, as well as the subject matter of his later art and his drawing style—Woody apparently watched the girls through the cracks in the pine and tin walls, observing how "their bodies moved with a sophistication that seemed beyond the comprehension of their blank childlike faces."[5] He made money doing cartoons and signs for a druggist and tried his hand at painting in oils around this time as well, spending "every cent he could on tubes of oil paint, canvas and fine sable brushes."[6] Unfortunately, nothing of this period remains. In fact, only two "finished" works in oil, a crude (perhaps paint-by-numbers) rendition of Abraham Lincoln dated 2/37 and a roughly massed landscape showing angled adobe dwellings and a vibrant sky, exist in a private collection.

The best known of Guthrie's artworks are the William Gropper–like leftist cartoons (figures 1 and 2) many of which accompanied his "Woody Sez" columns during the Depression (described by Klein as "funny in a sly political sort of way"), and a limited number of illustrations that have appeared in books by and on Guthrie, most notably *Born to Win* (1965) and *Pastures of Plenty: A Self-Portrait* (1990), an anthology of material edited by Dave Marsh and Harold Leventhal, which includes excerpts from Woody's diaries, columns, letters, and other texts, interspersed with drawings. As Woody wrote of his own talent in a 1940s notebook, these exhibit a shared approach: "a self-styled kind of writing and drawing— classic in its own little way."[7]

On the reverse of one of four atypically (and awkwardly) academic renderings of the male nude marked off in numbered squares as a guide to proper proportions (figure 3), Woody wrote himself the following notation in 1945:

WE PLEGE OUR
ALEGIANCE TO OUR
FLAG ...... AN TO WALL
ST., FOR WHICH IT
STANDS .....ONE
DOLLAR, UNGETTABLE
.....

FIG. 1. *"We plege our alegiance to our flag . . . ," circa
1939. Ser. 1, no. 3, brush/
touche tracing paper, 9 × 11
in.* COURTESY OF WOODY
GUTHRIE ARCHIVES.

FIG. 2. *"Boss watches hand
work till sundown," no date.
Ser. 2, no. 6, pen/brown
ink/wash, 28 × 21.6 cm.*
COURTESY OF WOODY
GUTHRIE ARCHIVES.

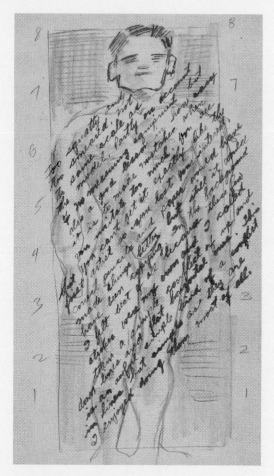

FIG. 3. *"Drawing of man on long paper,"* 1945. *Ser. 10, no. 1, graphite/newsprint, 92 × 21.5 cm.* COURTESY OF WOODY GUTHRIE ARCHIVES.

Dont surround light things with heavy line ? ? ?
  Dont draw movie stars.
     draw people not
     well known.
  A costume does not make
  a PICTURE. It should
  have some other interest
  besides a demonstration
  of technique. *mood.*
  action. story. Sentiment.
  message. Conflict.

In many ways, this recipe sums up not only Guthrie's approach to visual iconography, but to subject matter in general; folklorists and musicologists are in general agreement that his songs are far more interesting for the stories they tell than as examples of technical virtuosity.[8] Eschewing musical innovation, Woody frequently borrowed well-known folk melodies, endlessly repeating the same refrains. In a statement printed in *Hard Hitting Songs for Hard-Hit People* (published in 1967, but written in 1940), Woody explained what worked best for him. "It wouldn't have to be fancy words," he noted. "It wouldn't have to be a fancy tune. The fancier it is the worse it is. The plainer it is the easier it is, and the easier it is, the better it is—and the words don't even have to be spelt right."[9] He unwittingly foreshadowed avant-garde theories of music advocated in the 1950s by composer John Cage when he remarked:

I won't say that my guitar playing or singing is anything fancy on a stick. I'd rather sound like the cab drivers cursing at each other, like the longshoreman yelling, like the cowherds whooping and the lone wolf baying—like anything in this big green universe than to sound slick, smooth-tongued, oily-lipped.[10]

Guthrie carried this attitude over into the realm of the visual in his professed disdain for avant-garde art. As recorded by Richard A. Reuss, in a cartoon feature that ran in the 18 April 1940 issue of *People's World* (possibly figure 4), he "lampooned modern art, thereby provoking considerable pro and con discussion in the letters to the editors."[11] Not knowing, of course, where he would end up living most of his adult life, he wrote scornfully (and purposely ungrammatically) of the art capital of America in "Woody Sez":

New York is a big town for painting pictures. Least they call them pictures. Some of em look like you didn't get done with em.

Call em modern paintings. But I'm glad to see em in fashion. It makes everybody a artist. I mean when you can't get no other kind of job; why you get a hold of some paint and you're a artist.

I always did think that all of us was good for something—and now I see what it is. We're painters.

And if you can't tell what our pictures are sposed to be, we take down the $5 tag and put up a $50 one.

Paint—splatters on.[12]

In reality, Guthrie understood and probably appreciated modern art far more than this column implies; according to Klein, he took Lefty Lou (Maxine Crissman), his singing partner on Los Angeles radio station KFVD, to the art museum there and explained to her how paintings work (for example, he told her you had to step back to understand impression-ism).[13] Clearly, however, he remained suspicious of overintellectualiza-tion, of judgments of quality made by "the college boys [who] will study on it for a couple of hundred years and because they can't make heads nor tail of it, they'll . . . maybe call you a natural born genius."[14]

Carrying further the implications of the parallel drawn between Woody Guthrie and avant-garde music, it is interesting to note that, also in a naive, untutored Will Rogers kind of way, much of Guthrie's volumi-nous poetry and prose—and some of his later visual images (figure 5)—strongly resembles the modernist art and literature he said he despised. John Greenway has described Woody's "hypnosis with words," the curi-ous associations he found between simple terms that led him into "fan-tastic flights of imagery," his unrestrained metrical restrictions, diction filled with picturesque expressions, and extreme speed of composition.[15] *Broadside* magazine (issue 85) once published a list of two hundred allit-erative phrases written by Woody in the 1950s.[16] Stylistically such char-acteristics appear related to the late cubist paintings of Pablo Picasso and the writing of James Joyce (although their derivation from the devastat-ing symptoms of Huntington's chorea, the progressive genetic disease that led to Guthrie's death, is a more likely explanation). In any case, Woody's Joycean brand of talking blues, his "long, rambling intoxicated outpourings in an uninhibited stream-of-consciousness style" would have a strong impact on songwriters of the next generation, most notably Bob Dylan.[17]

Picasso once famously said something to the effect that it had taken him a lifetime to learn to draw like a child. Woody, who wrote numerous songs and drew many pictures for children—the majority created specifi-cally for his beloved daughter Cathy Ann (1942–47)[18]—affected a par-allel attitude toward creativity in both published and personal state-ments. For example, on 16 August 1947, he wrote rhetorically in his notebook, "Now as goes for the art of children let me remind you once more and all over again. The best kind of an artist that you can be is when your art runs out of you just like it runs from the kids." Earlier, in a "Woody Sez" column he had pronounced, "If I know anything worth knowing, or think anything worth thinking or working towards,—about half of it I picked up just by listening to the kids."[19] Claiming himself de-sirous of being "advanced into the noble state of the child," he scrawled to Cathy Ann (whom, as in figure 6, he depicted many times with a pencil or crayon in hand), "I figure our minds graze on the same pasture, swim the same rivers and jump the same fences," perhaps providing a self-justification for his apparently careless style and uninhibited, often un-predictable behavior.

FIG. 4. *"Modern Art," ca. 1939. Ser. 1, no. 8, ink/heavy tracing paper, 26 × 22.5 cm.* COURTESY OF WOODY GUTHRIE ARCHIVES.

FIG. 5. *"Old Thoughts Wash In," 1948. Ser. 15, no. 12, ink/type/bond, 18 × 13 cm.* COURTESY OF WOODY GUTHRIE ARCHIVES

FIG. 6. *"I'm Making A Bigger One," 2 November 1946. Ser. 17, no. 3, pencil/tablet, 30 × 22.5 cm.* COURTESY OF WOODY GUTHRIE ARCHIVES.

In a significant percentage of Woody's sketches, particularly those created during the Depression, the period of his first marriage and wandering minstrel years, the faintly autobiographical little stick men "with pointy knees and elbows" in his adolescent caricatures mutate into a recognizable skinny, wiry-haired, guitar-toting doppelgänger, depicted bumming rides, getting into fights, singing in bars, escaping from the cops, making love (figures 7–9). Obviously a Steinbeckian chronicle of his own escapades (real or imagined), these sketches bear a striking resemblance to many of famed regionalist painter Thomas Hart Benton's drawings, especially his linear illustrations created in the late thirties and early forties for Mark Twain's *Adventures of Tom Sawyer, Life on the Mississippi*, and *The Adventures of Huckleberry Finn*.[20]

Imbued with comparable populist values (although, after an early flirtation with leftist views, militantly anti-Communist),[21] Benton, who began his own career as a cartoonist for the *Joplin American*, became the most notorious American artist of the Depression, even appearing on the cover of *Time* magazine. Like Woody, Benton declared himself an anti-intellectual and antimodernist who created for the common folk. Both affected a similarly Whitmanesque sense of locality, favored an unpretentious (but certainly faux-naive) vernacular grammar and style, and often adopted a satirical approach to narrative subject matter. Both men were democratic nativists who were militantly anti–big city capitalism and identified with the dispossessed Okies and the working classes. Both were eccentric, insecure, and combative, often behaving in ways deemed by others coarse, vulgar, and opportunistic, and each strove instinctually to fight injustice through his art, projecting onto it a more utopian society.[22]

Rhythm played an important role in the conception of Benton's energetically swirling compositions, and he cared deeply about folk and country music, to the point of basing prints and paintings on specific hillbilly songs like "Frankie and Johnny" and "The Ballad of the Jealous Lover of Lone Green Valley." In 1942, Decca Records released a three-record 78 album, *Saturday Night at Tom Benton's*, which stemmed from the artist's famous weekend musicales in Manhattan, Kansas City, and on Martha's Vineyard, where he had a summer home.[23] In many ways, Thomas Hart Benton provides the perfect contemporary foil for Woody Guthrie: one was an artist who loved to play folk music (on the harmonica); and one, a folk musician who loved to draw. Both also wrote copiously, primarily autobiographical prose. Guthrie's books such as *Bound for Glory* (1943), *Born to Win* (1965) and *Seeds of Man: An Experience Lived and Dreamed* (written in 1947–48 but published in 1976), are paralleled by Benton's *An American in Art* and *An Artist in America* (printed in 1969 and 1983, but incorporating material that dates much earlier.)

FIG. 7. "*WG with foot on running board,*" *ca. 1942. Ser. 7, no. 40, ink/posterboard, 36 × 28 cm.* COURTESY OF WOODY GUTHRIE ARCHIVES.

FIG. 8. "*Don't Pick This Fruit,*" *April 1946.* COURTESY OF THE RALPH RINZLER FOLKLIFE ARCHIVES AND COLLECTIONS, CENTER FOR FOLKLIFE AND CULTURAL HERITAGE, SMITHSONIAN INSTITUTION.

FIG. 9. "*Woody's Dream,*" *ca. 1942. Ser. 7, no. 58, ink/posterboard, 28 × 36 cm.* COURTESY OF WOODY GUTHRIE ARCHIVES.

FIG. 10. *Thomas Hart Benton,*
Exterminate, *from* Year of Peril
series, 1942. STATE HISTORICAL
SOCIETY OF MISSOURI,
COLUMBIA.

Both Benton and Guthrie were also militantly antifascist during the
war years. Benton produced a caricaturish, overtly propagandistic set
of six large paintings, the *Year of Peril* series (figure 10), immediately
after the Japanese attack on Pearl Harbor, intended, according to art
historian Erika Doss, to be shocking and apocalyptic in contradistinc-
tion to the optimistic tenor of his more typical regionalist efforts.[24]
Meant as a "call to arms," these works received widespread national
distribution in the form of a pamphlet with an accompanying essay by
Benton underwritten by Abbott Laboratories, the wartime pharmaceu-
tical company that had purchased the gruesomely surreal and disturbing pictures.

In like manner, at the start of the war, Woody Guthrie scrawled in
blue paint across his guitar, "This Machine Kills Fascists," explaining in
a later diary entry (*Notebook from Cathy to Pete*, 1947):

> My guitar is anti fascist.
> It breaks down hate.
> But I've felt lots of times
>   like I hate something
> I guess I hate hate.

Proclaiming "I'm gonna whip these fascist rats," he had written a poem three years earlier for Cathy Ann in the same horrific vein as Benton's *Year of Peril* pictures:

What is a fascist? Would you like
to know?
I think I know and I will try to
show
These stinging lizards dressed in clothes
like us
Have crawled up from the cess pool
down below.

Their word is kill. Their job is
sneak and steal—
Their god is robbery and their
ideal
To rape and plunder murder thievery
and
Their mind thinks just one thought
and that is kill.

A fascist brain works for itself
alone
The hands to rape and when the
rape is done
Its face grins like a melted waxen
dummy
Upon the ground where some girls'
red blood run.

Like wolves and mad-dogs frothing
at the lips
This wild hyena 'cross the country
slips
Seizes a young girls hair and slits
her throat
And rapes her in the grass where
young blood drips.
. . . .

Each fascist really worships one thing,
greed
To kill your soul and take the
things they need
You do not have a soul or mind to
them
Your heart is just a thing to kill
and bleed.[25]

However, Woody assures his daughter just a few pages later, "WE'LL SMASH THE FASCISTS! . . . OUR LAND BELONGS TO EVERY WORKING MAN!"

Visualizing World War II in Marxist/Stalinist terms as part of a larger struggle against capitalist imperialism,[26] Guthrie began to write song lyrics with titles like "My Uniform's My Dirty Overalls" and "Talking Hitler's Head Off Blues." Earlier, in mid-1942, during the time Marjorie Mazia (who would become his second wife on 13 November 1945) was pregnant with Cathy Ann, Woody sent her a series of letters and postcards in which he visualized their unborn love-child as a union organizer and fascist fighter extraordinaire called "Railroad Pete."

Woody introduces Pete on a 1942 datebook page (labeled at the top "BLACKOUT TONIGHT 9:30") as a tough-looking kid with a shock of blond hair who proclaims, "I'm Railroad Pete—I'm just kind of a blur somewhere on Old Mama Nature—I aint old enough to make up my mind what I wanta look like—I aint born yet—but I wanta be quick so I can fight." Two postcards sent to Marjorie during the summer of 1942, starred Pete in his characteristic turtleneck sweater and stocking cap—this outfit had appeared earlier in Woody's drawings of "The Boom Town Kids"—walking through the city, hands stuffed in his pockets, expectorating. Encountering Adolf Hitler on 5 July, Pete knocks him out with his spit (figure 11); elsewhere he wipes out an entire Panzer division in a similar way. On two facing datebook pages that same year (7–8 August), Woody depicts Pete performing a complicated Rube Goldbergian action. Labeled "Pumtitchka doing his quadruble shotgun glance shot / The only man to ever perform this feat," this sketch shows Pete, blindfolded and

FIG. 11. "R.R. Pete spitting at Hitler," 5 July 1942. Postcard, ink/board, 3 × 5 in. COURTESY OF WOODY GUTHRIE ARCHIVES.

FIG. 12. "Cathy's Feets," 1943.
NB-1, no. 22, p. 181, ink on
tablet, 7.5 × 10 in. COURTESY OF
WOODY GUTHRIE ARCHIVES.

standing backward, ricocheting phlegm into a spitoon.[27] Woody later wrote to his baby daughter, "If you'd of been Rail Road Pete like everybody had guessed, I already had a book full of stuff wrote up for him. But then you fooled us all, you was Crosstie Cathy instead," and affectionately captioned a cartoon of her in her diaper and undershirt, wearing pointy slippers, her face covered with an oversized woolen hat, "Cathy's feets / That cap's Pete's" (figure 12).

In his biography of Guthrie, Joe Klein identifies Railroad Pete accurately as a symbol of the remarkable intimacy between Woody and Marjorie Guthrie. Although he married three women and was apparently unfaithful many times to all of his wives, Marjorie was clearly the love of Woody's life. In 1942, as part of an extended essay titled "Letter to Mama and Pete," Woody poignantly laid bare his inadequacies and insecurities (resulting, he notes, from "one hell of a one-man-personal rebellion against the world and all that's in it") and how much he needed Marjorie—who "had developed her mind along different lines and who was entirely different in outlook and approach than he was"—in order to function.

The daughter of Jewish immigrants from Russia and a dancer since 1936 in Martha Graham's avant-garde company, Marjorie Greenblatt (her stage name was Mazia) was nothing like any other woman Woody had known, especially his first wife from rural Texas, Mary Jennings. Describing himself in "Letter" as having lived "like a wild wolf in the canyons of NY for a couple of years,"[28] Woody proclaims that, in Marjorie, he had finally found a soulmate "whose mental make up supplies his missing link." Acknowledging that, whereas she "attaches great importance to good habits" and he himself has "acquired all of the bad habits known to man," he continues in loving detail to characterize Marjorie as his opposite, except creatively. For, even though she is "mostly interested in the graces of the body," and he dwells on "the hurts and hopes of the mind," he sees them both as "Artistic minds following a star. Loving the other for following a star."

According to Nora Guthrie, her father was mesmerized not only by her mother, but by every member of the Martha Graham dance troupe, attracted to their discipline, physical energy, independence of spirit, and above all, the beauty and fluidity of their bodies in motion. Woody had been introduced to the company in the spring of 1941 when the Almanac Singers collaborated with Sophie Maslow—one of Graham's dancers and a political radical who admired Woody's columns in *The Daily Worker*—to produce dance sketches set to his *Dust Bowl Ballads* (1940, Victor Records). Maslow subsequently asked Guthrie to narrate another experimental dance she was choreographing called *Folksay;* Marjorie performed in the work, which debuted early in March 1942.[29]

As Stephen Polcari has pointed out, Graham's dances and those of her protégés were based on a highly original conception of the expansion and contraction of the female body and its flow through space. Drawing on primitive and ritualistic sources, Graham emphasized her own and her dancers' innate rhythm, organic power, and physicality in "vitalist and expressive sequences of inward and outward motion," creating abstractly "a sense of the ebb and flow of human action" that seemed to originate from within the dancer's psyche. To Graham, "movement was a vehicle of expressive as well as structural and psychological form."[30]

The primal and visceral "kinetic dynamism" to which Guthrie was exposed when watching the Martha Graham ensemble (he spent so much time at rehearsals, he was "adopted" as their mascot) had an immediately strong impact on his artistic subject matter and drawing style. Woody's California radical friends of the late thirties and early forties, writer Ed Robbin and actor Will Geer, had been well aware of his sensuality, expressed even then in intensely lyrical and unexpurgated letters he wrote to women (a habit that would cause legal trouble for him in the future). Robbin likened Woody's erotic sensibility to D. H. Lawrence's in *Lady Chatterley's Lover;* Geer evoked instead *Leaves of Grass* by Walt Whitman, pointing out he had observed Woody pick it up and read it at his home.

According to Geer, like Whitman, who had a similarly "wide democratic feeling for his fellow men," Guthrie "loved to catalog the names and places as well as the bodies of men and women and all their parts."[31] However much he admired Whitman's poetry, Woody seemed to have an instinctive sense that his own agenda was different, remonstrating himself in his notebook, "From Cathy to Pete," on 10 August 1947:

> I got to steer clear
> of Old Walt Whitman's
> Swimmy Waters
> He didn't find a woman
> In all of his
> Leaves of Grass.

Believing "a man's most basic wants, hopes and needs come out of him in . . . poems and explosions,"[32] in response to his exposure to Graham's company, Woody began to create loosely articulated linear renditions of Marjorie dancing or making love as in the two expressively sexual drawings he bawdily labeled "Sugar In My Gourd" and "Like A Dog On A Bone" (figure 13).[33] A Young Folkways Series record dust jacket in 1947

FIG. 13. *"Like A Dog On A Bone,"* 23 April 1946. COURTESY OF THE RALPH RINZLER FOLKLIFE ARCHIVES AND COLLECTIONS, CENTER FOR FOLKLIFE AND CULTURAL HERITAGE, SMITHSONIAN INSTITUTION.

FIG. 14. *Insert for* Nursery Days—Songs to Grow On, *1947. Young Folksay Series Disc 605.* COURTESY OF WOODY GUTHRIE ARCHIVES.

featured a series of photographs of Marjorie and Cathy Ann (by now affectionately re-nicknamed Cathy Rooney and Miss Stackabones by her father) doing dance exercises on the beach (figure 14); examining these tender and graceful images clarifies how much and why Woody loved the female body.[34] Numerous drawings of Cathy Ann (who would soon die tragically in a fire) shown posing with her parents naked, in her mother's arms, or dancing alone for daddy, date right before and after these beach pictures.[35]

Woody's devastatingly short time with Cathy Ann was further limited by the exigencies of war. Service in the Merchant Marine and army had kept him away from her and Marjorie for most of 1945 and 1946. Apparently, it was during this solitary period (during which he often drew caricatures of his fellow servicemen) that he began to realize he probably also carried the gene for the disease that had seemingly driven his mother mad and led to her early death. Amazingly, over the next decade, he was able to father four additional children (three more with Marjorie and one with his final wife, Anneke) despite the fact that Huntington's chorea had indeed begun attacking his nervous system, destroying brain cells, creating severe mental agitation, erasing his inhibitions, and causing erratic and uncontrollable sounds and movements. Not surprisingly, a by-product of his illness was Woody's composition of increasingly disturbed and disturbing drawings, as well as his generation of poems and prose even more disorganized and fantastic.

The vast majority of Woody Guthrie's visual production between 1947 and 1956, the year he was permanently hospitalized, can be characterized

FIG. 15. *"Tears in Both Eyes,"* 1949. Ser. 22, no. 13, ink/construction paper/watercolor, 30.2 × 22.7 cm. COURTESY OF WOODY GUTHRIE ARCHIVES.

as involuntarily childlike, its loose, suggestive, shorthand style a metaphor for the way his own mind and body were spinning out of control (see, for example, figure 15). When he was first beginning to feel dissociated, he described himself in one of his diaries in the third person, as "beat back by an enemy he can't see, feel, get hold of, figure out, unsettle with nor fight." In a notebook of the later forties, Woody lamented further:

The old head I've got seems to be all cluttered up with trash and garbage and crazy moving pictures—that whirl around all of the time and never see anything quite clear enough—and never feels [sic] anything quite plain enough.

Never knows anything quite sure enough.

Maybe something ought to happen to me to make me be born again brand new.[36]

During what was apparently a more lucid interval in the early spring of 1951, Guthrie created a group of thematically related, more legibly composed drawings that reveals another facet of the effects of his losing battle with Huntington's disease. Despite the often dire circumstances they describe, many of his songs and writings had projected an ultimately positive attitude toward human potentiality. No trace of optimism remains in these works; all hope is submerged beneath a dark and pessimistic paranoia.

Props and characters from some of his Depression-era drawings—most notably the hangman's knot, Ku Klux Klanners, and the bullying Vigilante Man—are reprised in more viscerally menacing situations in numerous works Woody dated "March 1951." An unusually finished color drawing labeled "Jealous Love," shows a dark-haired naked woman (Marjorie?) astride a recumbent man (himself?), but the pointed dagger she wields converts the scene from one of ecstasy to murder. Another work titled "Southland Tourist" (figure 16) presents three "lousy Kluck Klucks," identified by their pointy hoods, in confrontation with another naked couple—the man has Woody's wiry hair—seemingly about to be lynched. Ominously signed in the lower left, "Woody Guthrie down here on earth," this work conflates politics and sexuality giving each a darker edge.

"Seeds of Man," similarly themed, features gun-toting vigilantes bearing down on a reclining nude couple who embrace in the grass (figure 17). Most famously used as the title of an autobiographical anecdote Woody converted during the late forties into a full-length novel (it details a partly real, partly fictional search by the menfolk in the Guthrie family for a lost silver mine), the phrase "Seeds of Man" was one he had marshaled at many junctures for different purposes. All were, of course, related to potency: his own, the earth's, society's; in this 1951 drawing, one of his last fully realized compositions, every ramification of this concept is placed in danger.

A key component of the seemingly ever-expanding Woody Guthrie hagiography is the romantic sense of destiny his persona so evidently embodies: Woody may not yet have known it in Okemah when Blanche Giles praised his cartoons, but pretty early in his life he obviously became convinced he was a man "bound for glory." Whether, despite his Communist sympathizing, he should be considered a living personification of "the American spirit" (Guthrie was described in these words by none other than John Steinbeck,[37] whose own quintessentially American novel, *The Grapes of Wrath*, Woody idolized to the point of naming one of his sons after Tom Joad) depends frankly on what kind of evidence is being used to make the judgment. Certainly, the content of Woody Guthrie's private writings, and so much of the art he clearly felt compelled to create,

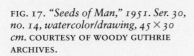

FIG. 16. *"Southland Tourist,"*
1951. Ser. 30, no. 18,
watercolor/drawing paper,
45 × 30 cm. COURTESY OF
WOODY GUTHRIE ARCHIVES.

FIG. 17. *"Seeds of Man,"* 1951. *Ser. 30,*
no. 14, watercolor/drawing, 45 × 30
cm. COURTESY OF WOODY GUTHRIE
ARCHIVES.

indicate that he was a man of many dimensions—some positive, some not—not just the caricature of the hard-travelin' hobo rambler "unfettered by life's burdens and woes" who fights injustice with song.

Assessing the parameters of his legend realistically has been made infinitely more difficult by the fact that Woody, as his friend Pete Seeger has pointed out, "scattered his genius" in so many directions.[38] But hundreds of drawings constitute ample evidence that Woody Guthrie was a visual as well as a verbal thinker; indeed he acknowledged the primacy of his ocular sense in *Born to Win* when describing himself as "nothing more nor less than a photographer without a camera."[39] There is no question that we need to correlate the visual element of Guthrie's creativity with the message of his songs and writings if ever we hope to plumb the depths of his unique talent.

NOTES

I thank Bob Santelli and Emily Davidson of the Rock and Roll Hall of Fame and Museum for suggesting that I investigate Woody Guthrie's art and write this essay. Amy Danielian and Nora Guthrie were extremely helpful in providing access to the drawings themselves and to unpublished materials in the Woody Guthrie Archives without which this essay could not have been written. Throughout my text, I have drawn on the insights into her parents and their relationship Nora was kind enough to share. I also appreciate the comments and encouragement given by Howard and Jay Landau and Henry Adams.

1. Diary entry from "Cathy's Book of Letters From All of Us Around Here" (1945), collection of the Guthrie Archives, New York. All subsequent material identified as coming from Guthrie's diaries and notebooks is also located in the Woody Guthrie Archives. Throughout this essay I have retained Woody's spelling, punctuation, and grammatical errors in all direct quotes from his writing.

2. Guy Logsdon, "Poet of the People," introduction to *Woody Sez* (New York: Grosset and Dunlap, 1975), xi.

3. Numerous extant drawings are either directly captioned or relate visually to known Woody Guthrie songs such as "Vigilante Man," "Worried Man Blues," and "Slipknot" (the latter is illustrated in Woody Guthrie, *Pastures of Plenty: A Self-Portrait*, ed. Dave Marsh and Harold Leventhal [New York: HarperCollins, 1990], 36). However I would estimate these to be a very small portion of Woody's total visual output.

4. Joe Klein, *Woody Guthrie: A Life* (New York: Knopf, 1980), 30. Woody's daughter Nora, relates that her grandmother (also named Nora Guthrie) encouraged her son's artistic talent as well, using scarce funds to buy construction paper and art pads for his use. (Interview with Nora Guthrie, New York, 19 December 1997.)

5. Ibid., 47.

6. Henrietta Yurchenko, *A Mighty Hard Road: The Woody Guthrie Story*

(New York: McGraw-Hill, 1970), 61–62. Yurchenko relates that Guthrie copied famous canvases, painting dozens of heads of Christ together with the "cops who killed him" as well as cheap signs for store windows, hotels, blacksmith shops, and funeral parlors. However, she points out that Woody loved music more than painting. "A picture you buy once," he remarked, "but you can sing a song and then sing it again."

7. "Letter to Mama and Pete" (1942), collection of the Woody Guthrie Archives.

8. In *Born to Win*, ed. Robert Shelton (New York: Collier Books, 1963), 72, Woody explains how he finds his subjects "everywhere you look, out of books, magazines, daily papers, at the movies, along the streets, riding buses or trains, even flying along in an airplane, or in bed at night anywhere." On 16 June 1947, Woody wrote in his datebook: "I think I've got a good ear and a good eye for a good story heard or seen." The best visual example of his storytelling ability is a set of drawings (see figure 2) that narrates novelistically sunup to sundown in the life of a "Hand" who has to punch the clock, toil, contend with his boss, and feed bread to his hungry children. Almost the entire story is illustrated in *Born to Win*, 106–14.

9. Alan Lomax, *Hard Hitting Songs for Hard-Hit People*, notes on the songs by Woody Guthrie (New York: Oak Publications, 1967), 19.

10. Quoted by John Greenaway, *American Folksongs of Protest* (Philadelphia: University of Pennsylvania Press, 1953), 276.

11. Richard A. Reuss, *A Woody Guthrie Bibliography, 1912–1967* (New York: Guthrie Children's Trust Fund, 1968), 28. Reuss lists nine letters to the editor published in the newspaper commenting on Guthrie's cartoon (numbers 134–36, 138–43 in his bibliography), 28–29. Unfortunately, I have not been able to gain access to these and read them, which is why I am not certain that the Chaplinesque cartoon illustrated as figure 4 is the one in question, although it seems likely that it is.

12. *Woody Sez*, 114–15.

13. Klein, *Woody Guthrie*, 43.

14. Lomax, *Hard Hitting Songs*, 19. In a 22 August 1947 diary entry, Woody wrote (to nobody in particular), "I don't feel welcome at your table of big long words."

15. Greenaway, *American Folk Songs of Protest*, 287–88. Pete Seeger's observations on Woody's prose sources are highly illuminating:

As a prose writer, too, I think him a genius. All of a piece. He wasn't pretending to be anybody else—he was just himself. He wrote fairly fast, and his big problem was that he had not learned how to rewrite and boil down later on.

He learned from everybody, and from everything. He learned from the King James Bible, he learned from the left-wing newspapers and publications; he had a devouring curiosity. I'll never forget the week he discovered Rabelais and read through a two-inch-thick volume, a relatively unexpurgated edition, in a couple of days. During the following weeks I could see him experimenting with some of the techniques of style that Rabelais used, such as paragraphs full of images, adjective after adjective, getting more and more fantastic.

See Seeger's *The Incompleat Folksinger*, ed. Jo Metcalf Schwartz (New York: Simon and Schuster, 1972), 54.

16. For example, in one of his notebooks (exact date not known) Woody wrote an alliterative bawdy nonsense "poem" titled "Shookspeare":

Shookahook Shakaspear
Shebolivar Shagnasty
Shefilthy Shefoulmouth
Shennanigan Shakeastick
Speakshake. Shookhook.
Spearasnatch.
Snatchaspeare.
What in the hell
was that feller's name
anyhow?

17. See Wayne Hampton, *Guerilla Minstrels: John Lennon, Joe Hill, Woody Guthrie, Bob Dylan* (Knoxville: University of Tennessee Press, 1986), 96. In a prefatory essay included in *Woody Sez*, viii, Studs Terkel relates the following anecdote:

I remember a night in 1941. [Woody] and three colleagues, Pete Seeger among them, were passing through Chicago. They were on tour, singing everywhere and anywhere. . . . Woody slipped off around 10 P.M. to a neighborhood tavern. About two in the morning—or was it three?—as though in a dream, I heard a rapid-fire tapping away on my portable. A few hours later, on awakening, I noticed the wastebasket rammed with foolscap, typed single-space. God, it was Joyceian, Burnsian, Wolfeian, O'Caseyian. Never had a neighborhood tavern been so overflowing with life and its wild comedy and its high hope. And so off-handedly chronicled. I have no idea what happened to that wastebasket, damn it.

Klein, *Woody Guthrie*, 151, reports that Alan Lomax also described Woody's prose style as analogous to Joyce, adding, "the sentences were sometimes almost a page long, . . . they had the looping grace and originality of the prose masters."

18. See, for example, Woody Guthrie with Marjorie Mazia Guthrie, *Woody's 20 Grow Big Songs* (New York: HarperCollins, 1992), a replica of an unpublished songbook written more than forty years earlier. "Riding in My Car" is probably the most famous of his children's songs.

19. The first quote comes from Woody's "Notebook from Cathy to Pete 1947," Brookylyne [*sic*], Two Four, New York, 93, collection of the Guthrie Archives. For the second, see *Woody Sez*, 42.

20. The Tom Sawyer illustrations were published in 1939 and Huckleberry Finn in 1942, both by the Limited Editions Club, Cambridge. See *Thomas Hart Benton's Illustrations from Mark Twain from the State Historical Society of Missouri Collection* (Mid-America Arts Alliance, 1976), introduction by Sidney Larson.

21. See Matthew Baigell, "Benton and the Left," in *Thomas Hart Benton: Artist, Writer, and Intellectual*, ed. R. Douglas Hurt and Mary K. Dains (State Historical Society of Missouri, 1989), 1–33, for a discussion of the impact of Benton's early flirtation with Marxism on his artistic career. A connection between Guthrie and Benton was their acquaintance with Mike Gold, editor of *The Masses* during the 1930s. I have no way of ascertaining whether Guthrie and Benton ever met, but Benton was a friend of Charles Seeger, Pete Seeger's father, with whom he played music in Manhattan before moving back to Kansas City.

It is unclear whether either Benton or Guthrie were ever actually card-carrying Communists. Benton told an interviewer in 1935, "Don't get the idea I have any hatred for Communists. I used to be one of them myself ten years ago, and I am still a collectivist" (quoted in Baigell, "Benton and the Left," 3.) Although Gordon Friesen (in "Bound for Glory," *Broadside*, no. 134 [January–March 1977], 24) maintains that Woody was "a member of the Village branch of the Communist Cultural Section and proud of it," the editors of *Pastures of Plenty* note that "one of the key unanswered questions about Woody Guthrie's life is whether he actually joined the Communist Party," as there is no proof of his membership. He did once write, "The biggest thing that ever happened to me in my whole life was back in 1936 the day that I joined hands with the Communist Party." Nonetheless, when applying in May 1940 to work for the Bonneville Power Administration, U.S. Department of the Interior, he answered no to the question "Do you have membership in any political party or organization which advocates the overthrow of our constitutional form of government in the United States?" (see *Pastures of Plenty*, 26, 163–64). His association with *People's World* and the *Daily Worker* as columnist and cartoonist caused problems for Guthrie during the war and the later McCarthy era.

22. In his essay, "Benton's Ballyhoo," in *Benton's America: Works on Paper and Selected Paintings*, exh. cat., Hirschl and Adler Galleries, New York, 19 January–2 March 1991, 11, Douglas Dreishpoon analyzes Benton's provocative personality. Dreishpoon could easily have been writing about Guthrie as well when he compared Benton and Twain, observing that "both had a journalistic bent and a streak of humor and satire in their work; both were humanitarian showmen; and both affected a character that straddled the fence between cultural sophistication and calculated naiveté."

23. See Alan C. Buechner, "Thomas Hart Benton and American Folk Music," in Linda Weintraub's, *Thomas Hart Benton: Chronicler of America's Folk Heritage*, exh. cat., Edith C. Blum Art Institute, Milton and Sally Avery Art Center, Bard College Center, Annandale-on-Hudson, New York, 1984–85, 68–77, for an excellent discussion of Benton's musical avocation. His last mural, *The Sources of Country Music*, was painted in 1974–75 for the Country Music Foundation in Nashville, Tennessee.

24. See Doss's *"The Year of Peril*: Thomas Hart Benton and World War II," in Hurt and Dains, *Thomas Hart Benton*, 35–63, for discussion of these works in the overall context of Benton's career.

25. From an undated notebook in the collection of the Guthrie Archives. On a subsequent page, Woody states that Cathy Ann is "the ripe old age of 3 weeks," so the poem (which he evaluates as "crappy") must have been written in February 1943.

26. Hampton, *Guerilla Minstrels*, 115. According to Hampton, Woody's version of World War II cast Franklin Delano Roosevelt and Joseph Stalin as the heroes and the American workers as warriors in a struggle to defend our land and freedoms.

27. In August 1942 Woody wrote a long letter to Railroad Pete in his diary (on the pages dated 19–31 January). In it he describes Pete's projected talent as "not just a useless, wishy washy kind of spitting . . . but an organized, socially significant kind." Not only would Pete be able to beat Hitler, but he could "walk into a town, look it over, shake hands with all of the workers; then spit, and the whole town organizes into one big CIO" (see *Pastures of Plenty*, 95–99). As so many of his song lyrics attest, Woody remained throughout his life a strong believer in unions as the salvation of the working man.

28. Woody wrote to Marjorie about trying to adjust to living in New York: I was pushed out of the main road pretty early and had to come up along the ditches and the mud and the weeds. . . . Now I'm picked up out of this kind of life and find myself camped along the trail of the intellectuals. . . . To put the matter mildly, I'm having a hard time. I hear their words that run like rainclouds and splatter a few drops across some hot Pavement—and the sun and the wind turn the words to steam and they go up in the air like a fog. (quoted by Klein, 251)
However, he wrote elsewhere in one of his notebooks that "New York is something thats alive to me. . . . Every house and building is a little cell in her body and in every little hall and every little street and every little old dirty alley you'll find little specks of real life, these are New York's little people. The little people that are really the living part of this big rocky iron town."

29. Interview with Nora Guthrie, 19 December 1997, and Klein, *Woody Guthrie*, 223–24, 227–29.

30. Stephen Polcari, "Martha Graham and Abstract Expressionism," *Smithsonian Studies in American Art* (Winter 1990), 13, 15.

31. Edward Robbin, *Woody Guthrie and Me: An Intimate Reminiscence* (Berkeley: Lancaster-Miller, 1979), 121–22. Clifton Fadiman once assessed Guthrie's talents as "a natural possession like Yellowstone or Yosemite," concluding that he was "a new Walt Whitman" (quoted by Logsdon, *Woody Sez*, xv–xvi.) However, Woody wrote on 5 August 1947 that, in his opinion, "Whitman makes glorious the works, labors, hopes, dreams, and feelings of my people, but he does not do this in the sorts of words my people think, talk, and dance and sing." He judges the writings of Sandburg and Pushkin similarly (see *Pastures of Plenty*, 180).

32. Excerpt from a letter written to Marjorie when Woody was in the army stationed in Las Vegas (quoted in Klein, *Woody Guthrie*, 303–4).

33. A datebook entry of 5 August 1947 seems to narrate this latter picture. In it, Woody wrote in part, "I and my wife made some loving today here on our couch in our newborn baby passion club [Arlo Davy Guthrie had just been born]. And I got worked up to such a flying point that I got up my nerves and asked her to do something she said she was too tired and sleepy to do. . . . It wasn't till away up in the middle of the day that we got to doing it all over again, and I got so full of sweet things my bitter stuff run out of me and stayed gone all day" (see *Pastures of Plenty*, 180).

34. An erotic poem by Woody Guthrie dated 13 August 1947 reads in part:
> I'll say to you, woman, come out from your home
> and be the / wild dancer of my breed.
> I'll say to my man come out of your walls and move
>   in your / space as free and as wild as my woman
> I'm married and wed to a dancer in my front line
> and the ways / she moves while I beat my skin
> drum would knock your / soul and your lights out
> . . . .
> Dance out to sing equal.
>   Dance up and be pretty.
>   Dance around and be free.
>   (*Pastures of Plenty*, 182–83).

35. To my knowledge, there are no extant drawings of Woody's first wife or

their three children, Teeny (Gwendolyn), Sue, and Bill. Nor are there any sketches of Nora and Lorina, his last two daughters (probably because he was too ill to make them). A handful of drawings of his sons Arlo and Joady with Marjorie are in the collection of the Guthrie Archives.

36. The description of himself as "beat back" was written in 1942 in "Letter to Mama and Pete." He also told his as yet unborn child, "I have dreams that tell me I'm not entirely as sane as is comfortable. . . . I don't know what kind of feelings are in me to cause me to write all the things I do. . . . It ain't Pete that's the baby in this family. Not by a longshot—NO, I really think I'm the baby in this family, don't you?" (see Klein, *Woody Guthrie*, 239).

37. Hampton, *Guerrilla Minstrels*, 94–95.

38. Seeger, *Incompleat Folksinger*, 58.

39. See "People I Owe," dated 13 March 1946, in *Born to Win*, 19.

PART three

This Land Is Your Land

CHARLES F. MCGOVERN

WOODY GUTHRIE'S AMERICAN CENTURY

Woody Guthrie has been a presence in American culture perhaps without parallel: a bard, an activist, a prodigious writer whose output far outstripped what was published during his lifetime, a figure who in many ways came to stand for the entire genre of folk music. He was an artist who seemingly ignored the notions and philosophies of art, a singer who sought to submerge his own voice in those of his audiences, the communities that sustained and nurtured his music. His work had a tremendous impact upon his peers and devotees, and he managed to attain a legendary status in his own lifetime. Who could compare with him? Among musical influences, perhaps only Louis Armstrong, Duke Ellington, Jimmie Rodgers, Al Jolson, Elvis Presley, and Bob Dylan come to mind; among American literary artists, perhaps only Walt Whitman and Will Rogers. Of these few, only Dylan combined both an artistic genius and a specific social vision plainly expressed through his own compositions. Yet such comparisons only obscure the individual in question. In part Guthrie was unique because he came along at a singular time in American history: he straddled the early twentieth century, when local traditions largely dominated American life, and the modern national and even global communications era. That historical setting gave his wedding of social activism and art its great power and helped make Guthrie an extraordinary and unique figure in American life.

The other essays in this collection speak directly to his art, his beliefs, and his long shadow of influence. Woody's art transcended his times, yet it is fitting to consider those times at length to appreciate their special import. He was a product of his age as well as a figure who spoke to the ages. This essay offers first a summary of United States history in Guthrie's times, the better to understand the ways in which the momentous changes in America during his life made Woody's own voice and vision so compelling. Next it considers Guthrie's cultural impact in its historical context, to show that his legacy was not only in music or social concern but was part of a sea change in American life that placed American culture itself—seen most distinctly as the experience and expressions of plain people, their communities, and their regional origins—as a central and defining aspect of American life.

The United States in Woody's Times

During Woody Guthrie's relatively brief lifetime, the United States became a world power, and the experience of everyday life changed for most of its inhabitants. The country evolved from primarily a rural to an urban and then suburban nation in less than fifty years. American society was transformed by a series of migrations that remade cities and settlement, population movements that altered the forms, accents, and concerns of American culture. Stunning technological changes in communication, transportation, and manufacturing combined to remake the American landscape, redefine work, refashion ideals, and reorder everyday experience. The country witnessed two separate sustained bouts of economic prosperity along with a fifteen-year era of depression, privation, and insecurity that had far-reaching consequences for its politics and popular aspirations. A broad democratic social movement encompassing both the New Deal in the 1930s and the Great Society in the 1960s, with working- and middle-class people at its core, revolutionized the country's political order by making government a principal agent in the welfare of Americans. In Guthrie's lifetime the nation became first a world influence and then the world's greatest power, participating in four overseas wars. The government developed and used a weapon of such destructive force as to threaten the existence of people on earth; the United States nearly faced a mutual destruction with another superpower over possession of nuclear weapons.

The advent of atomic power and the Cold War after World War II altered the country's mood and culture: the fear of Communism that stood at the core of American life censored critical thought and dissent fostering a cultural climate of fear and repression. It also led to government actions, most notably in the Vietnam War, that both shook the American people's belief in the moral goodness of their national ideals and their faith in their elected representatives. By the time Guthrie died in 1967 many Americans were questioning their once unshakable faith in material progress, in the purity of American institutions and ideals, and in their country's essential fairness and openness. While such skepticism and doubt (along with high ideals) had infused the American

Left, with which Guthrie had long been allied, these criticisms entered broad segments of the nation, perhaps never to be fully purged from the mainstream.

Guthrie lived to see the beginnings of this great change in American life, the waning of faith in progress that had long dominated most Americans' beliefs about their nation. In both his art and his political affiliations, he dedicated himself to offering open, honest testimony and protest about the world as plain people found it. By the time he died, that commitment had been taken up by thousands of Americans who were united by nothing other than a desire to speak out against what they perceived to be a grave series of wrongs in their society's customs and structure, and in their government's policies. How dissent and protest itself had become provisionally acceptable across so much of American life is beyond the scope of this essay, but we can trace that arc in Guthrie's times, and with it understand better how he himself participated in the general historical movements that remade America.

Guthrie was born in the Progressive Era, a period when American citizens began demanding that federal and local governments pay attention to troubling social conditions that were convincingly linked to the worst excesses of laissez-faire, robber-baron capitalism. The idea that government would be expected to note and in some way solve such problems seemed revolutionary at the time. While government had intervened in meliorating social conditions throughout American history, the decades bracketing the turn of the century saw the institutionalization of highly visible reform efforts in public health, political, economic, and judicial regulation, public utilities, and social welfare. With popular opinion rallying behind reform, legislators sought to temper the worst results of so-called free-market economic chaos through regulation and planning, and to address social unrest and instability through political reform and new social services for the poor, the immigrant, the injured, and the infirm.

Accompanying these efforts were new conceptions of society—grounded both in the urban experience and new academic disciplines—that stressed the interdependence of its members. Thus both moral obligation and social self-interest compelled Americans to address wide-ranging social inequities. Such ideas, fostered in the university as well as on the street, slowly displaced the beliefs in social laissez-faire that had until then dominated American public life, law, and business. Also, a growing appetite in popular middle-class media for representations of every facet of society focused attention on social conditions, especially the relatively new and unfamiliar settings of immigrant-filled cities. During the muckraking era in the early twentieth century, sustained reporting of social, economic, or political scandal often fostered reform efforts.

The relatively new technologies of the photograph and half-tone, the movie camera and sound recording, fostered a new investigative journalism to uncover troubling aspects of poverty, corruption, and despair in the country. While such social depictions would at first concentrate upon the squalor of the cities and great urban enclaves of the poor—tenements, dives, factories, and alleys—by the 1930s that attention would be turned to the entire country.

Communications and transportation revolutions altered both daily habits and choices for everyday Americans. The rise of the automobile remade American culture, landscape, and transportation. The automobile affected social relations, making possible different expressions of autonomy and freedom in everyday life. It is no small stretch of the imagination to call it "liberal individualism"—the ideal of self-determination on wheels. Courtship patterns and sexuality were famously altered with the auto: by providing a release from the confines of home or community, the auto offered opportunities for both sociability and sex. The auto changed habits of daily life, from labor to residential opportunities to the basic routines of commerce. It quickly became central to workers' patterns of mobility, as people, especially in rural areas, began using the auto to redefine the possibilities open to them. The car became central to American conceptions of what was possible or necessary in order to make a living or to pursue happiness. While the majority of American families did not own cars until after World War II, by the 1920s the auto certainly had become both a symbol of achievement and a necessity for Americans at virtually all levels of society. For people of Guthrie's station and experience the car was central to their changing economic fortunes. The Okies and the migrants whom Guthrie chronicled largely depended upon cars for their survival. Guthrie himself rambled not only on freight trains but in Model Ts and Buicks. The social dislocation of his subjects—Okies, hoboes, farmers, and others on the road—was seen as much through the back of an old Ford as a boxcar.

When Guthrie came of age in the Depression he became a witness to the worst economic and social privation the nation had yet seen. From 1921 to 1929, the nation had experienced extraordinary prosperity, as seen in rising real wages, a ballooning stock market, and the substantial growth of a consumer culture that featured a wide variety of mass-produced goods available to many, although by means to all. Not everyone enjoyed this boom equally: farmers and agricultural workers lost economic ground the entire decade, while the majority of factory workers lived at or near a bare subsistence level. Yet the Depression worsened things by erasing the gains of the more affluent industrial workers and the middle class by creating unsustainable downward pressures on wages and jobs. By 1931, within two years of the stock market crash, millions had lost their jobs, been made destitute, or become homeless, as industrial capitalism nearly ground to a halt. As its managers began a damage-control process that protected inventories, property, and profit margins, President Herbert Hoover struggled to reconcile his own belief in an economic order run by enlightened management with the increasing evidence that planning and managerial techniques alone were unable to stem the country's growing social and political emergencies.

Put another way, Hoover could not address the mounting evidence that the Depression's true crisis was not the fall of American production but rather the staggering costs of that collapse in human misery, insecurity, displacement, and shame. Industry, commerce, and agriculture generally proved unable and unwilling to sustain employment and wages, with little secure demand for their goods on the horizon. As people suffered and even died, business leaders maintained that the principal problem was one of faith: Americans lacked enough confidence in the economy, in America itself. Those without money, shelter, or hope were generally unavailable for comment.

Big business's response to the Depression, by and large, was to assert the prerogatives of capital and property over human life: the need to control costs by cutting labor, and to preserve price levels and profits. Their social responsibilities were secondary at best. These attitudes were compounded by a bitter hostility to the labor movement, which after the relative torpor of the 1920s again became a potent force in American life with Franklin D. Roosevelt's election in 1932. Throughout the decade business would again and again use its close connections to state power and local authority to fight, repress, or terrorize union activists, social protesters, and plain people who sought to better their own working and living conditions. Those struggles of unionists, whether miners, autoworkers, or farmworkers, became a central concern of the decade: even for those not directly connected, the labor movement symbolized the social changes that seemed imminent in the 1930s. Roosevelt's New Deal programs addressed capitalism's ills by (1) instituting real changes that placed business and the economy under much stricter regulation than in previous years, and (2) locating citizen welfare, particularly purchasing power, at the heart of economic reform. Yet the struggles of workers remained at the center of the decade's political and social upheavals. Those battles between the great numbers of poor and struggling workers on the one hand, and authorities—police, businesses, the government—on the other, became Guthrie's cause and gave him his life's work.

No social factor was more important in American society during Guthrie's prime years than migration, which remade the fabric of American society and transformed its population at the turn of the century. American cities swelled with new immigrants, mostly peasant peoples from southern and eastern Europe. Arriving in massive numbers from the 1890s through World War I, their influx was stopped only with the severe immigration restriction acts of the 1920s. Those peoples formed the core of both the ethnic urban working class and, with their children, the industrial union movement in the cities; in the 1930s they became the backbone of the New Deal political coalition that set the agenda for American politics until the 1960s. The migrants remade American cultural life as well. Both as creators and audiences they imparted their distinct accents and experiences to American films, popular songs, Broadway and vaudeville, the comics, and professional and amateur sports. Immigrant cultures heavily shaped the attitudes and appetites of midcentury America, the place where Guthrie's work had its immediate impact. But the foreign-born were not the only newcomers.

African-Americans had begun migrating from the rural South, where they had lived primarily, before 1920. By 1930 they had established important enclaves in most northern cities, with profound effects on American life and culture. In the 1930s the migration was intensified, as literally millions of families were thrown off the land. The collapse of the Southern crop-lien and sharecropping system, implementation of New Deal programs that favored large farms, and the exhaustion of land through unsustainable farming practices all drove Southerners of all races to the cities. African-Americans traveled to northern and western cities from the Deep and Upper South: to Memphis, Saint Louis, Chicago, and Detroit from the Mississippi Delta, to Los Angeles from Texas and Oklahoma, to Cleveland and Pittsburgh from the Upper South, to Baltimore, Philadelphia, and New York from the Piedmont and Eastern South. They were joined in those cities as well as the agricultural valleys of California by millions of white families, driven off by the same conditions. With the coming of World War II and the massive revival of large-scale industry for war production, even more left their homes on the farm to find steady work in the new world of the city.

This extended migration from the South throughout the country literally remade the social and cultural fabric of the United States. The great mass movements of Southerners to the north and west changed the cultural face of the country. Bringing Southern culture—music, political, and social attitudes—into the cities to mix in with that of the older established European immigrants, the great internal migration made possible important transformations in American culture. It enabled the birth and widespread acceptance of rock and soul music, contributed some elements to the many countercultures of the 1960s, and ultimately laid the foundation for some of the long-term realignments in American politics and values in the 1970s and beyond.

Guthrie's life was intimately bound up in those migrations. He moved west from Oklahoma and wound up working in and around the agricultural camps in the mid-1930s, after a broad social base of farmworkers had begun to organize and strike for a better life. As Michael Denning has pointed out in his book *The Cultural Front*,[1] Guthrie did not particularly identify himself in this context as an Okie (which was an epithet), but instead characterized himself as one of a great number of peoples who were all migrating to find a better life. For Guthrie migration was at the heart of the story of Dust Bowlers wherever they drifted and the many farmworkers from all over with whom he worked in California, where he first gained some prominence. Homelessness and the perpetual need to move for survival united all the peoples Guthrie observed and chronicled. Guthrie came to portray people on the road, set off on hard travelin' by drought, bad luck, and a corrupt, unfair economic system. He got caught up in what he called the "art and science of migratin'" transformed by his experience of living amidst thousands of people who were literally refugees in their own country.

In other words, Guthrie showed that the experience of displacement, movement, homelessness, and transit was not simply a condition but a fundamental fact of American life. He made the point that American society and laws were so unfair and skewed that millions had no home in the world, no place of rest, no place to make community or to labor for their own betterment. While some of the decade's proletarian literature and of course John Steinbeck's *Grapes of Wrath* (with which Guthrie was often identified) showed the centrality of homelessness and migration to the Depression, Guthrie's own songs of displacement, movement, resilience, and hope pointed to the deeper connections of migrancy and American life. With so much of the country literally unsettled, the movement for social justice to which Guthrie and so many others dedicated themselves was an inevitable result of such profound dislocation rather than a subversive challenge to the American way of life.

Arguments over the meaning of "the American way of life"[2] were critical to the politics of the 1930s. While the Left and Right fought over whose prescriptions were best for the country, both their platforms rested firmly on visions grounded in the American past, and a powerfully felt, if vague, conception of the American way of life. It received its most well-known mainstream form in its evocation of a stable middle-class life—of a property-owning, individualist family, bound to local community through loyalty, history, and affection. The vision of the American way of life held the individual responsible for his own destiny. When spread by the corporate advertising, marketing, and culture industries, it worked together with a powerful business propaganda[3] campaign to counter and discredit the New Deal's emphasis upon government's role in national prosperity. The corporate vision of the American way took for granted that individuals and families alone were responsible for their prosperity and safety, and argued that the best way to secure those ends was to loosen regulations upon business. This corporate vision flew in the face of FDR's overwhelming popular success, ignoring the powerful traditions of populism and collective action that were part of working-class and farm life, traditions that even then were fueling the rise of the CIO, the American labor and farm movements.

Guthrie's own American way drew upon these labor-based traditions. In the working culture's vision of America, working people had built up America: their hard work, not the inspired visions of capitalists, had made America the great nation it was. Communities of working people, united by background, class, common history, and common purpose, rather than individuals per se, held the key to the American way of life. Home, family, and community remained at its center, but Guthrie's vision held that the dignity of labor and the right to earn a decent living were more important than the sacredness of property or the right to liberty from government intrusion. The labor vision clashed fiercely with business's over the importance of the community in the life of the family and over the true ends of America as a nation.

It was over these deeply held, conflicting beliefs about America that the most important ideological and cultural battles of the Depression were fought. Long after the specifics of political reforms were forgotten, these cultural aspects of the Depression, which included ways in which political beliefs were stigmatized along cultural lines, remained fresh in the memories of the participants. Guthrie's emergence in the 1930s as an entertainer and chronicler of the Dust Bowl and agricultural migrants was grounded in these larger battles. Although he took his music and politics to the cities by the 1940s, its roots in the Depression battles over decent living standards and dignity for farm laborers and the dispossessed remained at the core of his own vision.

The war effort largely ended the Depression's economic malaise, but it accelerated further changes in American life, temporarily submerging the clash over the meaning of American life; those conflicts would reemerge with a vengeance in the radically different atmosphere of political repression during the Cold War. World War II had set even more families in motion, to seek new jobs or to follow kin in the service. Even as the country united for the common purposes of defeating the Axis and preserving freedom, the social clashes of the 1930s were only temporarily set aside.

Popular memory has largely enshrined World War II as "The Good War": many of those who lived through it have distinct and strong memories of the period as one of unprecedented social unity and commonality of purpose. Yet the war revealed that American society still suffered from long-untended wounds; social tensions visibly erupted on the home front, especially along racial lines. Riots over housing integration occurred in Detroit and numerous other cities during the war years. In 1943, servicemen in Los Angeles precipitated a massive race riot targeted at Chicanos. Facing rising inflation, skyrocketing prices, and frozen wages, and with strikes forbidden, labor became more frustrated and militant and tensions flared in dozens of workplaces. The euphoria over winning the war, the victory of freedom over tyranny, quickly dissipated in the new realities of the Cold War.

The years after the war saw a sobering change in American life. The fragile social coalitions that had united behind the war began to crumble. For example, 1946 witnessed the largest wave of strikes ever to hit American workplaces. The Cold War enshrined Communism as the greatest threat to American life, and fear of Communism took a horrible toll throughout American institutions. Censorship, political repression, and blacklisting all became common as American leaders in government and business sought to purge Communists from their midst, even as they could scarcely define what they were. Most troubling, even the most ephemeral personal associations became the test of an individual's character, as membership in organizations was used as evidence of subversive intent and moral fiber. The McCarthyist rush to judgment based on lists, letterheads, and unproved allegations served notice that the battles of the 1930s would be refought in the 1950s, but now without any protection for the right to dissent or to question the political order. In this environment the folk artists and activists of the Depression and war years faced blacklisting. Many were harassed or driven underground, even as members of a younger generation began discovering their work in the quest to find their own meaning of America.

The folk revival intersected with the rise of a series of social movements—civil rights, the antiwar movements, second-wave feminism, the counterculture—in the 1950s and 1960s. All these movements again placed plain people at the core of their activities and often made leaders not of the socially elite but of the rank and file as well. The young people who found their ways into these differing movements sought alternatives to the dominant culture. In great part they succeeded by seeking not only political power and social justice but by looking to cultural expression as an important part of their movements. They saw clear connections between institutions and everyday life, between politics and human experience. The role of everyday culture became central to the success of these movements; no form of expression was more important for them than music. In that sense these movements were all folk movements, and they remade the face of American public life. While Guthrie could not be involved with these postwar movements due to his illness, his own life-work had already shown the connections between folk movements and the mass society that the United States had become by the 1960s.

Guthrie and American Culture

Woody's life exemplified and influenced a number of the most important movements and directions in American culture over the century. His own career foreshadowed important trends in the course of American music, primary among them folk, country, and rock and roll. On a broad level, however, Guthrie resonated with important directions in American life and culture that transcended any specific genre of work. His own career offers an interesting window on the broadest origins of popular interest in folk culture, and on the desires for and debates over authentic expression that underpins much of twentieth-century American culture. By considering the relationship of commerce and popular art, we can see the tensions in American life that often mitigate the force of fierce individualism in art, while at the same time appropriating and making unforeseen uses of those visions.

First of all, Guthrie's emergence in the late 1930s as a voice of "the people" spoke to a broad appetite to view and understand American culture through individual figures. John Steinbeck's somewhat hesitant designation of Guthrie as their spokesman—"in a way, I suspect he *is* the people"—was part and parcel of a long search for America's cultural roots and the desire to find a representative type to serve as the template for the true American.[4] Since before the nation's founding, American critics at home and abroad bemoaned the absence of a fully grounded sense of past and tradition on the scale of Europe's—while often ignoring the traditions of native Americans already here. By the late nineteenth century, observers and critics alike had begun to locate "native" traditions in various cultural forms, inventing a past to suit their own worldviews.

In the urbanizing and modernizing world of the turn of the century, many intellectuals and critics were dismayed at the waves of immigrants flooding American cities, feeling that the foreigners challenged through sheer numbers the character and composition of cultural traditions practiced in the United States. These critics, notably Van Wyck Brooks and others, began to search for what they deemed the "authentic" roots of Ameri-

Sign for Woody Guthrie's performance at the Towne Forum in Los Angeles, California, 1941. PHOTOGRAPH BY SEEMA WEATHER-WAX. COURTESY OF WOODY GUTHRIE ARCHIVES.

can culture, by studying history and folkways, and in finding living examples of old traditions. Scholars, critics, and observers began to investigate the aspects of American culture that were seen as preindustrial holdovers from other times. They became greatly interested in so-called Anglo-Saxon forebears still keeping traditions that predated the United States itself, particularly in relatively isolated areas such as parts of Appalachia and New England. Dozens of interested scholars, antiquarians, collectors, and artists trouped into the Appalachians to study the folkways of mountaineers. They located in them wellsprings of traditions they wished to perceive as unchanged for decades or even centuries: some scholars even wrote of Appalachian people as speaking a variant of Elizabethan English. Ballad collectors scoured the hills for variants of songs that could be traced back over centuries, even as many mountaineers were adding the popular Tin Pan Alley songs of the day or previous years to their own repertoires.

As it happened, reality was more complicated, and the mountaineers hardly lived in a changeless, timeless society, even if it could not be deemed modern or urban. Other scholars and activists went to work with and "preserve" Native American peoples who lived very active and dynamic cultures, even as popular magazine pieces and perceptions indulged in the wishful thinking of Indians as a so-called vanishing race. Along different lines the settlement-house movement in the great cities placed strong emphasis upon recovering and teaching to second-generation youth the lost or suppressed arts, crafts, and traditions of their parents. The mainstream desire to embrace people whose culture actively resisted change had a curious effect: those seeking an unaltered past wound up ignoring the most vital aspects of these peoples' different cultures. In many ways folkloric interest in the Appalachians further marginalized them from American society as a whole.

Underlying all these diverse efforts was the assumption that cultural forms and practices had to be preserved and kept intact, that modern American life was inhospitable to the health of such traditions, and that their continuation was important for their communities, as well as the greater world outside. In this light, culture was a social balm, a means of easing the disruptive strains of the modern world. Second the investigations, accumulations, and observations all had one common assumption: the "true" American heritage was preserved by these peoples who were supposedly isolated from the modernizing mainstream with its commercial culture of dime novels, department stores, amusement parks, beer gardens, and its social ills born of industrialization—squalor, poverty, anomie. At the core, the search for an authentic American culture rested upon a belief in authenticity itself: that some experiences, expressions, and traditions had much stronger roots than others, and that they offered superior means of interpreting life. The quest for the "real," whether in pursuit of folk art pieces by monied collectors, or in the appreciation of a performer's sincerity and emotional force by a mass audience, has in this way dominated much of twentieth-century American culture.

During the 1930s that quest for the authentic drew in Guthrie. Although his own background was middle-class (definitions of the authentic generally focused upon the poor and working class as the only true sectors of authentic culture), the family tragedies that set him on the road at a young age and the suffering he witnessed among the migrants gave him the firsthand experience that enabled him to present himself and to be seen as an authentic bard of the people. The belief that some forms of expression were truer, purer, older, and morally superior to others—specifically to new forms rooted in the changing tastes of an urban-dominated marketplace—gave Guthrie's own art and musical vocabulary its character and fervor. The Weavers' Fred Hellerman noted at the American Music Masters conference on Guthrie that Woody was suspicious of musicians using more than three chords and any but the simplest melodies.[5] Guthrie's aversion to acknowledging other musical forms or pop traditions—an aversion shared by many—often ignored the remarkable adaptability and omnivorous appetites of traditional musicians for other types of songs. Yet the tension between a narrow interpretation of the authentic and a wider, more inclusive sense of traditional sources should not obscure that everyone involved believed in this most basic fact of authenticity: American culture was rooted in the experiences of plain people.

By the 1930s the search for the roots of American culture had coincided with what William Stott called the documentary impulse: the drive in American culture to record and to fix in time not only social conditions, but the cultural expressions of the common people.[6] The emphasis on plain folks' culture complemented the reportage of social conditions that flourished in Depression America. The emphasis upon the common people in part arose from a widespread popular curiosity that was fed by both the commercial culture industries—magazines, newsreels, movies, radio, serial fiction—and the state. This turn to common people in these years flourished in both fictional and nonfictional works. While plain people had always been represented before this era, the Depression cast a focus on everyday folks as both the victims of the Depression and those who defied it. The commercial culture industries made the most out of this: Hollywood films, for example, forsook the jazz era's focus upon flappers, romance, and historical epochs for an emphasis upon plain people, such as those in Frank Capra films and MGM's Andy Hardy series— or, in their pathological forms, those in gangster, vice, and crime movies. Similarly, such diverse entities as newsreels, marathon dancing, popular and pulp magazines, and above all, radio, centered on representations of ordinary folks in their daily lives. Radio especially exemplified this in that its characteristic and innovative forms of entertainment—soap operas, situation comedies, and even adventure serials—were all built upon representations of plain folks.

Similarly, the government built its cultural efforts of the decade specifically around the interests and legacies of common people. Many of the New Deal's cultural interventions were giant recovery and preservation efforts: oral history projects of ex-slaves, workers, and others; guidebook projects that were largely compilations of history and lore along with almanac-style information; photographic assignments to make a record of existing folkways along with social conditions. All these in effect documented the culture of everyday ordinary life. While other programs, most notably the public art programs and the Federal Theater, fostered the creation of new works very often linked to current social issues, the New Deal's general emphasis on the common people signaled a change that has remained with us ever since. Since the 1930s, the rhetoric of portrayal representation and focus on common people has been central to the culture industries. While extraordinary, powerful, and famous people and events continually remain important in commercial culture, the plain people have become both the symbol and the subject of American cultural distinction.

Guthrie was caught up in the shift in attention to the common people. As someone who wrote to chronicle and represent plain people, he forcefully and artfully staked a claim that America and the world should pay attention to the common folk's perspectives, dignity, and rights. Although his own hatred of pretense and falsehood would have made him ridicule many of the portrayals and discussions of the common people or labor issues in his era, he nevertheless participated in and benefited from the larger hunger in American life for understanding "the people." That hunger partly played itself out in sentimental idealized portraits of "the people," especially in the film version of *The Grapes of Wrath* (1940), where the harsh social conditions and brutal oppressions suffered by farmworkers and migrants under agri-capitalism were wrought into a sentimental depiction of a noble people in their suffering. For the millions broadly allied with the New Deal and the political coalition with labor (particularly the CIO), such portraits of suffering and discrimination were not simply objects of pity, they were working people looking at themselves. In other words, one of the sources of hunger for "the people" in fact was the tremendous appetite of the people for all the forms of commercial popular culture available throughout America.

Along with the desire for stories of the people, Guthrie tapped into another long-enduring cultural development in the United States, what might be called the vernacular or do-it-yourself ethos. Like so many blues and some folk artists, he wrote much of his own music; that is, he adapted old songs to new lyrics in many cases, and fashioned his own tunes along very simple lines, making them easily sung in groups and among people who were not trained musicians. While Guthrie was hardly the first folk, hillbilly, or blues artist to gain fame singing his own compositions, he was one of the first to become celebrated for his songs and songwriting abilities. The notion that it was possible to write "folk songs" out of one's own contemporary experience was critical to the folk revival and to its influence on rock and roll.

But do-it-yourself entailed more than just an emphasis upon participation: as amplified in rock and roll, do-it-yourself meant that the individual's own perspective, gifts, and voice—no matter how untrained, unorthodox, or untalented—were central to the force and significance of his or her work. In other words, Guthrie was a compelling example of an American appetite for voices and styles that did not reflect the orthodox training, particular refinement, or conventional notions of beauty. Here Guthrie's legacy to rock and roll was one with the legacy of the blues and country music: you didn't have to be a schooled musician or have a trained voice to communicate. Only that kind of belief would make it possible for rock and roll to appeal to millions who could just as easily have been the performer instead of an audience member. That aesthetic was essential for linking music and social change, a potential realized in the post–World War II era.

A mistake often made in talking about vernacular music is to assume that its practitioners had no training or were "primitive geniuses" lacking training and succeeding on unmediated talent and inspiration; many thought long and hard about their music, practiced it constantly, and could be quite articulate about it. That the first Count Basie Band relied on memorized rather than written arrangements only meant that the musicianship of the band came out in another form than sight reading. That Hank Williams read mostly comic books or was not a conventional lyricist did not make him any less of a craftsman, poet, or genius than Cole Porter. Guthrie himself was part of this very broad movement that redefined the entire scope and character of American popular music over the century. The European and southern migrants who made and remade America's cities created a culture that was an amalgam of their own voices, and it was their tastes and experiences as much as the artistry of their entertainers that recast American music in a series of decidedly working-class accents.

It was by and large those accents and orientations that became the foundation for rock and soul music. The do-it-yourself ethos made its centerpiece the unreconstructed self, making it possible for many young consumers and listeners to imagine themselves as performers and communicators. By eliminating the standards of training or beauty as necessities for music-making, the do-it-yourself ethos in fact broadened aesthetic and social connections and paradoxically opened ears to many different kinds of beauty and art. That ethos translated in the end to much more than music itself: it can be seen in film; in the dozens of sports and games that have sprung up in the post–World War II era; in underground comics; in the fascination for monsters and freaks; and in the general offshoots of culture that we now deem to be "punk."

The fierce independence that fueled so much of Guthrie's own art and social vision never existed in a vacuum: this essay argues that he was always a product of his times. But his career and work offer another insight about the connections of individual genius and the commercial apparatus that govern how Americans experience their culture. He was part of perhaps the last generation who enjoyed the ability to create outside a commercial system that continually feeds on novelty and seeks the marginal and dislocated as a principal resource of innovation. Guthrie lived out much of his life unknown to most of the world. The vast influence he exercised mostly happened through recordings and disciples whose paths were beyond his control. He recorded for Folkways, a small independent record company whose devotion to artists with a social vision was matched by its quirky presence in the marketplace. The company was almost thoroughly marginalized from the mainstream, and unknown to most record buyers.

Yet by the early 1960s, corporations made plain their interest even in the most marginal or suspect of artists and stances. The commercial success of rock and roll and its celebration of plain people in plain voices forced major corporations to rethink their strategies. If youth could hold the keys to large markets, then the marginal, the plain, the ugly, and the suspect were all ripe for sales. Even as the folk revival offered up well-scrubbed and clean-cut figures such as the Kingston Trio, the formerly blacklisted Pete Seeger was signed by Columbia Records. The company also signed Bob Dylan, scruffiest of all the new folkies and an avowed disciple of Guthrie's, and showcased him with the same graphics and publicity as they offered their mainstream, safe stars such as Barbra Streisand, Tony Bennett, or Mitch Miller's Gang. In another light, the do-it-yourself ethos had proved so successful that little would be outside consideration by the mainstream corporations. The subsequent tensions among dissent, protest, and resistance and their commercial doubles erupted throughout the 1960s and have simmered beneath American life ever since.

Guthrie's American Century held within it the promise of social renewal and regeneration by plain people seeking and securing justice and recognition from their government and from a society that largely exploited them. Within that century as well, American life has come to be defined here and abroad by the cultures of those plain people. Woody Guthrie's own legacy and influence in those movements has yet to be fully understood, but he remains central to any assessment of the folk in American life. It seems clear at this point in time that American civilization may ultimately be judged on its honoring and recognizing the interests and culture of ordinary Americans in their diversity as well as their commonality. As long as that remains true, Guthrie will remind us of our nation's tremendous potential, our serious responsibilities to all its inhabitants, and our accountability for how we respond to their claims upon us.

NOTES

1. Michael Denning, *The Cultural Front: The Laboring of American Culture in the Twentieth Century* (New York: Verso, 1996), 272.

2. For preliminary discussions of the American way, see Warren I. Susman, *Culture as History: The Transformation of American Society in the Twentieth Century* (New York: Pantheon, 1985), 150–210.

3. For more detailed discussions of the business counterattack in public relations, see Roland Marchand *Creating the Corporate Soul: The Rise of Public Relations and Corporate Imagery in American Big Business* (Berkeley and Los Angeles: University of California Press, 1998), 202–47.

4. Steinbeck quoted in Denning, *Cultural Front*, 270.

5. Fred Hellerman, quoted at Hard Travelin': The Life and Legacy of Woody Guthrie conference held on 28 September 1996 in Cleveland, Ohio.

6. William Stott, *Documentary Expression and Thirties America* (New York: Oxford University Press, 1973).

DAVID R. SHUMWAY

YOUR LAND
The Lost Legacy of Woody Guthrie

He's a poet, and he's a picker.
He's a prophet, and he's a pusher.
He's a pilgrim and a preacher
and a problem when he's stoned.
—Kris Kristofferson, "The Pilgrim—Chapter 33"

On his album *The Silver Tongued Devil and I*, Kris Kristofferson introduces "The Pilgrim—Chapter 33" by naming a list of performers who inspired the song. They include Dennis Hopper, Johnny Cash, Bobby Neuwirth, Jerry Jeff Walker, Paul Sieble, and Ramblin' Jack Elliott, but the prototype is not named. All of these men follow in the footsteps of Woody Guthrie. "The Pilgrim" describes a figure "wasted on the sidewalk / in his jacket and his jeans / wearing yesterday's misfortunes like a smile." This figure, as the title suggests, is both a wanderer and a believer—though not in any traditional religion. He is defined by his loneliness, his marginal position relative to social norms and public acceptance. Kristofferson gives us no sense of where the person he describes came from, but Joe Klein, Guthrie's biographer, gives us a good idea. He shows that Elliott began his career by hanging around Woody and imitating him: "He could imitate Woody perfectly. It was downright eerie, and Woody would shake his head and giggle: 'He sounds more like me than I do.'"[1] And Jack Elliott was just the first Guthrie imitator. Klein describes the horde of young folksingers who would congregate on Sunday afternoons in Washington Square Park, "whanging away at their guitars, singing, 'Goin' down the road feelin' bad . . .' with all the grit their adenoids could muster. Many of them affected—uncannily—a certified Guthrie slouch, ratty old clothes, facial stubble, and aroma."[2] Klein suggests that

most of these young wannabes didn't know very much about Guthrie,
and that what he represented to them was the freedom of the road, freedom from parents and school. What's missing from these imitators' sense
of Guthrie is politics: what Guthrie believed and his deep to commitment
to those beliefs.

Historically, of course, there was only one Woody Guthrie, but a particular image of him was "canonized," an image that largely excluded the
radicalism of his life and songs. Why has the creation of the "pilgrim"
personality been Guthrie's most familiar legacy? The radical politics of
his songs are certainly not unknown, especially to insiders, aficionados,
and scholars, but they have often been obscure to the larger public. It is
reported that President Lyndon Johnson once said that "This Land Is
Your Land" should be the national anthem. One can only assume that
Johnson made this remark without awareness that the song explicitly op-
poses private property. It is true that the most radical verses of the song
were probably unknown to the President just as they were, and still are,
to most Americans. Still, the song's socialist agenda should have been
clear to anyone who cared to pay attention to the words or who knew
some of Guthrie's other lyrics. It was more than the particular oppression
of the 1950s that kept the politics of Woody Guthrie's songs from being
understood. Rather, conditions endemic to American culture render it almost impossible for genuinely radical positions to be recognized or remembered—except when they are demonized. In what follows is a care-
ful look at Guthrie's songs to show just how radical they are. I shall then
explore how the image of the romantic individualist came to supplant a
fuller picture of Guthrie that included his politics.

Not all of Woody's lyrics are explicitly radical, of course. He wrote
children's songs, songs that celebrated the engineering feats of Bonneville
Power Administration, songs that celebrated and lamented life on the
road. Moreover, many of Woody's more explicitly political songs were
not released on record until long after they were recorded in the 1940s.
The albums *Struggle* and *Ballads of Sacco and Vanzetti*, for example,
contain material largely unfamiliar even to the folk music audience. Still,
many of Guthrie's more familiar songs, including those from the only significant album of his to appear during his performing days, *Dust Bowl
Ballads*, make his radical politics very clear. This is material that
Guthrie's imitators and fans might reasonably be expected to have
known.

Perhaps the most striking fact about Woody Guthrie's oeuvre is the sa-
lience of class in so many of his songs. This is striking because class is
something that American culture constantly denies to itself. F. Scott Fitz-
gerald made class an issue in his fictional depictions of America in the

Woody Guthrie and Burl Ives in the park reading HoBo News, *1940.* COURTESY OF WOODY GUTHRIE ARCHIVES.

1920s, but people ever since have had trouble taking him seriously. Walt Whitman, the poet of democracy and the people (according to F. O. Matthiessen's influential reading) is more typical. He is, perhaps, a garden-variety American populist, one who speaks of the people in such a way that the term includes everyone. Jazz, rhythm and blues, and rock and roll, have all claimed at different times to be the music of the oppressed, but they have seldom articulated that oppression explicitly, much less expressed it in class terms. It was racism that these forms may to some extent have challenged or opposed, but even this was not done explicitly. As Michael Denning has argued, the 1930s saw the emergence of a new working class that began to reshape American cultural production, even as it reshaped American industrial relations and tried to reshape American politics.[3] Guthrie is one of these "organic intellectuals" in whose songs class oppression comes across not as an element in a theory, but as part of his experience of America.

In bourgeois literature and song, class is usually represented in terms of various markers of status and identity. The novel of manners, of course, distinguishes classes by reference to codes of conduct and taste defined by bourgeoisie. Popular songs (Cole Porter's for example) are filled with references to the commodities that distinguish the rich from the poor. Class in Guthrie's songs, on the other hand, is almost always portrayed as conflict. One repeated motif is the poor individual or family whose home has been taken by the rich. The motif is present in many of the songs of *Dust Bowl Ballads*. In "Dust Can't Kill Me," the singer loses his homestead to the landlord and his house to a tractor. In "Pretty Boy Floyd," the singer remarks that you won't ever see "an outlaw drive a family from their home." "Tom Joad," which tells a version of *The Grapes of Wrath*, describes the Joads as being "tractored out by the cats." But it is, not surprisingly, "I Ain't Got No Home" that makes the most of the loss of one's dwelling. As in the other songs, a "Rich man took my home and drove me from my door," the singer tells us. But we also get more information about his relations with the ruling class. When the singer had his home, he was a sharecropper who was "always poor" and whose crops he "laid in to the banker's store." He concludes that the world is a funny place where "the gamblin' man is rich and the working man is poor." As this song makes clear, homelessness for Guthrie is not a matter of happenstance, whether climatic or social, but the very condition of being a worker. The singer is radically dispossessed, not just of property, but of his social being, his belonging to place and community.

The world Guthrie's songs depict is structured by constant, violent class conflict. The violence is primarily what workers experience at the hands of the bosses, and their henchmen, cops, and thugs. "Vigilante Man," from *Dust Bowl Ballads*, is about the latter type, men of the sort who carry clubs and shotguns, who roust the homeless taking shelter from the rain, and who kill Preacher Casey for saying "Unite, all you working men," an incident also mentioned in "Tom Joad." "I Ain't Got No Home" tells us that "the police make it hard wherever I may go." The law in Guthrie's lyrics is always on the side of the bosses and the rich. "Hangknot" (a.k.a. Slipknot), from *Struggle*, asks "Who makes the law for that hangknot," and then suggests that merely asking questions can get you on the wrong end of one. The song connects hanging as a punishment for escaped slaves to lynching (They hung him from a pole / and they shot him full of holes. / Left him there to rot on the hang knot), and both to legal execution. *Ballads of Sacco and Vanzetti*, of course, is a prolonged exploration of an instance of "justice" serving the interests of the rich. In "You Souls of Boston," we hear that Judge Webster Thayer could not "allow / The Morelli Gang's confession to stop him now. / Sacco and Vanzetti are union men. / And that verdict, guilty, must come in." The songs on *Struggle* deal primarily with the death and misery perpetrated by capital against labor both on the job and on strike. "Waiting at the

Gate" describes a mine explosion that occurs because the company ignored an inspector's warning. The title of "Union Burying Ground" speaks for itself. "Ludlow Massacre" and "1913 Massacre" are detailed narratives of organized violence against striking workers, their wives, and children. There is no question in these accounts of the violence being inadvertent or unplanned. The strikers and their families are class enemies that the bosses will go to any length to defeat.

While Guthrie's songs often deal with workers' defeats, they are not defeatist in any sense. Many go beyond descriptions of oppressive class relations to support organized opposition to them. "Union Maid" is probably Guthrie's most famous organizing song: "Oh, you can't scare me I'm sticking to the union / Sticking to the union, till the day I die." Besides "Union Maid," the songs on *Struggle* might be the most forthright in their calls to organize. Even the stories of the horrific massacres are concluded with uplifting calls to arms. "Union Burying Ground" asserts that every death will bring one hundred more members. "Buffalo Skinners" describes the revenge workers take on a boss who lured them out into the wilderness and then refused to pay them. There is less talk of unions on *Dust Bowl Ballads* than one might expect, but Guthrie's "Tom Joad," as Denning has pointed out, echoes "Joe Hill" by having Tom assert as he leaves his mother that "Wherever men are fightin' for their rights / That's where I'm gonna be, Ma."[4] A number of songs on *Ballads of Sacco and Vanzetti* include calls to organize or to fight, as for example, "Two Good Men": "All you people ought to be like me, / And work like Sacco and Vanzetti; / And every day find some ways to fight / On the union side for workers' rights." One of Guthrie's most popular songs, "Pastures of Plenty," sung in the voice of the migrant agricultural worker, claims that "we fight till we win," and that "My land I'll defend with my life, if it be / 'Cause my pastures of plenty must always be free." Klein describes these verses as "patriotic," but they could just as easily be read as a defense of the migrant's claim to the land.[5] This meaning becomes more plausible in light of the way private property is treated in "This Land is Your Land."

While many listeners today know that "This Land is Your Land" was written as a left-wing response to Irving Berlin's "God Bless America," the song continues to be reprinted in collections of patriotic songs (which ironically often include Berlin's song as well). I'll address the general question of the patriotism of Guthrie's songs below, but this practice clearly seems to take "This Land" to be patriotic only when it is stripped of any oppositional content. Nonetheless, this seemingly innocuous celebration of the American landscape is the most radical of all of Guthrie's songs. The fact that the song's radicalism was lost was not entirely the fault of an uncomprehending public. The first recording of the song, issued in 1951, included only four verses, omitting the two or three explicitly radical ones. Given the Red Scare then in progress, it makes sense that this safer version should have been released, and it was this version that was recorded by numerous others, few of whom, as Klein puts it, "could have realized that they were singing a song originally intended as a Marxist response to 'God Bless America.'"[6]

Clearly the context of the 1950s militated against it, but the song's radical meaning could have been understood by anyone who sought to discover it. Indeed, the song's chief message lies in its title and opening line, "This land is your land / This land is my land." What is being claimed here is nothing less than common ownership of the American land. The land is not the landlords', not the bosses', not the rich people's, but yours and mine. We, the workers, the migrants, the poor, the landless, own this land. This interpretation is inescapable once one hears the following omitted verse:

> Was a big high wall there that tried to stop me
> A sign was painted said: Private Property.
> But on the back side, it didn't say nothing—
> This land was made for you and me.

By specifically rejecting the sign's claim of "private property," Guthrie makes clear the radical message of the song as a whole. Private property is the fundamental right asserted by capitalism, the foundation of the inequality that it seeks to promote and perpetuate. In the United States in particular, property rights have often been the only rights the government has been willing to protect. Labor struggles, for example, until the New Deal, almost always turned on the government's willingness to use force to defend the owners' property rights against the workers' rights to assemble, to express themselves, and to protect their jobs. Many of Woody's other songs deal with the power of the propertied over the propertyless. The first verse of "Do Re Mi," for example, deals with the illegal blockade that the Los Angeles police established at the California border to keep out those without money during the Dust Bowl. The second verse expands the lesson to living in California, "a paradise to live in or to see / But believe it or not, / you won't find it so hot / If you ain't got the do re mi." "This Land" claims the moral right of all to share America's land and its property. Another of the suppressed verses describes the reality of life in the United States, where not only is the land not common property, but the barest necessities of life are not available to many:

> One bright sunny morning in the shadow of the steeple
> By the relief office I saw my people—

> As they stood there hungry,
> I stood there wondering if
> This land was made for you and me.

The most striking thing about this verse is its difference in mood from all of the others. While the "private property" verse is defiant, this one is skeptical of the assertion made throughout the rest of the song. That may be the reason that, while the "private property" verse is now often sung by left-leaning performers—probably as a result of Arlo Guthrie's efforts (see Klein)—this last verse is not. Yet it is, I would argue, an important part of the whole. It explains why the song's central assertion is not mere rhetoric, mere nationalist celebration. It is because there are hungry people in the midst of plenty that it is necessary to claim the rights of all to common ownership of the land. Nor is this merely a condition of depression, as the liner notes to the first volume of the Smithsonian's new series of Asch Collection recordings contends. It is rather an observation that could be made today, when, in spite of good economic conditions, the number of hungry Americans continues to grow. What this verse suggests is that a struggle is necessary if poor Americans are to claim their rights to their land.

It is only in the "relief office" verse that "This Land" sounds at all like a protest song. Elsewhere, its tone *is* celebratory. Like "America the Beautiful," which it to some extent echoes, "This Land" extols the American landscape: "As I went walking that ribbon of highway / And saw above me the endless skyway / And saw below me that golden valley." Another verse speaks of a Whitmanian voice "chanting" "This land was made for you and me."

This celebratory tone raises the difficult issue of this song's and Guthrie's patriotism. It has always been difficult for the American left to make effective use of patriotic imagery and sentiments. When left-wing positions are expressed in patriotic terms the positions often go unnoticed. Consider Ronald Reagan's attempt to appropriate Bruce Springsteen's "Born in the U.S.A." as an endorsement of his regime. The reason for this, I believe, is that patriotic sentiments, which in some nations are most strongly attached to place, are in the United States usually bound up with a particular ideology. Garry Wills has observed that the Declaration of Independence is often treated as if it were a secular scripture defining what it means to be an American: "If there is an American *idea*, then one must subscribe to it in order to be fully American. . . . To be fully American, one must adopt this idea wholeheartedly, proclaim it, prove one's devotion to it."[7] The American idea is usually assumed to be inconsistent with the radical vision of Guthrie's songs, but so powerful is the identification of this ideology with America, that Guthrie's celebration of its landscape is nevertheless read as an endorsement of that ideology. Even those who recognize the radicalism of Guthrie's songs often seem unable to resist the dichotomy between the left-wing vision and love of country. For example, according to Robert Cantwell

[Guthrie's] lived consciousness of the gulf between rich and poor, shaped in the peach orchards of California could, without grave distortions, easily adapt itself to a Marxist analysis of capitalist society; or, at least, could be put to service in the various projects to which the [Communist] party dedicated itself in the thirties. But as his own songs—"This Land is Your Land," "Pastures of Plenty," "Ramblin' Round," "Hard Travelin' and many others—suggest, Guthrie's vision was closer to Whitman than to Alfred Hayes, "an intoxication," wrote Robert Shelton, "with the richness and breadth, the variety and the promise of the American soil and character."[8]

Cantwell's invocation of the "party" alerts us to another obstacle to the appreciation of Guthrie's politics. Ronald D. Cohen's essay in this volume attempts to settle the question of Guthrie's relationship to the Party, but regardless of whether he was a Communist, Guthrie was strongly identified with the Party, often writing and performing on its behalf, and, as Klein shows, willingly adopting the Party line through its torturous changes during World War II. The problem is not Guthrie's association with the Communists, but the absolute identification of left-wing radicalism of the 1930s with the Party. Denning has suggested a more accurate account of American radical politics of this era, one that does not deny the Communists a significant role, but that argues for a larger social and cultural movement, the Popular Front. Rejecting the usual assumption that the Popular Front "was made up of Communists and fellow-travelling liberals," Denning sees instead "a historical bloc, in Gramsci's sense, . . . a broad and tenuous left-wing alliance of fractions of the subaltern class."[9] The base of this bloc was the labor movement, especially the CIO, which successfully organized new industrial unions in manufacturing and mining. What developed from this base was not only a political movement but a cultural one, and Woody Guthrie is one of Denning's chief examples of the latter. Indeed, for Guthrie, Denning's analysis works better than the traditional one: union organizing was the political activity that first attracted him and in which he was consistently involved. What Denning's perspective shows is that Guthrie's radicalism should be understood as indigenous to America, not something preached by Moscow.

Of course, left-wing radicalism during the 1950s was understood precisely as something emanating from Moscow, so the folk music revival of that period, as Cantwell shows, had to bury its political roots. This accounts for some of the ways Guthrie came to be understood, and taken together with the more general failure of American culture to recognize the possibility of a native radicalism, the failure to recognize Guthrie's politics may seem wholly explained. But one must also add another factor to this mix, the influence of *Bound for Glory* on Guthrie's imitators and the larger public. *Bound for Glory* contains many of the same radical themes as Guthrie's songs, but they are not dominant in the book. It is certainly not the story of a political education; in fact, Guthrie's political activities are barely mentioned. Instead, the book gives us the story of the same sort of character whom Kristofferson describes in "The Pilgrim." The Woody Guthrie who emerges from *Bound for Glory* is very much the individual, and not a representative member of class. We get to know him as one who has overcome significant misfortune, one who has had experiences and adventures not shared by most members of the middle class. The latter makes the book of a piece with much other American prose of the mid-twentieth century, including the fiction of Hemingway and Kerouac. The Guthrie of *Bound for Glory* represents the possibility of escape from the routines and responsibilities of post–World War II America. In this guise Guthrie fits with Davey Crockett, Elvis Presley, and other icons of the 1950s more than he does with Tom Joad or Paul Robeson.

If Kristofferson's introduction to "The Pilgrim" leaves out the first in the series, it also fails to mention the most significant of the subsequent examples, Robert Zimmerman of Minnesota, who changed his name to Bob Dylan and claimed Woody's mantle.[10] Dylan was certainly the most political of the performers who followed in Guthrie's footsteps, but he was more attracted to Woody the romantic individualist than Woody the singer of the people. According to Anthony Scaduto, it was reading *Bound for Glory* that really captured Dylan's imagination. Before reading it, Dylan knew little of Guthrie, but "*Bound for Glory* knocked Dylan out, and he was quickly caught up in the whole romantic hobo life that Guthrie had lived and written about. . . . He became Woody Guthrie."[11] Like Ramblin' Jack Elliott, Dylan adopted Guthrie's personal and musical styles, and sometimes appropriated his Okie heritage, but he developed significantly different politics. This was perhaps inevitable; the struggle of Dylan's moment was the civil rights movement, and unions no longer seemed radical. Class is thus a theme that is largely absent from Dylan's corpus. Dylan's politics were always more liberal, more focused on individual freedom than structural oppression. Moreover, Dylan's aesthetic trajectory, which took him away from overtly political songs by the mid-1960s, is much more in keeping with the romantic individualism celebrated in "The Pilgrim," than with the Guthrie of *Dust Bowl Ballads* or *Sacco and Vanzetti*. Dylan wanted to be an artist and not merely a singer of the people's songs. Moreover, in the long run Dylan seems to be the ultimate "believer" in Kristofferson's sense, one who keeps shifting from creed to creed so that finally one finds it hard to take any of his positions seriously. Like the other followers, Dylan did not ultimately help keep Guthrie's political legacy alive.

The image of Woody Guthrie as a romantic individualist probably made it possible for him to reach an audience in the 1950s and later. I don't mean merely that this image helped to keep Guthrie's songs from being blacklisted during the McCarthy period, but that it even today remains a much more acceptable role for a singer-songwriter to play. This would be true even if Guthrie expressed more popular political positions; politics in general are not regarded as the best material for songs. But if we are to understand Woody Guthrie's place in our cultural history, we can only do so by acknowledging the indigenous radicalism of his songs.

NOTES

1. Joe Klein, *Woody Guthrie: A Life* (New York: Knopf, 1980), 364.
2. Ibid., 421.
3. Michael Denning, *The Cultural Front: The Laboring of American Culture in the Twentieth-Century* (London: Verso, 1996), 7–8.
4. Ibid., 270–71.
5. Klein, *Woody Guthrie*, 196.
6. Ibid., 434.
7. Garry Wills, *Inventing America* (New York: Doubleday, 1979), xxii; emphasis in original.
8. Robert Cantwell, *When We Were Good: The Folk Revival* (Cambridge, Mass.: Harvard University Press, 1996), 136, quoting R. Shelton, "A Man to Remember: Woody Guthrie," *Newport Folk Festival Program* (1960).
9. Denning, *Cultural Front*, 5–6.
10. I heard Kristofferson in concert say in introducing "The Pilgrim" that "he wouldn't dare write a song about Bob Dylan."
11. Anthony Scaduto, *Bob Dylan* (London: Helter-Skelter, 1996), 41.

RONALD D. COHEN

WOODY THE RED?

Woody Guthrie has long been a national treasure, with "This Land Is Your Land" the country's unofficial anthem, familiar to most elementary school students as well as their parents. His musically productive years spanned only about a decade, starting in the late 1930s—but what a decade! Woody's moving paeans to the country's natural richness and industrial potential, his funny, sprightly children's songs, his love songs to friends, family, and the human spirit have all garnered deserved attention. Yet his overtly political songs are less known, and understandably so, for they deal with concerns seemingly long dead and buried: labor struggles, corporate greed and cruelty, issues of war and peace, racism, and a faith in grassroots democracy. Many of these issues were connected to struggles championed by the Communist Party at the time, a frightening, unsavory, and faint memory for most Americans by century's end.

Woody was certainly linked to the Communist Party, but how, to what degree, and to what end? And what difference does it make in coming to grips with his contributions and legacy? Stephen Whitfield, in his otherwise admirable study *The Culture of the Cold War*, labels all Communists by the 1940s as "Stalinists": "They habitually offered alibis for mass murder and denounced as 'slander' the effort to expose Soviet crimes. To call them Stalinists is also a reminder to readers that American Communists were enemies of civil liberties, which they disdained as 'bourgeois' but which they invoked in their own behalf when opportune. They themselves remained mini-totalitarians." Carrying through with this impression, he later remarks: "Woody Guthrie had proudly cultivated an ardent pro-Communism by the late 1930s and did not waver thereafter . . . 'This Machine Kills Fascists' was inscribed on Guthrie's guitar. During the Korean War, however, he did not conceal his support for the North Koreans and Chinese forces." Seemingly because of his extreme political views, this "unabashedly Stalinist" musician was out of favor in the 1950s. Yet a decade and more later, "This Land is Your Land" had been recorded by Bing Crosby, Connie Francis, Paul Anka, and the Mormon Tabernacle Choir, as well as used in advertising jingles by Ford Motor Company and United Airlines; "all of whom were thus pouring into mainstream culture a Marxist rebuttal to 'God Bless America,'" Whitfield concludes.[1] But how do terms like "Stalinist" and "Marxist" help to understand Woody and his substantial contributions to America's musical life and cultural spirit? And what were his politics?

Dave Marsh has a much softer, more positive view of Woody's political milieu. "Meetings were never his metier," Marsh explains. "The few he attended, he did his utmost to turn into parties of the opposite kind. But Guthrie lived in a community suffused with socialism, in which whatever of its principles could be enacted without state power were put into practice. Most important, Woody Guthrie wrote his greatest songs and stories while living among people who believed in and worked toward a high and mighty goal outside themselves." Marsh's description is quite a distance from Woody as Stalinist dupe.[2]

Before exploring the specifics of Woody's political views and affiliations, it is necessary to have some grasp of the history of the Communist Party. Scholars have been grappling with this issue for decades, with no consensus in sight despite the demise of the Cold War. Socialist and other left-wing parties and movements in the United States date from the early nineteenth century, and they visibly proliferated in the decades following the Civil War. Various radical parties had emerged by World War I, striving to achieve economic equity and power for the downtrodden.

The tumult of war and revolution, with the splintering of the dominant Socialist Party, the domestic Red Scare, and the triumph of the Communist Party in Russia, led to a domestic reshuffling of radical allegiances. The Communist Party of the United States soon emerged, committed to fomenting revolution at home and abroad. Party members and associates viewed the Soviet Union as the beacon of freedom and equality, a workers' paradise, and there was a close relationship between Moscow and the Party leadership in various countries throughout the world. With a shrunken membership, the Party limped through the 1920s, then emerged in the midst of the Depression with an invigorated agenda and escalating membership, spurred by the rejuvenated labor movement, the struggle against European and homegrown fascism, and a strong homegrown commitment to racial justice. The fluctuating membership included hundreds of thousands by decade's end, heavily concentrated in foreign language units and within organized labor, as well as among intellectuals and those in show business. The Party's cooperative attitude toward others within labor/Left movements created a heady period of growth and creative fervor.

Party members struggled with issues of war and peace as World War II loomed, however, partly confused by the Nazi-Soviet nonaggression pact in August 1939, until the German invasion of the Soviet Union in June 1941 and the subsequent Japanese attack on Pearl Harbor in December. During the war the Party dissolved itself, solidly backing President Franklin Roosevelt and the war effort. At war's end it emerged into an atmosphere of escalating anti-Communism and Cold War hysteria, which reached a frenzy by the early 1950s. Woody Guthrie's experiences with the Party took place during this time of political peaks and valleys, ranging from the revolutionary optimism and Popular Front days of the late 1930s, through patriotic antifascism, to the fearful times of the later 1940s and the splintering of the old coalitions.

While historians agree on the general outlines of the history of the Party, they disagree violently on its meaning and substance, particularly whether Party members and sympathizers were "loyal" Americans or dupes, perhaps even secret agents, of a nasty foreign power, led by Stalin, a sadistic megalomaniac out to conquer the world. Recently two rough camps have emerged: those who prefer stressing Party members' links to Moscow and their untold nefarious deeds versus those who generally interpret members' actions as conscientious and well-meaning, perhaps even contributing to the country's economic, political, and cultural health. Among the former, Harvey Klehr and John Earl Haynes emphasize the Party's centralized structure; they thus refer to a generic Communist: for example, "American Communists sought nothing less than revolutionary transformation of society into a perfect egalitarian socialism," or "American Communists pursued their goals with remarkable energy," or "American Communists coupled their idealistic devotion to the movement with hatred of their opponents." In another context, Haynes has qualified his stance somewhat: "There is no doubt that many individual Communists thought they were creating a heaven on earth even while they were creating something much closer to a hell." But generally, Klehr, Haynes, Whitfield, and numerous others, mirroring popular attitudes during the height of the Cold War, have focused on the Party's centralized leadership shackled to villainous Moscow despots, with little concern for the thoughts, actions, and contributions of the rank-and-file members and numerous fellow travelers, such as Woody Guthrie.[3]

Recently, a growing number of scholars have focused on those individuals laboring in the political trenches of the Old Left, with an understanding, if not totally sympathetic, approach. Michael Denning, for one, in his massive cultural study of the 1930s, argues that the Popular Front—the alliance between the Communist Party and members of the labor/Left through the latter half of the decade—was a "radical social-democratic movement forged around anti-fascism, anti-lynching, and the industrial unionism of the CIO." Concerned about a broad range of left-ist cultural and political issues, an exciting band of highly creative artists, not only in New York but throughout the country, made their marks in literature, music, art, theater, movies, and dance. An activist, non-Communist Left had also emerged during the 1930s, often in an uneasy alliance with the Communist Party until the Nazi-Soviet pact finally exploded this odd quasi-partnership. Student radicalism, fueled by the peace movement and a strong dose of antifascism, added to the political ferment.[4]

Woody emerged as a performer and pundit during this time of electrifying cultural and political dislocations. Moreover, he connected with the Communist Party in Southern California, led by political mavericks a significant three thousand miles away from Party headquarters in New York. After considerable roaming, Woody settled in Los Angeles in 1937 and soon appeared on local radio station KFVD. Particularly troubled by the plight of proliferating migrant workers, he took a turn toward political songs even before he met Ed Robbin, Los Angeles editor for the daily *People's World* (the West Coast equivalent of the *Daily Worker*), who had a radio show just after Woody's. Robbin asked Woody to sing at a Communist-sponsored meeting, while warning him of the radical politics. Woody responded, "I sing my songs wherever I can sing 'em. So if you'll have me, I'll be glad to go," and go he did. With some hyperbole, this about sums up Woody's politics at the time, and later. Robbin became Woody's agent, booking him at political meetings and fundraisers, which quickly adjusted to having a folk singer, any folk singer, but particularly one of his character and ability.[5]

About this time Woody also wrote:

Franklin D. says a third of us is ill this, ill these, ill those. If I had a car that was one third this broke down, I'd be willing to gamble on a new kind. . . . But we just jump up and innocently and ignorantly happen to discover the breakdown and being good sports and hardworkers, just sort of offer to help fix it, or to make a new one. This of course is what they hire the [Martin] Dies Gang (HUAC) for to keep you from spotting anything that's wrong, and to flail the daylights out of you for not putting out a big smile, and just setting there in the middle of the road, not moving a dadburn inch in either direction—with a big silly grin on your face, nodding gently and sweetly to all the folks, and waiting for the damn thing to take you somewhere to dinner. It just aint done.[6]

Robbin was also instrumental in introducing Woody to the actor Will Geer, who became a lifelong friend, and connecting him with *People's World* editor Al Richmond, after Woody expressed an interest in writing for the eclectic paper. "We took on this unknown hillbilly as a regular columnist, without pay, to be sure, but with some frontpage fanfare, and also without serious examination of his political credentials or antecedents, let alone an ideological screening test," Richmond has written in his autobiography.[7] Such faith in the maverick quickly appeared justified. Woody's *People's World* column, "Woody Sez," running daily, was launched in mid-May 1939, initially lasting until early January 1940; he also had a daily cartoon from May into September. After he moved to New York and began writing for the *Daily Worker*, he again contributed to the *People's World*, from March to November 1940.

Introduced to the paper's readers as an Oklahoma rustic, Woody continued the guise, peppering his columns and cartoons with folksy themes and telling anecdotes, yet with no hint of sectarian politics: "I ain't a communist necessarily, but I been in the red all my life." Concerning Woody and Will, "Neither was a political theorist. Neither bothered about what was the correct line to follow," Robbin believed. "Both Guthrie and Geer had always known which side they were on. . . . He and Geer both had always been on the side of working people, of the poor and the oppressed." This was enough for Robbin, who was later blacklisted, along with Geer and so many others. Woody and Will for a while traveled through the state's migrant camps, entertaining and organizing the downtrodden. "I drew pen sketches for the *People's World* and learned all I could from the speeches and debates, forums, picnics, where famous labor leaders spoke," he proudly recounted a few years later. "I heard William Z. Foster, Mother Bloor, Gurley Flynn, Blackie Myers [all prominent Communists]. I heard most all of them and played my songs on their platforms."[8]

Following the Nazi-Soviet pact, Woody took a strong antiwar position, believing, as he wrote at the time, "WAR is [a] game played by maniacs who kills each other. It is murder, studied, prepared and planned by insane minds, and followed by a bunch of thieves. You can't believe in life, and wear the uniform of death. . . . As long as the pore folks fights the rich folks wars, you'll keep a havin' pore folks, rich folks, and wars." While he would later strongly back intervention and throw himself wholeheartedly into the war against fascism, there is no reason to question his prewar neutralist stance. According to Joe Klein, Woody's biographer, following August 1939, the "doubters fell away and after the purification ritual, all that was left [in the Communist Party] was a hard core of true believers able to construct brilliant, elaborate rationalizations in defense of the romantic vision they chose to believe was a 'scientific' truth, but unwilling to ask themselves any of the basic questions that even a fledgling scientist must." Perhaps, but such a sweeping statement hardly incorporates the feelings of Woody—although Klein labels him a "professional innocent, still the adult child"—and many of his friends.[9]

Woody moved to New York in early 1940 and swiftly merged into the developing folk music scene, which was strongly laced with Left politics. In March he appeared at Will Geer's "Grapes of Wrath Evening," a benefit for the John Steinbeck Committee for Agricultural Workers, joining with Alan and Bess Lomax, Aunt Molly Jackson, Lead Belly, the Golden Gate Quartet, and Pete Seeger. Representing what seemed an authentic strain of midwestern rural radicalism, he appeared alongside the few other performers—Lead Belly and Aunt Molly among them—who connected eastern intellectuals with confirmed members of the rural working class. While Woody played up his romanticized role as Okie bard, the image was not too far off, although he certainly exaggerated for effect. "As long as a natian [sic] is run by Money Rule, you got rotten politicians, rotten banks, rotten crops, rotten clothing, rotten gangsters, and rotten ever thing," seemed to sum up his general politics. "I dident know I was so smart," he added.[10]

Always the maverick, he yet resented any questioning of his patriotism or attempts to fasten him into an ideological straitjacket. "They called me a communist and a wild man and everything you could think of but I dont care what they call me," he confessed to Alan Lomax in September 1940, reacting to recent slurs in the New York press following some positive publicity. "I aint a member of any earthly organization[.] My trouble is I really ought to go down in the morning and just join everything. I registered in California as a democrat and changed it one day to a progressive just because I was passing the lady[']s house. I done that on a dare more or less from a girl I was out walking." So much for sectarian politics.[11]

Woody traveled continuously. Passing through Oklahoma, he met "Bob and Ina Wood, the organizers of the Communist Party in Oklahoma. They gave me as good a feeling as I ever got from being around anybody in my whole life," he would testify. "They made me see why I had to keep going around and around with my guitar making up songs and singing." Returning to New York, Woody connected with the Almanac Singers, which partially defined his political and musical potential at the time, although he was never a secure member of the group, often preferring to go his own way. Pete Seeger, Lee Hays, and Millard Lampell had formed the loose assemblage in late 1940, and were soon joined by Bess Lomax, Pete and Butch Hawes, and later Sis Cunningham, hoping to foment a singing labor movement. Woody was not around when the group recorded their antiwar album *John Doe* in the spring of 1941, nor does he appear on the *Talking Union* album. But he recorded with them the labor-oriented "Song For Bridges" and "Babe O'Mine," then the two nonpolitical folk albums, *Deep Sea Chanties and Whaling Ballads* and *Sod Buster Ballads*, in early summer. With the German invasion of the Soviet Union in late June, the Almanacs, along with Woody and the rest of the Old Left, buried their antiwar ditties. Pete Seeger later explained, referring to the Almanacs' antiwar period and much else, "Should I apologize for all this? I think so. At any rate, today I'll apologize for a number of things, such as thinking that Stalin was simply a 'hard driver' and not a supremely cruel misleader." Woody never really apologized or explained, just moved ahead.[12]

Writing to Pete, Lee, and Mill from Portland in early July 1941, Woody partly summed up his populist feelings: "And it is our job if we claim the smallest distinction as American Folk Lorists, to see to it that the seeds are sown which will grow up into free speech, free singing, and the free pursuit of happiness that is the first and simplest birthright of a free people." But freedom was an uphill struggle against the almost overwhelming forces of monopoly capital. "For with their songs chocked and their pamphlets condemned, their freedom will be throttled down to less than a walk, and freedom of going and coming, of meeting and discussing, of course, freedom will just be a rich man's word to print in his big papers and holler over his big radio, it wont be real, it will only be a word. As now the case about 90% of the time." The battle against oppression had now to be fought on two fronts, at home and in Europe.[13]

Woody plunged into the war effort, musically and physically. Working with the Almanacs, he penned "The Sinking of the Reuben James," his paean to innocent lives lost, then "Boomtown Bill" and "Keep That Oil A-Rollin" for the Oil Workers International Union, where he connected fighting fascism with a strong labor movement. "And now we're fighting in a war, the oil has got to flow / And the best way to beat Hitler is to join the C.I.O.," he urged the workers in "Boomtown Bill." Looking ahead to the postwar years, he dreamed: "C.I.O. is the place for me / When this war is over, I want to be free / That company union made a fool out of me / I'm a union man in a union war / It's a union land I'm a-fighting for." Always weaving the two together—organized labor and defeating fascism—Woody's commitment propelled him into the Merchant Marine in 1943, along with his singing partner Cisco Houston. The story has been humorously documented by their traveling companion Jim Longhi.[14]

Longhi carefully, wittily captures not only Woody's odd personality and ludicrous antics, but also his fierce dedication to worker solidarity, particularly through his membership in the radical National Maritime Union (NMU). Rehashing one shipboard political discussion during their

Woody Guthrie and Cisco Houston performing at a communist political association rally, 1944. COURTESY WOODY GUTHRIE ARCHIVES.

first voyage into the North Atlantic, Longhi notes: "Woody said that true freedom consisted in the right of every person to have a decent job, as well as the freedom to say his piece, and that socialism might be the way to guarantee that." The only mention of Stalin was by Woody's antagonist, Davey Bannanas, who yelled, "They're *all* motherfakkers! Marx, Engels, Lenin, Stalin." Another time, on another ship, Woody, responding to a question, explained he was writing an article for the *Sabbath Employee*. "Never heard of it," his shipmate responded. "Its official name is the *Sunday Worker*," Woody continued, only to be confronted with, "The *Sunday Worker*? That's a no-good fucking Communist newspaper!" "Told you you'd get mad," said Woody. "It's the only paper that printed my stories about the Okie fruit-picking camps." And that is what mattered, not its Communist affiliation. Still, according to Longhi, after Woody returned to the States, the FBI seized his seaman's papers because of his article in the *Sunday Worker*. "'I'm fighting them,' Woody said." Klein makes no mention of FBI problems, but in any case Woody was not too radical to avoid the army draft, which oddly came in May 1945, despite his being in his early thirties and having numerous dependents.[15]

Woody, Pete Seeger, Mill Lampell, Lee Hays, Cisco Houston, Jim Longhi, and their friends were homegrown radicals, proud of their heritage and trying to make the country benefit everyone. While they perhaps saw the Soviet Union as somewhat of a model for the good society, even the source of world revolution, they had no real interest in any allegiance to a foreign power, or even in visiting Moscow, for that matter. Their attitudes toward President Franklin Roosevelt fluctuated, depending on circumstances. Woody gladly joined the Roosevelt Bandwagon in the fall of 1944, a musical tour supporting his reelection. "I speak for the union people that see a union world," he wrote in December. "I speak as a singer for the AF of L, CIO, Brotherhoods and Sisterhoods and all of the kids and childhoods and all of the other hoods but I fight against the white hood of the Ku Klux Klan because I hate them and their gizzards and their whizzards and their lizzards. . . . I speak for the human beings of this human race."[16]

Woody struggled for racial justice as he fought for economic equality and workers' rights. Reviewing a new Asch album by Huddie "Lead Belly" Ledbetter, an old friend, accompanied by Sonny Terry, he praised Lead Belly's hard life as well as his artful music: "They know the cause and the cure for the blues. Their folks have the high price blues. The no money blues. No clothes blues. No man blues. No woman blues. No nothing blues. The no vote blues. . . . If there come jobs, then along comes the biggest blues of them all, the Jim Crow blues." Connecting racial and class discrimination, Woody struggled to put the talents of Lead Belly, Sonny, and so many other rural musicians "to work on the union side. Let them help to get union people out to union meetings and affairs." Whatever their racial, ethnic, or geographic origins, people were people, needing a decent shake.[17]

Although Woody normally had little use for organizational structures, or anything that smacked of sectarianism, which violated his fierce individualistic streak, he could sacrifice his independence in the pursuit of loftier goals. Toward the end of the war a struggle broke out within Communist ranks over the current status and future of the Party. The Party had transformed itself into the Communist Political Association in 1944, throwing its support behind Roosevelt's reelection and the domestic prowar alliance. With Germany's defeat the following spring, the rejuvenated Soviet Union urged its Communist allies throughout Europe and the United States to begin a rebuilding campaign, sharpening their attacks on capitalism. The more militant W. Z. Foster pushed aside party chief Earl Browder and officially reestablished the Communist Party.

These battles energized Woody's political sensibilities. In a rather rare exploration of such matters, on 4 July 1945, as he languished in the army, Woody explained his position. "I have rolled the whole thing over in my mind and have come to believe that we need to have the CP back again," he thoughtfully argued. "And especially now that our Party Principles are actually taking a shape at the election booths all over Europe and Asia, we need here in our U.S.A. the most solid form of an elective, politically active, Communist Party." Linking domestic and foreign political agendas, not Stalinist rhetoric, Woody sought to continue the progressive home he had previously known. "I felt when we had our Party that I had found the one organization I could stand up and feel proud of," he concluded. Joe Klein quotes a few other letters from this period with similar sentiments, including one in which Woody seems to praise Stalin: "The whole world cannot trick Joseph Stalin because he is too scientific for them." Yet he gives no hint of approving, much less knowing, of either Stalin's purges before the war or his ongoing repressions, and Woody shuddered at any forms of dictatorship.[18]

Again a civilian in December 1945, Woody plunged into a new attempt to stimulate a singing Left/labor movement—his prime ambition. Pete Seeger and Lee Hays, with considerable support, launched People's Songs on the last day of the year. "The reason for Peoples [sic] Songs is to shoot your union the kind of a song or songs when you want it and fast," Woody explained. "It is through such music firms as this that your people will know my people, know each others [sic] plans and hopes and our past struggles and fights." Woody preferred education, rabble-rousing, and performing to sectarianism or political rancor. His postwar columns in the *Sunday* and *Daily Worker* as well as *People's World* dealt with domestic matters, strolls around New York City, Ingrid Bergman, whatever struck his fancy. He described a Westinghouse strikers' rally in Pittsburgh in March 1946, where he performed with Pete and Lee: "We sang 'Solidarity Forever' and the papers said the rally started off with a communist song. Oh. Well. Any song that fights for the case of the workhand is a communist song to the rich folks. . . . If I had been a sick man at the early start of this day I would have got well awful quick. There was so much of that electric surge of life in the air that it would make a new person out of you if you would let it take hold of you."[19]

A favorite of *Worker* readers, Woody still had to pass political muster. His short story "Us Kids" about his experiences with Cisco Houston and Jim Longhi in Sicily during the war, was rejected by the paper. "Our short story committee read this story and checked with several of our GIs who had fought through Sicily during the war," Associate Editor John Pittman informed him in July 1948. "It was their idea that the story did not give an accurate picture either of the war in Sicily or of the Sicilian people, who actually had the worst record of all Italians insofar as resistance to Hitler and Mussolini was concerned." Pittman added, "We expect that you'll be sending us some others in the future." Subsequently, for whatever reason, Woody had very few articles in the Party press.[20]

Preferring the uphill struggle for union and civil rights to electoral politics, Woody understood the mounting threat of anti-Communism when he threw himself into the quixotic 1948 third-party presidential campaign of Henry Wallace, formerly Roosevelt's vice president and Truman's secretary of commerce. Stalin, Moscow, the Comintern—all were abstractions, with little meaning in daily life, art, politics. But the escalating Cold War and domestic Red Scare were concrete realities, necessitating plans and strong reactions, finally a national campaign for the presidency. "If your work gets to be labeled as communist or even as communistic or even as radically leaning in the general direction of boleshevism, then, of course, you are black balled, black listed, chalked up as a revolutionary bomb thrower, and you invite the whole weight of the capitalist machine to be thrown against you," he wrote to Moe Asch in July 1946. "I know that there are thousands of office holders, and just ordinary workers, trade union leaders and members of the potential millions that are branded already by the capitalist investigators as 'communistic.' I have decided, long ago, that my songs and ballads would not get the hugs and kisses of the capitalistic 'experts,' simply because I believe that the real folk history of this country finds its center and its hub in the fight of union members against the hired gun thugs of the big owners." Two years later, with growing domestic repression, it seemed all the more necessary to battle the system.[21]

Abandoned officially by the CIO, red-baited, and undercut by Truman's "progressive" shift, Henry Wallace suffered an ignominious defeat, garnering a little more than one million votes, less than three percent of the national total. Somewhat daunted, Woody continued to champion various unpopular causes, often connecting with Communist Party issues, daring the red-baiters to do their worst. In mid-1949, in a long piece in the *Worker Sunday Magazine*, Woody reminisced about his first encounter with the Party while traveling around California (although misdating the event 1936, rather than the proper three years later), particularly about carrying a pocket-sized "Constitution of the Soviet Union, U.S.S.R." He preferred the clause, "You are guaranteed a good job as long as you live." "My last few months over KFVD I dedicated to all of you trade union workers," he vividly recalled. "I wore that little ten-cent blue book out carrying it around in my shirt pocket. The best thing I did in 1936, though, was to sign up with the Communist Party and start turning the open pages of some thicker books. I bought and give away about a dozen of those little USSR Constitution books since 1936." Again he emphasized the dream, rather than any reality, of Communism, which he conflated with socialism.[22]

Escalating anti-Communism by decade's end, paralleling and fueling shrinking Party ranks, fed growing paranoia on both the Left and Right. Woody continued his attack on what he perceived as rising fascism and the general refusal to confront domestic problems. The cure for the country's ills is "socialized healing. Socialized medicine. Socialized living, socialized working, socialized thinking, and socialized resting, sleeping, seeding, breeding, which you may or may not be fearful about," he wrote to Tom Clark, the country's very conservative attorney general, in January 1949. "If you are full of fears of about socialism, sir, then you are surely spreading your killing fears through your own self and through the whole civilized world." For Woody, Communism represented socialism, not vice versa. A few months earlier he had written favorably about Eugene Debs, the founder of the Socialist Party at the turn of the century: "Every hand that did worry very much about how to best help the folks that do the hard work in this world and around this world has wrote down the name of Gene Debs, or spoke about Gene Debs or sung some song about Gene Debs. Gene Debs is a pure cross between Jesus Christ and Abe Lincoln. A lover. A man to think. A man to fight. . . . And he died easy like a man in high peace."[23]

Woody's last effort for the *Daily Worker* was a September 1949 review of Charter Records. Initiated by Mario "Boots" Casetta in late 1946, Charter became People's Songs' unofficial record company, first in Los Angeles and later in New York. "Our best folksong & ballad players and singers are like ball players, the very top crop step up sometimes and fan out," Woody explained. "The ones that stay closest to the troubles, fights and ups and downs of the trade union worker are most apt to turn out the best stuff and to have the finest, highest type of an audience. The mother lode of the folk vein is the battle of the trade union worker," which People's Songs, recently defunct, had preached. Aside from records by Pete Seeger and singer Betty Sanders, Charter also issued a two-sided record about the riots in Peekskill, New York. The first concert with Seeger and Paul Robeson in Peekskill slated for late August proved stillborn, as an angry mob, shouting "Dirty Commie" and "Dirty Kike," threatened the performers. The following week the concert, guarded by a cordon of trade unionists and war veterans, did take place, but the screaming, rock-throwing mob attacked the audience as they left the grounds. "Charter's director, Boots Casetta, was riding Pete's Jeepwagon when it got smashed by the Nazi rocks at Peekskill," Woody explained.[24]

Peekskill portended swelling political repression, which mounted in the mid-fifties, all but destroying the Communist Party, which had a plethora of internal and external problems. Woody reacted as he could to the situation, but Huntington's disease increasingly took its toll on his body. In 1951, he railed against those who are "not born and bred nor raised up to be what you call an outright labor parader, picketer, shouter, leader, nor partaker in strikes, rallies, meetings, etc., militant scenes and struggles, such as I saw, for example, up there on those golfing grounds around the town of Peekskill." The searing pain of that event marked a symbolic turning point in Woody's, and the Old Left's, political sensibilities.

But Woody could no longer participate in any uphill battles for union solidarity and the implementation of socialism at home and abroad. His increasingly erratic behavior soon landed him in the hospital. "I can't help but hate to see all of us wiggling around in rooms like [Joe] McCarthys trying to suit & satisfy his dictatorial mind when he cuts off all of our most gifted and our highest talented minds and he keeps them from being useful for the rest of us," Woody wrote in 1954, with the utmost difficulty. "If I am dying and some communist doctor and nurse can save me I say go ahead and cut—but I hear all my new crops of new generations of kids growing up to ask me if I lose it when some dimwit alleges communist." And then he was basically silent, for his remaining thirteen years.[25]

From his first contacts with the Communist Party in the late thirties, until his prolonged hospitalization fifteen years later, Woody identified with the Party's basic domestic goals, while resisting any slavish obedience to Party doctrines or dictates. In this he was typical of most rank-and-file members or camp followers, initially attracted to the Party during the Depression, and he remained committed to the promise of socialism and worker solidarity, with some notion of Moscow, Stalin, or world communism. Like the majority, Woody had no connection to the Party hierarchy, no desire to move (or even travel) to the Soviet Union, no hunger for dictatorship or a bloody revolution. Debs and Lincoln, more vibrant and meaningful than Lenin or Stalin, were their heroes. For Woody and his friends, the Communist Party, at least through the forties, represented hope for a better world. Expressing himself through his creative, lyrical songs and unending prose, Woody Guthrie captured well this longing for equality, democracy, and a peaceful world. It is impossible to separate his political views from the rest of his artistic, often chaotic, life. He was a Red, but of his own stripe—no contradiction in a political climate where anything was possible, as Woody demonstrated.

NOTES

I would like to thank Nora Guthrie, George Arevalo, and the staff of the Woody Guthrie Archives for their assistance and support; also Barry Ollman for his cooperation.

1. Stephen J. Whitfield, *The Culture of the Cold War* (Baltimore: Johns Hopkins University Press, 1991), 3, 201, 203.

2. Introduction to *Pastures of Plenty: A Self-Portrait, Woody Guthrie*, ed. Dave March and Harold Leventhal (New York: HarperCollins, 1990), xxi.

3. Harvey Klehr and John Earl Haynes, *The American Communist Movement: Storming Heaven Itself* (New York: Twayne, 1992), 177–78; John E. Haynes, *Red Scare or Red Menace? American Communism and Anticommunism in the Cold War Era* (Chicago: Ivan R. Dee, 1996), 6. For an overview of the literature, see Michael Kazin, "The Agony and Romance of the American Left," *American Historical Review* 100, no. 5 (December 1995), 1488–1512.

4. Michael Denning, *The Cultural Front: The Laboring of American Culture in the Twentieth Century* (New York: Verso, 1996), xviii; on dance, see Ellen Graff, *Stepping Left: Dance and Politics in New York City, 1928–1942* (Durham: Duke University Press, 1997). See also, Michael E. Brown et al., eds., *New Studies in the Politics and Culture of U.S. Communism* (New York: Monthly Review Press, 1993); Judy Kutulas, *The Long War: The Intellectual People's Front and Anti-Stalinism, 1930–1940* (Durham: Duke University Press, 1995); Fraser M. Ottanelli, *The Communist Party of the United States: From the Depression to World War II* (New Brunswick: Rutgers University Press, 1991); Robert Cohen, *When the Old Left Was Young: Student Radicals and America's First Mass Student Movement, 1929–1941* (New York: Oxford University Press, 1993).

5. Ed Robbin, *Woody Guthrie and Me: An Intimate Reminiscence* (Berkeley: Lancaster-Miller, 1979), 32. On Woody's life, the starting point is Joe Klein, *Woody Guthrie: A Life* (New York: Knopf, 1980). On the Party in California, see Dorothy Ray Healey and Maurice Isserman, *California Red: A Life in the American Communist Party* (1990; Urbana: University of Illinois Press, 1993); Al Richmond, *A Long View From the Left: Memoirs of an American Revolutionary* (Boston: Houghton Mifflin, 1972).

6. "Woody Sez," *Mainstream* 16, no. 8 (August 1963), 17. The House Un-American Activities Committee (HUAC) was organized in 1938, mainly to root out Communists and others on the Left.

7. Richmond, *A Long View From the Left*, 280

8. Woody quoted in Klein, *Woody Guthrie*, 126; Robbin, *Woody Guthrie and Me*, 99; Marsh and Leventhal, eds., *Pastures of Plenty*, 7.

9. Woody Guthrie, *Woody Sez*, comp. and ed. Marjorie Guthrie et al. (New York: Grosset & Dunlap, 1975), 62–63; Klein, *Woody Guthrie*, 130, 133.

10. Guthrie, *Woody Sez*, 154.

11. Woody to Alan [Lomax], 19 September 1940, Woody Guthrie Archives, New York City, printed with permission.

12. Marsh and Leventhal, eds., *Pastures of Plenty*, 9 (the Woods were soon after jailed and their radical bookstore shuttered for "subversive" activities); Pete Seeger, *Where Have All The Flowers Gone? A Singer's Stories, Songs, Seeds, Robberies* (Bethlehem, Penn.: Sing Out Corporation, 1993), 22. For all of the Almanacs' recordings and many other matters, see Ronald D. Cohen and Dave Samuelson, authors and comps., *Songs For Political Action: Folkmusic, Topical Songs, and the American Left, 1926–1953* (ten CDs with a book, Bear Family Records, 1996).

13. Woody Guthrie to Pete, Mill, and Lee, 8 July 1941, Woody Guthrie Archives, New York City, printed with the permission of the archives.

14. Jim Longhi, *Woody, Cisco, and Me: Seamen Three in the Merchant Marine* (Urbana: University of Illinois Press, 1997).

15. Longhi, *Woody, Cisco, and Me*, 60, 247, 271.

16. Woody Guthrie, *Born To Win*, ed. Robert Shelton (New York: Collier Books, 1967), 226. On the Communist Party during World War II, see Maurice Isserman, *Which Side Were You On? The American Communist Party during the Second World War* (1982; Urbana: University of Illinois Press, 1993).

17. Woody Guthrie, "Leadbelly's New Album of Songs," *Daily Worker*, 25 April 1944. On Woody's relationship with Lead Belly, see Charles Wolfe and Kip Lornell, *The Life and Legend of Leadbelly* (New York: HarperCollins, 1992).

18. Woody Guthrie [to Moe Asch, Marian Distler, Herbert Harris], 4 July 1945, original in possession of Barry Ollman and used with his permission; Klein, *Woody Guthrie*, 318. For Woody's relationship with Moe Asch and his record companies, see Peter Goldsmith, *Making People's Music: Moe Asch and Folkways Records* (Washington, D.C.: Smithsonian Institution Press, 1998).

19. Marsh and Leventhal, eds., *Pastures of Plenty*, 14, 174. On People's Songs, see Richard A. Reuss, "American Folklore and Left-Wing Politics, 1927–1957," Ph.D. diss., Indiana University, 1971; Robbie Lieberman, *"My Song Is My Weapon": People's Songs, American Communism, and the Politics of Culture, 1930–1950* (Urbana: University of Illinois Press, 1989); and the notes accompanying Cohen and Samuelson, authors and comps., *Songs For Political Action*.

20. John Pittman to Woody Guthrie, 13 July 1948, original in author's possession. The essay finally appeared in Guthrie, *Born to Win*, 92–98.

21. Marsh and Leventhal, eds., *Pastures of Plenty*, 197.

22. Woody Guthrie, "My Constitution and Me," *Worker Sunday Magazine*, 19 June 1949, 3, 12.

23. Guthrie, *Born to Win*, 68, 212–13.

24. Woody Guthrie, "Woody Guthrie Sounds Off On Charter Records," *Daily Worker*, 29 September 1949. On Charter Records and Peekskill, see Cohen and Samuelson, authors and comps., *Songs For Political Action*.

25. Woody letter to Jolly Robinson, 1951, quoted in Gordon Friesen, "The Man Woody Guthrie," *Broadside*, no. 57 (10 April 1965); Marsh and Leventhal, eds., *Pastures of Plenty*, 245. On the Cold War and associated Red Scare, see David Caute, *The Great Fear: The Anti-Communist Purge Under Truman and Eisenhower* (New York: Simon and Schuster, 1978); M. J. Heale, *American Anticommunism: Combating the Enemy Within, 1830–1970* (Baltimore: Johns Hopkins University, Press, 1990); and particularly Ellen Schrecker, *Many Are the Crimes: McCarthyism in America* (Boston: Little, Brown, 1998).

ROBERT CANTWELL

FANFARE FOR THE LITTLE GUY

Think, every time you pass the greasy alien on the street, that he was born thousands of years before the oldest native American; and he may have something to communicate to you, when you two shall have learned a common language. Remember that his very physiognomy is a cipher the key to which it behooves you to search for most diligently.
—Mary Antin, *The Promised Land* (1912)

The army must have been running out not only of men but of uniforms by March 1945, when it drafted Woody Guthrie for the third time (his two stints in the Merchant Marine not apparently having satisfied its thirst for his patriotism), because it couldn't find a uniform small enough to fit him. Most of us have seen the photograph of the new inductees at Fort Dix in May 1945, where a wiry long-necked fellow with a bushy head of black hair, at thirty-two visibly older than most of the rest of the men, looks as if he has got his suit on backward. Like some impish impostor, he is attempting to fill the shoes and trousers of some real long-legged, barrel-chested soldier who has been swindled out of his clothes and who is shivering in his underwear in the barracks behind the group.

Measured against the fifty-odd other fresh-faced, scowling, or overearnest young fellows extending across the frame, most of them filling their fatigues quite handsomely, nothing could be clearer than that Woody Guthrie didn't really belong. He seems almost to have sneaked into the picture, like the barber or the cook, or to be a kind of trick of it, like those wiseacres in group photographs who used to dart behind the old panoramic camera ahead of its arc so as to appear, in the final image, at both edges of the picture at the same time.

Woody Guthrie's cultural proportions are large, even great, as great certainly as those physically more imposing men such as the athletic Paul Robeson or the lanky Pete Seeger, whose personal presence, in the many situations where the embodied man must for better or worse contend

Woody Guthrie and others in front of army barracks, 1945. NORA GUTHRIE COLLECTION. COURTESY OF WOODY GUTHRIE ARCHIVES.

with the public persona, generally affirmed, or even enlarged, the authority and power already granted to them. Robeson was big, like his voice, very big; and Seeger stood, and stands, tall, as one who has made a career of principled opposition and indomitable (if at times insufferable) protest, must do. All politics is local, said the bearish and overbearing Tip O'Neill—as local, perhaps, as the few square feet of ground we require to stage a single interpersonal encounter. A mere handshake, a nod, a name enunciated—each is a subtle but seminal social moment that might first establish, and then endlessly reproduce, a routine of power that will ultimately manifest itself in movements, parties, elections, and regimes. No one knows this better than the professional politician.

If the personal is political, then at this irreducibly local level it is ineluctably true that the political is personal. At this level the personal is not merely a sluice through which subjectivity flows along its accidental meandering and ahistorical way, but a site at which the various streams of historical affiliation and collective experience, the social tributaries of the personal, converge with a kind of half-intelligible political meaning to which precisely because we cannot know it we must unconsciously submit. Struggle as we might in whatever way to extricate ourselves from the structures of power we remain mired in the personal, which is itself obdurately grounded, like it or not, in history.

Hence a relief map of social power, advantage, and preeminence, could it be laid upon the map of personal beauty, stature, and presence, if not quite congruent with it, would conform to it with startling regularity. Precisely at the point at which personal forces convert history into fate, and social forces gather fate up again into history, lies race—that most arbitrary of arbitrary signifiers that like all signs awash in culture and embedded in the thickness of history most unarbitrarily refuses to be dislodged from its significance. Race, as the nineteenth century knew, is located not in this place or that place, but everywhere, like culture; for "culture," in the anthropological sense, was what was then meant by the term; in the days before virtually instantaneous communications and global transport, race and culture appeared to grow up together, in the same human medium. That's why race, evolutionary theory, and social class could be combined to produce the weird science of phrenology, essentially a biological justification of the social hierarchy, implicitly inflected

Woody Guthrie in army work clothes, 1945. COURTESY OF WOODY GUTHRIE ARCHIVES.

by race. Race was never what we thought it was, a class or a category, but rather a kaleidoscopically shifting human manifestation that marks the pauses and the densities of the social process as culture and history have shaped it. So various, elusive, and dynamic is race, as much so as today's configuration of clouds, that we sometimes yield to the temptation to distribute its properties as if they were fixed and permanent to people and cohesions of people for whom race, in the eye of time, is only a shadow that passes over, a rumor that passes through and is gone—as if race had an essence, an origin and an end, when in fact it has only formations, and endless transformations. Race, like music, is nowhere and nothing; and yet, like music, it always belongs to someone, someplace; migrate about as it will, it finds itself burdened with meaning everywhere.

If race is so perfectly meaningless in itself that we overburden it with meaning, somehow finding in its myriad accidental associations and metaphorical resonances patterns of effects whose actual causes are long decayed and in any case buried in the past, it is because race, in a sense *is* history, an unconscious, yet visible, history. From it springs the dream-imagery whose neurotic agitation haunts all our personal associations with unease and misgiving, stirs us with inexplicable attractions and repulsions, obscurely signifying where there is nothing significant. Hence it is full of signification, a kind of empty syntax ready to absorb to itself all the meanings of conquest, caste, and class, of peoples and their migrations, of specific historical enslavements, exploitations, and segregations, concentrations and dispersals that it both records and perpetuates. Despite our attempts to isolate it, to hold it up for scrutiny, as a biological, social, or political fiction, as an instrument for making—symbolically or actually—a better democracy or a poorer one, it remains tangled together with place and position, with allegiance, alliance, and belief, and hence with class, nation, and state, as a factor in human identity. All of these forms of human social cohesion, insofar as they have histories, bring with them, however subtly or elusively, the racial markers that both indicate and have helped to produce and secure them.

The binaries of the racial semiotic inevitably accumulate at the sites of long-standing oppositions: Gentile and Jew, Western European and Eastern, Occidental and Oriental, White and Black, Anglo and "Other," and it is out of such binaries that we form the idea of race. But literary and pictorial traditions, with our happy complicity, have evolved a subtler racial language, where complexions fair and dark, features coarse and fine, statures tall and slender, short and squat, noses long and sharp or round and bulbous, lips thick or thin, eyes wide and narrow, brows low and high, voices shrill or deep have communicated as much social and moral information as would otherwise require whole treatises to elucidate.

While in some respects a system of conventions peculiar to narrative or to drama, race is also a vernacular language in which meanings derived from one context may be recombined in new contexts to produce new and original meanings.

A French Canadian nose, for example, an Irish brow, and an Italian name (I am thinking of a character in a late nineteenth-century novel called *The Cliff Dwellers* by a smug Anglo-American named Henry Fuller) may summon in a few phrases an incorrigible and dangerous villain, while an African mouth, a patrician Anglo-Norman nose, and thick black Latin hair might produce an exotic sexual paragon (I am thinking of a Gap model). The traditional European systems of class, ethnic, regional, and national relations that were the milieu in which this racial language formed have in America been disrupted and scattered; from the minstrels and popular phrenologists of the nineteenth century to our own novelists, filmmakers, illustrators, photographers, and especially advertisers, we have been seeking as a culture to bring into alignment our European-derived racial language with our shifting power arrangements, to make intelligible on the landscape of American raciality the topography of dominance and submission, resistance and accommodation, center and margin, that have made and are making it.

None of us really escapes racial marking; it is only that we are more evidently "racial" as race more transparently implies a social location. In this context "race" and "ethnicity" are of course simply alibis for sociopolitical exclusion. By a kind of social trigonometry, these ideas reduce the complex fields of social distributions, of cultural, material, and actual capital, into chronic alignments both conceptual and actual whose essence is violence. Here white and nonwhite, advantage and disadvantage, power and powerlessness all mean the same thing, so that "race"—as in "race records" or "the race"—becomes, not merely an evasion, but a kind of tautology: that is, you only have it if you are it, you are it if you have it.

Hence it is the racial anomaly, and its challenge to our system of racial understanding, that most fascinates us, especially, it seems, in the age of the reproducible image in which it is nearly impossible to dissociate the public figure from her image, where, indeed, in some realms at least, the celebrity or politician or even the author or musician may be said to be pure image, or *only* an image. Whatever our estimate of Elvis Presley as an artist, for example, surely the dark Mediterranean softness of his face, arrestingly and improbably yoked with the gestures and expressions of the working-class rural South, clowning, mocking, unprepossessingly "racy," wrought a mystery and magnetism utterly resistant to any easy racial description. Somehow in him, the youthful and innocent was also urbane and exotic; Neopolitan nobility mixed, as in a foundling's tale, with Irish peasantry; the smooth matinee idol was also the hicksville movie usher, the millionaire playboy, the crunchy sharecropper's son, the baseball pitcher and the supperclub crooner, the maître d' and the bus-boy, congregated in one body. In the language of American raciality he was, and is, an utterly original expression, a living testament to the awe-some significatory power of race.

We celebrate Woody Guthrie for his political conviction and his poetic genius. But others have evinced the same who have not been enlarged, as he has, to the scale of myth. Let us consider, then, that his myth has in it a racial aspect more difficult to fathom, and at the same time more dur-able and more fascinating for the deep unsolved symbolic riddle it poses, than the antic energy of his prose and the simple eloquence of his songs. If "Mr. Guthrie defines an essential character in the American dream," as a *New York Times* reviewer once claimed, then that essentiality, and that character, must at least partially inhere not only in his intellectual but in his corporal nature, not only in his life and work, but in *him*.

Woody was a skinny little feather-boned guy with a head of springy black hair, a high-sloping intelligent brow, sharp-hooded, sometimes heavy-lidded scrutinizing eyes, a nose and mouth coldly faceted as if by a smith's hammer and yet, in the pronounced bow of his upper lip, touched with sensuality. He was, in a sense, homely, and in another, beautiful. His hands, moreover, his lifelong guitar-picking notwithstanding, were plump like a woman's, languidly relaxed, possibly lovely. He had light, quick, animated movements, like Charlie Chaplin's, as if he had been cut from paper, with a quality of subtle self-caricature that accelerated the expressive tempo and sharpened the quality of his presence. His wide rec-tangular forehead and wiry hair gave him an elfin, childlike aspect, as if his entire body were made of intelligence. In sum, he was a sort of featherweight Robert Mitchum, transforming the slow irony buried in Mitchum's massive composure into a sparkling satirical energy.

On first glance you might have figured him, from his sometimes starved and arid features, a child of rural poverty, bred out of the red clay at the end of some overgrown lane; and yet these same features, with a shift no more pronounced than a shift in the direction of a breeze or the intensity of a shadow, might be utterly transfigured, imparting to him a sensitive, generous, vulnerable quality, as if tears had started to his eyes. His was a face and form that, like an actor's, might play many parts. Not only could he absorb the moral atmosphere around him; he could model its expression to others. Guthrie was a metaphor-maker in that syntax of human identity that articulates us all as individuals, as types, as classes and races, that locks us into histories we have not lived and locales in which we have never lived, as well as the ones in which we have. It was this same quality that allowed such young men as Jack Elliott, Bob Dylan, and even Bruce Springsteen—no, not to transform themselves into Woody Guthrie—but to transform Woody into themselves.

I speak of course not of the real, but of the mythopoetic Woody Guthrie, who belongs to a social imaginary usually more associated with literature and the arts than with ordinary social intercourse, but one that nevertheless is always ready to push through the social surface of things to lend its mystery, charm, and danger to real men and real women. These are the charismatic people who often find themselves gravitating as if by some irresistible interpersonal urging onto the stage, or before the movie camera, or into public life, precisely because their presence and their person work in marvelous and irresistible ways upon others, arousing some obscure attraction or fascination, preoccupation, infatuation, or love. They are not always beautiful, but they are always striking, full of obscure and impregnable import. Many become the victims of their own interest and beauty, of which there are too many well-known examples to name; some learn very early in life their own power of manipulation and make careers of it; and some, like Woody, growing gradually into a full sense of their own social puissance, use it as we would use any talent or skill—not opportunistically, but tactically, as an instrument of adaptation and survival.

In the mundane, as against the mythopoetic world, Woody Guthrie was extraordinary not so much in his origins as in the events that thrust him out of them. There is no need here to recount the sad litany of misfortunes that unraveled the weave of his early years and turned him into an orphan, a refugee, even an outcast—but let us at least note that he was born of respectable and aspiring, if not exactly prosperous parents, and that if he could not ultimately enjoy the blessings of the middle-class standing he was born to, he had at least been decently educated, was a curious and eager reader, brilliant with words, and as a young man could reasonably imagine himself becoming, as he sings in "Ramblin' Round," a "man of some renown." In his work he aligned himself with working men and women of every stamp; but as Gordon Friesen reminded him, he had never harvested a grape in his life. Woody was essentially a poet and intellectual at a time when a nationalist embrace of grassroots imagery and expression, mixed up with an urban romantic conception of an heroic American People in whom one might detect the unquiet ghost of a revolutionary proletariat, had prepared a place for him, as Steinbeck observed, in a sense to *be* that People.

Guthrie was a westerner, out of the old Indian Territories, with Scots-Irish (read "hillbilly") roots, and like his hillbilly-musician brethren, he had a knack for the African-American way of diddling a tune, especially on that down-home, make-do, hip-pocket instrument, the harmonica. Once transplanted to New York, however, the "clever little man," the "bantam rooster" as his friend Jimmy Longhi called him, the "real Dust Bowl refugee" and "the great American frontier ballad writer" could never again be seen in his mundane aspect, or even as a man with any history of his own; instead he would inevitably be woven into an essentially mythic web of a socialist heroic, replete with images and ideas of a glorified working people, of labor union triumphalism, Wobbly millennialism and, especially out of this last, the still unsung frontier epic we seem to glimpse in Woody's songs. In this story, cowboys and hoboes, wheatfield gleaners, peach pickers and grape harvesters, loggers and fishers and builders of giant dams are all toiling under the vast bright Western sky on behalf of a stolen dream. It is *your* hops we gather, he sings in "Pastures of Plenty," *your* beets we pull from the ground, *your* vines from which we pick the grapes, addressing the song rebukingly to the privileged classes; out of California, Arizona, Oregon, he conjures a nation of workers laboring "to set on your table" in some faraway city "your bright sparkling wine." A strange concatenation of abundance and privation, pride and resentment, alienation and fascination, Guthrie maps it like degrees of rainfall onto the great expanse of the continent.

It is the paradox evident in all of Guthrie's work—an imagery that loves, reveres, and glorifies, a language that points, exposes, rebukes—and one that time, where history is always transformed into romance, has largely resolved, sifting out of the ideologically inflected times in which he wrote and sang the essential ore of his idealism. Whether this is a reading or a misreading of the Guthrie legacy is not, I think, so much at issue as that it has happened at all.

Whether he liked or disliked "middle-class bourgeois people," in Moe Asch's phrase, and despite the rancor, resentment, and righteous indignation that, if not everywhere in his songs, is often the nub of their meaning—"some'll rob you with a six-gun, some with a fountain pen"—the fact is that Guthrie's *own* meaning lies neither in the singer nor the song but in the tension between them. Transfigurations of memory working upon his image and his images have finally yielded up a new Woody Guthrie for a new political moment. In the truth-vacuum that corporate capitalism has made of political discourse, a Guthrie revival is shaping itself out of a strange mix of nostalgia and revisionism, where the very collapse of a progressive politics seems to have created an opportunity for its renewal, and where the exhaustion of a musical strain seems again to demand a return to, which is always a creation of, the roots.

No one, I think, captured Guthrie so imaginatively, with a precision as outrageous as it is uncanny, as his most vigorous champion and promoter

Alan Lomax, who called him a "pureblood Neolithic Pict." This riveting and ineradicable bit of nonsense, more poetic than anthropological, and smacking of nineteenth-century racial fantasy, points irresistibly to what we mean when we say Woody Guthrie.

First, *Pict*. What is Pict? The Picts, as all the dictionaries say, and the Roman language tells us, were "painted people": warriors, with paint on their faces, with spears and arrows and coverings of animal skins, dark little tangleheaded savages from the north of Scotland whom early explorers to America could not help comparing to the little swarthy naked painted people they found here, drawing them into their sketches of the American Indian to help the European imagination to get itself around what was not yet, but was in the process of becoming, the idea of a noble savage.[1]

Who were they? They are the people "about whom little is known," and much is conjectured, but above all a "race," a mixture of an invading Aryan "stock" and an unknown aboriginal people who at some immemorial time occupied all of Britain—that is, they are the original, no, the more than original, the native, the autochthonous people—ultimately to be displaced by the Britons, whose Celtic language overmastered their own unknown non–Indo-European tongue. The Picts, being warlike, carried on sporadic border skirmishes with the Romans, joined with Irish raiding parties to assist the Saxons in conquering their own conquerors, were converted to Christianity by Saint Columba in the fifth century A.D., and by the seventh century had established their own Pictish kingdom in the north. By the ninth century they had come under the dominion of Kenneth I, a Scot, himself an invader from Ireland, and were absorbed into what would become the Kingdom of Scotland. The Roman historian Eumenius mentions them in A.D. 297 as invaders of Roman Britain; Tacitus, too, alludes to a dark-skinned people small of stature, of western Wales but possibly of Pictish origin, whom he distinguishes both from the Gaelic Scots and the Gallic Britons, tall and fair-haired and speaking the Celtic language.

Thus far the dictionaries and encyclopedias. But folklore has elevated the darting, elusive, thrice-conquered Pict to a peculiar niche in the ecology of imagination, where in the glens, the thickets, the woods, and watercourses the "little people," with their tiny voices and their elaborate courtly nocturnal convocations from time to time make their presence in human affairs known with enchantments, gifts, and the occasional wayfarer's tale, sometimes leaving behind a birthmark or a lazy-eye, or recovering a long-lost finger-ring, to say they've been there. There is a vaguely druidical cast about them, a ghostly presence that forms where history, memory, and dread meet in twilit forests and morning mists.

Whatever else may be said about this imaginary figure, the pureblood Neolithic Pict, it is certain that he is not well represented in, say, political office, among chief executive officers or elected officials, appointees to the directorships of federal agencies, among the military brass, or partners in Wall Street or K Street law firms; nor is he much revered in Hollywood, unless it is as the occasional character actor. Neither, for that matter, is he much found among crew foremen or factory-floor managers or union officers or in less official positions of working-class leadership. Very occasionally you might find him in the U.S. House of Representatives—but almost never in the Senate.

The Pict is, by definition, the "little guy." He resides in the hinterlands, literally and/or figuratively, because ages ago someone pushed him back there. He knows his own smallness, his obscurity, and speaks of himself as such, the little guy. Only a generation ago he might, though white, have been called a "boy," especially if he carried water for a road crew or a sports team, and like his cast-iron blackfaced counterpart, the cast-iron livery boy, might be vaguely associated with the stable, horse racing being the one sport in which, as a jockey, he has excelled.

He might be in the trades, or even the professions, he might keep a store, but he knows that his strength and his survival must lie in cleverness, shrewdness, skill with words; however physically powerful he may be, however intense his personal presence, it is useless to attempt to impress himself upon others in these ways. His Pictish nature, he knows, has for better or worse always been a factor in the history that brought him to his beleaguered position. Deserved or not, he has a reputation for pugnacity. From his point of view, life has been a never-ending negotiation with a superior race, or at least a race that likes to think of itself as such. To them, to whom he is at once real and imaginary, he *is* elusive, and in a sense magical, having sprung it seems out of those long-lost miniature ages when the sleeping berths of sailing ships were the size of dresser drawers and the tombs of great armored knights could be mistaken for footstools.

I myself have encountered him once or twice, always under somebody else's eye or thumb, in his ill-fitting clothes: once on a highway construction crew, leaning on a shovel, where he called me "Bawb" and again and again asked me whether I thought I was going to "get to like it"—meaning the work (but the phrase had come from his wartime service in the Pacific)—and, most memorably in a pub in the north of England, near the Scottish border. I had asked the barman where I might get a bite to eat nearby, his own kitchen having shut for the night, when a little fellow next to me with a head of curly black hair and a pair of Buddy Holly glasses, who looked astonishingly like Woody Guthrie, recommended a place around the corner called Cheney's.

What was that? I asked. He peered up at me, his head no higher than my shoulder—and, reader, I am no lanky fair-haired Anglo-Norman, but a man of very medium build and medium height with a conspicuous ethnic marker in the middle of my face I am not altogether pleased to call my nose—and repeated, "Cheney's, richt arooned tha' coorner."

"Cheney's?" I repeated, finding a scap of paper on which to spell it out, "Cee, aitch, heee, enn..."

"Nair," he corrected me, 'Chey-neeze, chey-*neeze*!"

I had had a pint or two and was thicker than usual; but at last I got it. "Oh," I cried, balancing my eyeballs on the edge of their sockets as if I were trying to prevent them from falling out and rolling across the floor, "you mean Chi*nese*."

"Aye." He nodded, apologized profusely for his Scottish "broooghe," came, it seemed, within an inch of curtseying and pulling on his forelock (though he didn't really have a forelock), and together we laughed at the miscommunication over another pint of bitter. It was New Year's Eve, and later, full of egg noodles and Mu-shu chicken, I spotted him and his two equally elfin mates lurching along the street, singing merrily and gallantly accosting the occasional pretty girl with admiring phrases and a few stolen pinches and squeezes through their winter overcoats.

A pureblood Neolithic Pict if ever there was one.

Lomax's grossly unscientific assertion, then, once untangled, exposes the web of symbolic relations in which the respectable small-town Oklahoma boy orphaned in the midst of the Great Depression who became a hillbilly singer, radio personality, political columnist, railroad tramp and sign-painter betimes, and finally a "great frontier ballad writer" still has meaning for us. For that web is, after all, cultural, and still trembles when the bright ephemeral creatures of the social world blunder into it, their own substance drawn into the social imaginary to be spun again into fibers of weightless but absorbing illusion. Lomax's phrase inoculates one world with another, evokes and shatters the categories of which it is itself made, metaphorically infusing the present with the past. Like all metaphors whose fascination consists in the eerie intimation of their rational basis, it demands we entertain, even if we cannot ultimately grant, its literal sense.

Guthrie's story is one of class and class slippage, of class as it is bound up with regional, ethnic, and ideological difference, of class as it is obscurely bound up with race, and finally of race as a conceptual stand-in for the cultural temporalities to which all of this ultimately adds up; the Pict's story is one of nativity, tribe, and nation, of conquest and reconquest, subjection, marginalization, oppression, and resistance. Guthrie's is a story of the industrial age in postagrarian capitalist America, where social stratification, theoretically, follows the moraines of market flows through history's shifting social mass; the Pict's is of a feudal kingdom forming out of imbalances and equilibriums of martial force in the competition for protected spaces and fruitful lands, where social differentiation is made visible both on the earth's and in the human face. Guthrie's is of workers and bosses, the Pict's of warriors and kings.

In the most superficial sense, Lomax's complex metaphor simply figures Guthrie as an exotic, a kind of exile or refugee from the past, like Ishmael or Ishi the last man of a lost world; he asks us to imagine, not that Guthrie is *like* a Pict, but that he *is* one. Thus Guthrie cannot be in the social sense "white"; that is, he is neither entitled to nor capable of the range of material, social, and cultural privileges that constitute "whiteness" in Western culture. Consequently in a certain sense he must be, if not exactly "black" (though some have speculated as much), certainly somehow "other," where that otherness is precisely the register of disadvantage for which it is the figure, the more pronounced as it challenges its own status with special gifts, a certain political agenda, or simply by his failure to observe the protocols of otherness. Set at large in society he is, like the minstrel or *jongleur* of the Middle Ages, a landless, lordless, unaffiliated man, both and neither peasant nor noble, as at home in the court as on the highway, at once master and mendicant, a near archetypal figure whose descent reaches on the one hand to the blind court singers of antiquity to Shakespeare's Tom O'Bedlam to the hired hermit of the eighteenth-century landscape garden with his hourglass, his beard, and his Bible, figures in whom the negation of social identity at once confers the privilege of emancipation from it and compels contemplation of the "poor, bare fork'd animal" we know ourselves to be in the absence of it.

But this is only so much fairy-dust, the mere touch of a wand, until we attempt to make the Pictish metaphor intelligible in relation to the historical Woody Guthrie, of Okemah, Oklahoma, especially in the image-charged urban setting in which he at once achieved and was granted his mythopoetic status. Guthrie enlarged inestimably the power of his social critique by placing it in a context of bright hopes and unconquerable faith, an idealism just that much more violated and tarnished by failure and betrayal. Keepers of Guthrie's flame are quick to remind those who would like to turn "This Land Is Your Land" into the national anthem that the song was born in anger as an answer to Berlin's pious "God Bless America," and in addition to the now familiar celebratory verses included this one:

Was a big high wall that tried to stop me
A sign was painted said: Private Property.
But on the back side, it didn't say nothing—
God Blessed America for me.

And this one:

One bright sunny morning in the shadow of the steeple
By the relief office I saw my people—
As they stood there hungry,
I stood there wondering if
God Blessed America for me.[2]

But what is original in the song, and what song tradition has favored, is its ribbon of highway, its endless skyway, its golden valleys, and waving fields of wheat. It is very nearly picture-scrapbook snipped from one of the commercial picture-magazines of the period, where domed parlor cars, rubber tires, and farm machinery are tying corporate enterprise to a populist-patriotic paean to the continent. The prick of cruelty, and the ironic cut, are sharp—but have proved transient. Embodied as it is now, in Guthrie's total story, as it has accumulated in various writings, representations, recognitions, and imitations (including Guthrie's own autobiographical prose), this tension between a promise and its disappointment, a kind of wounded love, takes on a troubling new dimension. Woody Guthrie embodies, not an eventual triumph over injustice and inequality, but the awful depth and tenacity of them in the human scheme; even as we thrill to his moral idealism and the luminosity of his vision we feel, as a kind of instinct, with the example and the person of Guthrie before us, the impossibility of any realization of them. Conduct border raids as we might, harry the rulers with infinite tiny vandalisms, even ally ourselves temporarily with invading barbarians—we sense that nothing much, finally, is going to change.

We are the Picts, they are the Scots.

Our fascination, love, and admiration of Woody Guthrie as with all such minstrels and balladeers must inevitably be entangled with the contradictions inherent in the interplay of identity and identification: the one a fact of our social location and the other an imaginative tendency arising from it; the one a structure of ideas, conditions, affiliations, and associations whose fixity and integrity we struggle to maintain against odds, the other a capricious and restless testing of the self against the whole register of social possibility in which it finds, loses, and finds again its own place. Without the power of identification, there would be no identity, no way to convert the intersections of subject and social place into the material of a lived experience; without identity there would be no identification, that is, no social place from which to experience and assess the otherwise unreflected social aspects of the self.

Our Woody Guthrie—the Woody Guthrie of the Left in New York, of the folk song movement and the folk revival, even the scruffy bohemian and finally the stricken Guthrie of Washington Square, as against the western Guthrie of Oklahoma and California, the hillbilly radical—like his forebears in literature, on the stage, and in the landscape garden, morally strengthens and enlarges us with a message severely toxic to the status quo but whose very delivery of it confers, homeopathically, a certain immunity to its effects. The inspiration, even the mighty inspiration, we take from Woody's moral courage and independence has its basis in the refuge we enjoy, and know we enjoy, from the implications of them; we are moved by his orphanhood, stirred by his days on the highway, the railroad, in the labor camps—but, as Lomax tacitly conceded, mostly in relation to our own relative comfort, security, and safety. We are high-minded; we want to feel and think the immense promise of democracy as Woody sings of it, and rouse ourselves to indignation at the insults to it that he catalogues. But the figure of the little Pict in whom we take this essentially aesthetic pleasure offers unspoken reassurances; though the hayricks may be set on fire, the granaries raided, and the sheepfolds thrown open, nothing is likely to overthrow the edifice of power and advantage whose foundations are not in justice and right, but in history and—even more fundamentally, it is almost possible to believe—in race.

We are the Scots, they are the Picts.

That might be the end of the metaphor, were it not for the fact that the class consciousness fundamental to the political tradition in which Woody Guthrie somewhat cryptically included himself arises, as Marshall Berman brilliantly argues,[3] first in the wide new public spaces of the mid-nineteenth-century city, out of the glancing social encounters of an emergent class of respectable little men, the vanguard of the urban bourgeoisie, with officers and aristocrats on the one hand, the poor and the indigent on the other, in a new social theater. For the first time in history identity becomes conscious of itself not only as a social locus but as a public and hence ultimately a political performance open to the gaze of the socially, economically, and politically other. These characters, actuaries and clerks and scriveners, in patent-leather shoes and morning coats, white collars "mounting firmly to the chin" and neckties "asserted by a simple pin," as yet without social identity or political visibility, essentially anonymous and faceless, becoming aware of themselves as individuals and as a class in the promenades, arcades, cafés, and parks of Paris and

London, in Saint Petersburg's Nevsky Prospect, felt the stirring of a sense of self actuated to the dynamics of power relations and to the flux of historical change.

It was out of these multitudinous episodes of self-conscious social encounter that the idea of class struggle, wherein history endlessly produces and reproduces Picts and Scots in endlessly novel incarnations, finally emerged. Melville's Bartleby, Dostoyevsky's Underground Man, Eliot's Prufrock, even Joyce's Bloom are their literary reflections; cinema culture expressed the type in Charlie Chaplin—who, it is said, enacted some of his funniest scenes backward in order to achieve the inimitable movements that appear when the film was run forward—a pure artifact, that is, of the cinematic process. Hence the "Little Tramp," haplessly caught up in the machinery of social protocol, of constabularies, bureaucracies, factories, municipalities, indeed of machinery itself, like Guthrie not only performs but also embodies his own comic predicament. At the same time, he unwittingly engineers his own comic evasions of it—escaping the machinery of the modern by delivering himself up to it.

It does not need to be reiterated the direction in which the central stream of bourgeois sympathy flowed and still flows: toward the glistening surfaces of ruling class life and social, political, and moral reaction. But to those for whom that project seemed shallow or empty, or to whom it was essentially closed off,—most notably, intellectuals, Jews, and, pre-eminently, Jewish intellectuals—identity sought its reflected self, and its role in history, at the other end of society. In America, at a time when political and cultural elites were looking socially outward and downward for the vernacular energy that could resuscitate the collapsed economic and social system, they turned to the worker: figured, as all the heroic imagery of the period shows, as an impersonal regimental mass, a worker army, or as a godlike paragon of physical strength, wrestling with vats of molten steel or wielding nineteen-pound hammers, or as a sturdy farmer toiling behind a horse-drawn plow, or exercising his right of free speech on the courthouse steps, or facelessly presiding over the family table where all heads are bent in prayers of thanks.

But where in this epic synthesis was the urban little man with his frayed white collar? Where was the immigrant shopkeeper, tailor, or machine operator, or his son or daughter, upon whom the Depression had fallen with a wretchedly personal and private weight, who felt most keenly the betrayal of the promise he'd hoped to realize for himself or his children or his children's children, to find his own revolutionary image? Was it in the "folk?"—the rural poor who unlike himself were not creatures of capitalism but whom capitalism nevertheless had ruined, as near to indigence as himself, in whose exhausted face he saw his own terror of penury and dispossession? Who were not, like him, mere human refuse used up and thrown away in another financial-industrial storm-cycle but lean and hungry native stock, rooted in the soil, in the rights and freedoms the Founders had assigned to it and ready by temperament and tradition to declare those rights and freedoms?

Yes, but the "folk" could not strictly be identified either with the socialist worker-hero or with the images of stark submission and defeat with which much of the documentary photography of the period had marked the rural poor. Rather it was the Pictish zeal and pluck, springing out of wild hoedown fiddles and wicked comic songs, in outspoken blues ballads and cryptic workchants smoldering with anger, that one caught the revolutionary tone. In this setting no one better than a "real Dust Bowl refugee," his social conscience pricked by visible injustice, his verbal gift unsheathed by moral outrage and sharpened with satiric wit, his music rooted in a poor white rural tradition of Scots-Irish and African-American origin, a man whose own physical nature and personal endowment placed him among the ever-dominated, never-defeated outlander race, could have been ushered into the place, and taken on the role, of America's "great frontier ballad writer."

"Our class struggle," Marx wrote to Engels, "you know very well where we found it: we found it in . . . the story of the war of races."[4] In Woody Guthrie the comic majesty of hope plays continually in and against the tragedy of history. Like Chaplin, he was one with his medium, in effect *made* of it. His blood, mythopoetically speaking, is a mingling of the blood of all those conquered and exploited generations in whom the conqueror has searched out the sources of his own life. His *embodied* politics go deeper than the ground of things, the social and technical installations of production, to the living substance of flesh and blood, where injustice, inequality, and oppression are infused, and in which history has left a visible record of their expression. Hence the paradox of his songs is the paradox of him, and its very irresolution is what carries both his idealism and his realism, his rhapsody and his irony, beyond ideology and even poetry to what in postmodernity can perhaps no longer be called myth but which, like myth, can lend density and solidity to our specular and unreal world—not so much to enunciate belief as to lay a foundation for its possibility.

On a trip to Washington recently I happened in an idling moment to pick up from somebody's coffeetable a newsletter published by one of those property-rights think tanks on Seventeenth Street. I can't explain the context—I didn't really read it—but my eye fell on this sentence, or something to this effect: "We don't want a 'This land is your land, this land is my land' sort of society."

If I am not mistaken, this egregious misreading of Woody's sentiment quite coldly exposes the fortress mentality—essentially the cowardice of conquerors—that has arisen again in one of capitalism's intermittent periods of retrenchment. There isn't enough to go around, apparently. If the little fellow in the crumpled outfit has come back to us out of America's racial unconscious, it is perhaps because in postmodernity, under an oppression so vast and unreachable that we scarcely know what it is or what to call it, or what it is evolving into, we are all little guys again. Perhaps if the invisible legions of a new race, somehow more than human, fabulously rich and powerful, with unheard-of ability to communicate, to mobilize resources, to administer on a global scale, are emerging to dominate the old human race, and to efface once and for all with glamorous new lies the memory of the spacious and fruitful land that was our birthright. Maybe Woody has come to refresh that memory, and to arouse our Pictish indignation at its dishonoring.

NOTES

1. I am indebted to my colleague Philip Gura for this suggestion.

2. Quoted in Joe Klein, *Woody Guthrie: A Life* (New York: Knopf, 1980), 141. This version of the song appears in Guthrie's original manuscript; Guthrie recorded the song with the more familiar "This land was made for you and me."

3. See his *All That Is Solid Melts Into Air*, parts III and IV (New York: Penguin, 1988), 131–284.

4. Quoted in James Surowiecki, "The Care of the Audience," *Lingua Franca* 7, no. 7 (September 1997), 23; Michel Foucault had used this passage from Marx in a lecture.

DAVE MARSH

DEPORTEES
Woody Guthrie's Unfinished Business

> Next we won the slavery war, some other folks and me
> And every slave from sea to sea was all turned loosed by me
> I divorced old Madam slavery, and I wed this freedom dame.
> And that's about the biggest thing that man has ever done.
> —Woody Guthrie, "Biggest Thing That Man Has Ever Done
> (The Great Historical Bum)"

By far the most interesting "new" story about Woody Guthrie that emerged from the 1996 American Music Masters conference is the yarn told by his Merchant Marine shipmate Jimmy Longhi during the panel "Woody and Race." Longhi tells the identical tale in his book, *Woody, Cisco, and Me* and on the album *That's Why We're Marching*.[1] Longhi's command of the story's inherent humor and drama, and of its remarkable details, is best encountered in his own voice. But in outline, Longhi recalls being with Woody and Cisco Houston aboard a Merchant Marine ship carrying American troops across the Atlantic for the D-Day invasion. One night, they enter waters where a German submarine attack is expected. But rather than going on deck, where survival would be more likely, Woody, Cisco, and Longhi—in order of increasing reluctance—descend into the bowels of the ship, to entertain the troops in the hold. While there, they hear remarkable harmony singing coming from nearby and go to investigate. They find a company of black soldiers quartered in a toilet. The black soldiers insist that the white folksingers "don't belong there." Woody replies, "Wherever anybody's singing the way you're singing, that's *exactly* where we belong." Woody and friends bring the two groups of soldiers together, despite the objections of a colonel determined to maintain segregation in the face of death. By the end of the

Woody Guthrie performing for a group of African-American soldiers, ca. 1940. COURTESY OF WOODY GUTHRIE ARCHIVES.

night, the music has become so hot and joyous, the colonel dances with a black soldier.[2]

It's a great story, exactly analogous to the discovery of the Parses on the Pequod in *Moby Dick*—though Woody turns Ishmael into an activist, standing up to Starbuck and to hell with Ahab and his intentions. When Longhi told this story at the panel, he offered it to buttress the point Joe Klein, author of the standard Guthrie biography, *Woody Guthrie: A Life*, was making, "This was never much of an issue for Woody, or in his life," Klein remarked, echoing the substance of what he says in his book. (Interestingly, Klein tells a portion of Longhi's story in his book but omits any mention of the black soldiers.)[3]

Both Klein and Longhi meant their interpretation as a compliment to Woody. In this version, he was born color-blind, not only free of race hatred but of the patronizing liberal condescension that, Klein remarked, "was in many ways the standard operating procedure on the Left, in those days." In short, they maintained, Woody Guthrie was an entirely singular American who had escaped the most fundamental prejudice of his nation's culture. He simply saw no difference between the "races."

Furthermore, he had come to this perspective as a result of instinct, not reason: "There was never a point where, I think, he had this flash of revelation and realized, 'Oh! They're the same as we are,'" Klein commented.[4]

Not only experience but Klein's own rendition of Woody's history makes that interpretation unlikely. Okemah, Oklahoma, where Woody grew up was, in part, cotton country, an adjunct of the segregationist South; the town next door to Okemah was "an all-black town," Klein told the panel, which suggests that segregation was strong there, too. Klein also said that racial terror was a regular occurrence in Okemah and surrounds, and that Charley Guthrie, Woody's father, "participated in several lynchings."[5] Nor was Woody immune to his culture. In his book, Klein describes racist songs—both antiblack and anti-Japanese—Woody wrote and sang while he was a Los Angeles radio performer in 1937. When he received a letter from a black listener criticizing his antiblack song, Guthrie apologized on the air, and "ripped all the 'nigger' songs out of this book."[6] Perhaps the insight did not "flash," but flashing is not the only, or the most valid or permanent, way of arriving at valuable insights.

Guthrie manager and associate Harold Leventhal's position on how the "race" issue played itself out in Woody's life strikes me as closer to the mark. "I think it was Will Geer who 'educated' Woody in respect to the racist question in respect to the political scene of that era," Leventhal said. "He was also influenced in that sense by Cisco Houston." This process began while Woody still had his Los Angeles radio show. At least one of Woody's intimates found the change startling: "Mary [Woody's first wife] . . . didn't like the fact that he was hanging around with black people," according to Leventhal. Elsewhere, Leventhal has said that she attributed the breakup of their marriage to his change of attitude on the "race" question. Perhaps this is what is implied in what Woody wrote in about 1940: "I was parting in those days from my first wife, Mary, who's [sic] head got stuck so full of catholic [sic] religious notions that she hated all my new books and new friends and my newfound thought with a poison in her belly that killed everything I tried to learn and to work at faster even than I could tell her about them."[7]

For the American Communists of the late 1930s, who gave Woody his political education, opposing American racism was fundamental. This was essential, as racial division was, according to doctrine (and fact), the principal means of social control of the working classes. Racism pervaded every American institution, including the labor movement. Most unions did not admit blacks, and even the most "progressive" ones often had separate black and white locals. It's not insignificant that Woody made common cause with the black members of the National Maritime

Union, according to Woody's daughter, Nora Guthrie. But there's no evidence, on the other hand, of any contact between Guthrie and the most important black union of the period, A. Philip Randolph's Sleeping Car Porters.

Folksingers were hardly exempt from the force of the "race" issue. "The whole popular music scene at that time was riven with racism," Leventhal recalled. "If Duke Ellington, for instance, played at a white club, which he did, he couldn't sit down with people in the club. He could not socially mix. And this was typical all over. It was *not* typical, of course, within the circle of the folk movement at that time. There was every attempt . . . for the question of the unity of blacks and whites, which was a very important political struggle at that time. Woody was very much part of that."[8] As a leading light of the Popular Front, which meant to make cultural works of the common man more honored and respected (if only as a tool for revolution), Woody could hardly have been otherwise. It would strain the imagination of even the most dedicated believer in Woody's innate ability to express human universals to imagine that Communism and the Popular Front had no effect on his perceptions or that he responded so strongly to Communism only because it confirmed what he already knew.

It's notable that Woody, who more than anyone became the voice of the Okies (to those who believed such people were entitled to or capable of possessing a voice), went out of his way to express racial solidarity whenever he could. This is clearly evidenced in Woody's best-seller, the novelistic memoir *Bound for Glory*. Its first sentence: "I could see men of all colors bouncing along in the box car." Its first tumultuous incident comes when Woody aids a Negro hobo in escaping a beating in a box car. In the later sections, the black spiritual "I Shall Not Be Moved" becomes a theme, albeit in its labor incarnation as "We Shall Not Be Moved."[9] (It was this collective-noun version that became famous in the civil rights movement of the 1950s and 1960s.) In the course of the book, Woody makes it a point to express his solidarity with not only blacks, but also Indians and Mexicans, and makes a special point of opposing anti-Japanese racism at a time when it was rife because of the war.[10]

It was only as World War II grew nearer and nearer to both the United States and the Soviet Union that such antiracist efforts as organizing the sharecroppers' union came to be abandoned by Communists. (It would be inaccurate to describe Woody's political connections as belonging simply to the "Left." There is no record of his associating intimately with Trotskyites, anarchists, socialists, or social democrats. Whether he was or wasn't a "Communist," it was with Communists that he associated.) World War II could basically be construed as a war against racism:

Hitlerism was explicitly about the creation of a "master race," and Japanese fascism was certainly tinged with similar ideology. Not that America had solved its "race" problem, either. As black soldier Nelson Peery wrote, "We agreed that Hitler was the main enemy and had to be fought. We also agreed that we weren't going to knuckle down. We would fight fascism where we found it and we knew it was closer than Germany or Japan."[11] In his journals, Guthrie utters remarkably similar sentiments: "The slave war was fought and little pieces of it are still being fought," he wrote in a 1942 piece called "Big Guns."[12]

Still, it is true as I said in introducing the panel, that "Woody did not write that many songs that directly commented on 'race' issues in the United States." In searching the songs collected in Woody's lifetime (about 175 by my count),[13] this seems to be the case. The eleven that do touch on "race" are "Better World," "The Biggest Thing That Man Has Ever Done (The Great Historical Bum)," "Buoy Bells from Trenton (Got My Ship to Beat the Racial Hate)," "Death Row," "Deportees (Plane Wreck at Los Gatos)," "Hangknot" (a.k.a. Slipknot), "The Hour Cometh," "This Could Never Happen in My Dear Old Sunny South," "Vanport's Flood," and two arguable cases, "I Ain't Got No Home," because of its reference to sharecropping (although only most—not all—sharecroppers were black) and "Vigilante Man," although that song is sometimes interpreted as being about strikebreakers. (Knowing about Okemah's history of racial lynchings, and Charley Guthrie's participation in them, settles that question for me.)

Of these songs, the one that is today best known, "Deportees," was found as a lyric only after Woody had lost the ability to finish his work; the music is attributed to Martin Hoffman. That song is not about the main current of American racial oppression—black people as chattel slaves, peons, and the most disenfranchised of urban proletarians—but about Southwestern anti-Mexican racism, which is here presented as a function of the overall oppression of migrant farmworkers, a job that Woody himself once held. "Death Row" is hardly known at all, although its fourth verse speaks in terms that might be included in any contemporary discussion of the issue:

If you're white you've some chance to beat this Death Row;
If you're white you might get loose from off this Death Row;
But a man that's partly black, partly dark, chocolate brown
He ain't got an earthly chance to beat this Death Row.[14]

"The Hour Cometh," which is equally obscure, devotes part of its three central verses to "race" issues;[15] most of the other songs in this group mention "race" only in passing, and often express only the most oblique "all men are brothers" sentiments. The exception is "This Could Never Happen in My Dear Old Sunny South" which is not dated but seems to take its theme from the trial of the Scottsboro Boys in 1931. The case, which amounted to the legal lynching of nine black youths accused of raping two white women in a railroad siding, became a national cause célèbre for the next seven years.[16] Everyone in America was aware of the case, not only because it was lurid and controversial by itself, but because "Free the Scottsboro boys!" became a banner cry among the then-burgeoning American Communists. In 1937, just when Guthrie first began to write for the Communist press, the Supreme Court turned down the Scottsboro appeals. Unless Woody read nothing in *People's World* other than his own column, he could hardly have been unaware of it. This further buttresses the case for Guthrie's antiracist attitude as a position arrived at consciously rather than merely God-given.

But there is little or no reference to the struggles of black people or other minorities in the extensive recording Woody did with Alan Lomax for the Library of Congress.[17] Even when Woody sings "Boll Weevil Song," which is certainly black in origin, he presents it as being about migrant farm laborers and Okies. This may reflect Lomax's interest, although Woody would not have been shy about interjecting the topic, had it been foremost in his mind. Probably, at that time, Woody had more interest in writing and commenting about the Dust Bowl and its refugees than anything else. There's nothing illegitimate about this: the Dust Bowlers were as impoverished as any group of people in America, and Woody's direct personal experience tied him closely to their struggle. Throughout the late thirties and early forties, in his political songs, Woody mostly wrote about Okie topics, in favor of unions and the little man, and against fascism and capitalism. After his period of hard traveling, Guthrie's connection to black Americans seems to have come mostly from his association with black musicians, most importantly Lead Belly, Sonny Terry and, to a lesser extent, Brownie McGhee. (He did once write a virtual mash note in the form of an open letter after seeing a Paul Robeson performance.)[18]

In this regard several other factors come into play. For various reasons having to do with the ideology of the Popular Front, folk musicians had very little contact with popular black musicians. Neither did the sort of music that Woody Guthrie performed have much, if any, black audience. Because Woody, like any entertainer, tended to talk and sing about things held in common with his audience, this situation increased his tendency

Woody Guthrie and Sonny Terry, ca. 1940. COURTESY OF
WOODY GUTHRIE ARCHIVES.

to talk about "race" issues in the abstract—or as part of the entire American class system.

Second, great as he was, Woody Guthrie, like any other artist, worked within his own limitations. One of these was that he spoke most often, and certainly most comfortably and adeptly, in his own voice. This was true in his prose, and perhaps truer still in his songs: there are characters in his songs (Juan and Rosalita in "Deportees," the men of the *Reuben James*, Pretty Boy Floyd, and so on) but the narrator is always the singer himself. In a situation of limited contact with black people, this did not leave Woody with a whole lot to talk about. After the war, he did attempt an interesting dramatic piece, set in a Long Island coffeeshop where three soldiers are refused service with ugly results. But mostly he wrote about

unionists, hoboes, farmworkers, and the land itself. In part he chose
those themes because they were what he knew best and understood most
deeply. But in equal measure, he wrote and sang about some of those
things because he was part of a movement, which took the name of Communism (even if it could be argued that, in several respects, the ideology
of the Communist Party U.S.A. was not strictly communist at all, but
threaded with all sorts of other tendencies, most notably anarcho-
syndicalism, which was probably what enabled it to tolerate someone
like Woody Guthrie as much as it did). In the places where Woody Guthrie lived and worked from the late thirties through the early fifties, this
movement for social justice centered around issues other than ending segregation. It can, and probably ought to be, argued that this was a mistake. But as part of that movement, Woody and his work tended to flow
along the movement's lines (if not always the Party line).

To my way of thinking, then, one of the most important reasons that
there aren't many important Woody Guthrie songs that attack racism
and the whole Jim Crow enterprise is that Huntington's chorea cheated
us out of them. The movement to end de jure segregation in the United
States began picking up steam in the late forties, but it did so alongside
the continuing labor struggles and, equally important, the vicious ram-
page of the red-baiters and the rise of their anti-Communist blacklist.
Woody, whether he was ever a Party member or just a similarly inclined
comrade, would certainly have been blacklisted just as severely as Pete
Seeger and the Weavers, whose pop chart career was ended because of
their listing in *Red Channels* and Pete's brave refusal to cooperate with
the House Un-American Activities Committee. Woody avoided blacklisting only because, by the end of 1952, the disease had so far overtaken
him that his creative life had all but ended. By 1954, he wrote in huge led-
gerbooks, and even then had neurological symptoms so severe that he
was lucky to get an entire phrase on one page.[19] *Brown v. Board of Education*, the Montgomery bus boycott, and the other momentous events
that launched America's greatest postwar social movement passed by
while Woody was on the run from the reality of his illness, or hospitalized
because of it.

Woody had just turned forty in 1952. Given normal health, he had a
good twenty or thirty years of work left in him. If he'd had Pete Seeger's
constitution, he might have been able to continue working for another
decade or so past that. Certainly, without the intervention of
Huntington's, Woody would have become as deeply involved in assisting
the civil rights movement as was Pete, who not only contributed the secular version of "We Shall Overcome," but became a key inspirational figure and an important fund-raiser as well. Involvement with the civil

rights movement almost certainly would have produced a very different batch of Woody Guthrie songs. He was, after all, a great American propaganda artist, of similar stature to Tom Paine, Harriet Beecher Stowe, William Lloyd Garrison, W. E. B. Du Bois, and the Henry David Thoreau of *Civil Disobedience*. Indeed, with his instinct for rabble-rousing and cutting, irreverent humor, Woody anticipated the style not only of Bob Dylan, Phil Ochs, and the other "urban folkies," but even of black leaders like Malcom X and Bobby Seale.

It's intriguing to imagine what Woody Guthrie might have contributed to the civil rights movement, had his ability to create survived—what he might have added to "We Shall Overcome," how he might have adapted songs like "This Land Is Your Land," the different kind of inspiration he might have been able to lend to the new topical songwriters. That Woody would have become a militant supporter of the movement, there can be no doubt; that he would have turned his energies to writing for and about the movement, there is no question. We cannot know whether he would have had the personal impact that Pete Seeger had, or whether he could have matched such Dylan songs as "The Lonesome Death of Hattie Carroll" and "Only a Pawn in Their Game" in their insights into the system of white supremacy and class manipulation. Perhaps he could have come up with something even more sardonic than Ochs's "Here's to the State of Mississippi." We can only know that neither Seeger, nor Dylan, nor any of the other topical songwriters would have done their work in anything like the same way if there had never been Woody Guthrie.

For me, in the end, this is the final evidence that the implications of the American racial crisis were inherent to Woody Guthrie's work. If the topic is not dealt with explicitly as often as one would hope, it's nevertheless true that for several generations now, American songwriters, from Seeger, Dylan, and Ochs to Bruce Springsteen, Ani DiFranco, and Steve Earle, have drawn similar conclusions from hearing it. Those conclusions have always been in favor of justice and social equality—and in America, once you start thinking about those things, you are going to be drawn into questions about "race" and racism.

In a way, Klein and Longhi are correct about Woody's ability to transcend "race" in his personal dealings. But that ability, which many others have also remarked upon, didn't come out of some essential nature. It emerged from hard work, from dialogue, and from conviction. This conviction was, in the end, about something broader than "race." Woody believed that no man should be anonymous. Trying to render human beings invisible aroused his greatest rage: if there is any slogan of the contemporary period that sounds like something Woody might have coined, it is Jesse Jackson's "I am somebody." Woody demanded this stature for himself, but he also wanted it for every man and woman. Racism achieves its hideous ends only when it is able to render human beings so totally anonymous that they seem not even to be human any longer.

In this sense, just about every great song Woody Guthrie ever wrote stands in opposition to racism. Not by nature and not by accident, his work finally achieves the grand dimension W. E. B. Du Bois ascribes to black "Sorrow Songs" (spirituals and folk-blues) in *The Souls of Black Folk*: "Through all the sorrow of the Sorrow Songs there breathes a hope—a faith in the ultimate justice of things. The minor cadences of despair change often to triumph and calm confidence. Sometimes it is faith in life, sometimes a faith in death, sometimes assurance of boundless justice in some fair world beyond. But whichever it is, the meaning is always clear: that sometime, somewhere, men will judge men by their souls and not by their skins. Is such a hope justified? Do the Sorrow songs sing true?"[20]

NOTES

N.B. I have placed the word "race" in quotation marks throughout because, of course, there are no "races," but one human species, indivisible except by pseudoscience.

1. Jimmy Longhi. *Woody, Cisco, and Me: Seamen Three in the Merchant Marine* (Urbana: University of Illinois Press, 1997); *That's Why We're Marching: World War II and the American Folk Song Movement* (Smithsonian Folkways Records, 1996).

2. Jim Longhi from unpublished transcript of "Deportees: Woody and Race" panel, Guthrie conference held on 28 September 1996 at Case Western Reserve University, Cleveland, Ohio.

3. Joe Klein, conference transcript; Joe Klein, *Woody Guthrie: A Life* (New York: Knopf, 1980), 277.

4. Klein, conference transcript.

5. Ibid.

6. Klein, *Woody Guthrie*, 95.

7. Woody Guthrie, *Pastures of Plenty: A Self Portrait*, ed. Dave Marsh and Harold Leventhal (HarperCollins, 1990), 69.

8. Leventhal, conference transcript.

9. Woody Guthrie, *Bound for Glory* (1943; New York: Plume, 1983).

10. Ibid., 268.

11. Nelson Peery, *Black Fire: The Making of An American Revolutionary* (New York: New Press, 1994), 151.

12. Guthrie, *Pastures*, 78.

13. Woody Guthrie, *The Nearly Complete Collection of Woody Guthrie Folk Songs* (New York: Ludlow Music, 1963), 3–5.

14. Ibid., 35.

15. Ibid., 203.

16. See Dan T. Carter, *Scottsboro: A Tragedy of the American South*, rev. ed. (Baton Rouge: Louisiana State University Press, 1979).

17. Woody Guthrie, *Library of Congress Recordings*, Rounder CD 1041/2/3; recorded 1940, released on CD 1988.

18. Guthrie, *Pastures*, 66.

19. Ibid., 244.

20. W. E. B. Du Bois, *The Souls of Black Folk*, Library of America ed. (New York: Vintage Books, 1990), 188.

Woody Guthrie Biblio/Discography

GUY LOGSDON

Research was made possible by the National Endowment for the Humanities, Research Materials Division, and the Smithsonian Institution, Office of Fellowships and Grants.

Numerous individuals have given me information and assistance essential to the compilation of this biblio/discography, and I deeply appreciate the friendship and assistance of Jeff Place, Smithsonian/Folkways Recordings and Smithsonian Institution–Center for Folklife and Cultural Heritage; and Joe Hickerson, Archive of Folk Culture, Library of Congress.

PRIMARY ARCHIVAL/MANUSCRIPT COLLECTIONS

Guthrie, Woody. Woody Guthrie Archives, New York, New York.
> Personal and family papers, recordings, photographs, films, television shows, drawings and illustrations by WG, and ephemera

Library of Congress, Archive of Folk Culture, Washington, D.C.
> Guthrie/Lomax recordings, letters, manuscripts, radio shows, and ephemera

National Archives, Washington, D.C.
> Bonneville Power Administration documents and discs assembled by William Murlin

Reuss, Richard, Papers, Indiana University, Bloomington, Indiana
> Reuss was a scholar/collector of Woody Guthrie's life and materials; documents, letters, and taped interviews.

Smithsonian Institution, Center for Folklife Programs and Cultural Studies, Washington, D.C.
> Moses Asch/Folkways Records Collection, Woody Guthrie Collection, and Lee Hays Collection, recordings, master recordings, manuscripts, photographs, line drawings and illustrations, one oil painting by WG, and ephemera

TRO Richmond, New York, New York
> Song manuscripts and taped recordings

Additional items are in private and institutional collections across the nation.

BOOKS AND JOURNALS

Compiler's note: This is a bibliography of books and journals that contain songs written by Woody Guthrie; it is not intended to be an update of the Reuss bibliography (1968). I have included a few titles that are important to use in studying Woody Guthrie's songs even though they don't contain song texts.

Almanac Singers, The. *America Sings for American People's Meeting April 5–6, N.Y.* New York: American Peace Mobilization, n.d. (ca. 1941).

———. *Anti-Fascist Songs of the Almanac Singers.* Detroit, Mich.: The Almanac Singers, 1944.

———. *Songs of the Almanac Singers, Book 1.* Compiled by Bob Miller. New York: Bob Miller, Inc., 1942.

Brand, Oscar. *The Ballad Mongers: Rise of the Modern Folk Song.* New York: Funk & Wagnells, 1962.

Cantwell, Robert. *When We Were Good: The Folk Revival.* Cambridge, Mass.: Harvard University Press, 1996.

Carawan, Guy, and Candie Carawan, comps. *We Shall Overcome!* New York: Oak Publications, 1963.

Cohen, Ronald D., ed. *"Wasn't That a Time!" Firsthand Accounts of the Folk Music Revival.* Metuchen, N.J.: Scarecrow, 1995.

Cohen, Ronald D., and Dave Samuelson. *Songs for Political Action: Folk Music, Topical Songs and the American Left, 1926–1953.* Hambergen, Germany: Bear Family Records, 1996 [this is the 212-page book that accompanies the ten-disc set by the same title].

The Collected Reprints from Sing Out! Vols. 1–6, 1959–1964. Bethlehem, Pa.: Sing Out Corporation, 1990.

The Collected Reprints from Sing Out! Vols. 7–12, 1964–1973. Bethlehem, Pa.: Sing Out Corporation, 1992.

Denisoff, R. Serge. *Great Day Coming: Folk Music and the American Left.* Champaign: University of Illinois Press, 1971.

Dunaway, David King. *How Can I Keep from Singing: Pete Seeger.* New York: McGraw-Hill, 1981.

Green, Archie, "Woody's Oil Songs," in *Songs About Work: Essays in Occupational Culture for Richard A. Reuss,* edited by Archie Green, 208–20. Bloomington: Folklore Institute, Indiana University, 1993.

Greenway, John. *American Folksongs of Protest.* Philadelphia: University of Pennsylvania Press, 1953.

Guthrie, Woody: *Woody and Lefty Lou's Favorite Collection Old Time Hill Country Songs.* Gardena, Cal.: Spanish American Institute Press, ca. 1937 (two earlier editions were mimeographed and mailed to their fans).

———. "Woody & Lefty Lou's One Thousand and One Laffs and Your Free Gift of One Hundred and One Songs." April 1938, 104 pp.; manuscript in private collection.

———. "Songs of Woody Guthrie." 1941, 203 pp. typescript, "prepared by Archive of Folk Song [Library of Congress]." Two copies in the Archive of Folk Culture, Library of Congress.

———. "My New Found Land." "A collection of song texts and poems, mostly typewritten, *circa* 1941." Microfilm copy in the Library of Congress.

———. "Hard Hittin' Songs." "Collected by the Almanac Singers and written by Woody Guthrie; music transcribed by Peter Seeger [ca. 1942]." Microfilm copy in the Library of Congress.

———. *Bound For Glory.* New York: Dutton, 1943. New edition with a Foreword by Pete Seeger and a Tribute by Stewart L. Udall, 1968; Dutton paperback, 1968; Signet paperback, 1970; Dolphin Books paperback, n.d.; Plume paperback, 1983; reprinted in numerous foreign languages. Audio cassettes, read by Arlo Guthrie (Berkeley, Cal.: Audio Literature, 1992).

———. *Ten of Woody Guthrie's Songs, Book One.* New York: Woody Guthrie (mimeographed by WG), 1945.

———. *American Folksong*. New York: Moe Asch, 1947.

———. *Three Songs for Centralia*. New York: People's Songs, Inc., 1947.

———. *American Folksong*. Edited by Moe Asch. Reprinted from the 1947 original. New York: Oak Publications, 1961. Melody lines are added in this edition.

———. "A Child of VD." Words and music by Woody Guthrie, written in 1949, sung by Arlo Guthrie on "VD Blues," WNET, New York, and Educational Broadcasting Corp., published in *VD Blues* (New York: Avon Books, 1972). [This book is the "entire script of the TV broadcast plus the extraordinary HOTLINE reaction to the history-making program" presented by the Educational Broadcasting Corp.]

———. *California to the New York Island: Woven into a Script suitable for a Concert, Clambake, Hootenanny or Community Sing*, by Millard Lampell. New York: Guthrie Children's Trust Fund, 1958, 1960.

———. *Woody Guthrie Folk Songs: A Collection of Songs by America's Foremost Balladeer*. Introduction by Pete Seeger. New York: Ludlow Music, 1963.

———. *Born to Win*. Edited by Robert Shelton. New York: Macmillan, 1965.

———. *A Tribute to Woody Guthrie*. Woven into a script by Millard Lampell. Music edited and transcribed by Hally Wood. New York: TRO Ludlow Music in association with Woody Guthrie Publications, Inc., 1972.

———. *Woody Sez*. Compiled and edited by Marjorie Guthrie, Harold Leventhal, Terry Sullivan, and Sheldon Patinkin. Preface by Studs Terkel. With a biography by Guy Logsdon. New York: Grosset & Dunlap, 1975.

———. *The Woody Guthrie Songbook*. Edited by Harold Leventhal and Marjorie Guthrie. New York: Grosset & Dunlap, 1976.

———. *Seeds of Man: An Experience Lived and Dreamed*. New York: Dutton, 1976. (Pocket Book edition, 1977).

———. *101 Woody Guthrie Songs, Including All the Songs From "Bound For Glory."* New York: TRO Ludlow Music, 1977.

———. *"Roll on Columbia:" The Columbia River Songs*. Edited by Bill Murlin. Portland, Ore.: Bonneville Power Administration, 1988; new edition, Bethlehem, Pa.: Sing Out Publications, 1991.

———. *Pastures of Plenty: A Self-Portrait*. Edited by David Marsh and Harold Leventhal. New York: HarperCollins, 1990.

———. *Songs by Woody Guthrie*. Expanded edition. Edited by Judy Bell. New York: TRO Ludlow Music, n.d. (ca. 1990).

———. *Woody Guthrie Songs*. Edited by Judy Bell and Nora Guthrie. New York: TRO Ludlow Music, n.d. (ca. 1992), second printing has a different cover (1994).

Guthrie, Woody, with Marjorie Mazia Guthrie. *Woody's 20 Grow Big Songs*. New York: HarperCollins, 1992.

Halker, Clark D. *For Democracy, Workers, and God: Labor Song-Poems and Labor Protest, 1865–95*. Champaign: University of Illinois Press, 1991.

Houston, Cisco. *900 Miles: The Ballads, Blues and Folksongs of Cisco Houston*. New York: Oak Publications, 1965.

Jaffe, Eli. *Oklahoma Odyssey: A Memoir*. Hyde Park, N.Y.: Eli Jaffe, 1993.

K-6 Wranglers, The. *A Jack Guthrie Song Book*. Tacoma, Wash.: Western Entertainment Enterprises, 1946.

Klein, Joe. *Woody Guthrie: A Life*. New York: Knopf, 1980.

Lieberman, Robbie. *"My Song Is My Weapon:" People's Songs, American Communism, and the Politics of Culture, 1930–1950*. Champaign: University of Illinois Press, 1989.

Logsdon, Guy. "The Dust Bowl and the Migrant." *American Scene* 12 (March 1971), entire issue.

———. "Jack Guthrie: A Star That Almost Was." *Journal of Country Music* 15 (1993): 32–38.

———. "Woody's Roots." *Music Journal* 34 (December 1976): 18–21.

Lomax, Alan, comp. *Hard-Hitting Songs for Hard-Hit People*. Notes on the songs by Woody Guthrie. Music transcribed and edited by Pete Seeger. New York: Oak Publications, 1967.

Longhi, Vincent "Jim." *Woody, Cisco and Me*. Champaign: University of Illinois Press, 1996.

Nearly Complete Collection of Woody Guthrie Folk Songs, The. This is the cover title for *Woody Guthrie Folk Songs*. Ludlow, 1963.

Noebel, David A. *The Marxist Minstrels: A Handbook on Communist Subversion of Music*. Tulsa, Okla.: American Christian College Press, 1974.

———. *Rhythm, Riots and Revolution*. Tulsa, Okla.: Christian Crusade Publications, 1966.

Reprints from Sing Out! Vols. 1–12. New York: Oak Publications, 1959–73. (see also *The Collected Reprints from Sing Out!*)

Reuss, Richard A. *A Woody Guthrie Bibliography, 1912–1967*. New York: Guthrie Children's Trust Fund, 1968.

Richmond, Al. *A Long View from the Left: Memoirs of an American Revolutionary*. Boston: Houghton Mifflin, 1973.

Robbin, Edward. *Woody Guthrie and Me: An Intimate Reminiscence*. Berkeley, Cal.: Lancaster-Miller, 1979.

Schmid, Will. *A Tribute to Woody Guthrie & Lead Belly: Student Text*. Reston, Va.: Music Educator's National Conference, 1991.

———. *A Tribute to Woody Guthrie & Lead Belly: Teacher's Guide*. Reston, Va.: Music Educator's National Conference, 1991.

Seeger, Pete. *The Bells of Rhymney and Others Songs and Stories from the Singing of Pete Seeger*. New York: Oak Publications, 1964.

———. *Henscratches and Flyspecks*. New York: Putnam, 1973.

———. *Where Have All the Flowers Gone: A Singer's Stories, Songs, Seeds, Robberies*. Bethlehem, Pa.: Sing Out Publications.

Seeger, Pete, and Bob Reiser. *Carry It On!* New York: Simon and Schuster, 1985.

Silber, Irwin, ed. *Lift Every Voice!* New York: Sing Out Inc., 1957.

———. *Reprints from the People's Songs Bulletin*. New York: Oak Publications, 1961.

Terkel, Studs. *Talking to Myself: A Memoir of My Times*. New York: Pantheon Books, 1977.

White, Wava (Guthrie). *Jack Guthrie Memorial Album*. Sacramento, Cal.: Wava (Guthrie) White Publishing, 1950.

Willens, Doris. *Lonesome Traveler: The Life of Lee Hays*. New York: Norton, 1988.

Yates, Janelle. *Woody Guthrie: American Balladeer*. Staten Island, N.Y.: Ward Hill, 1995.

Yurchenco, Henrietta, assisted by Marjorie Guthrie. *A Mighty Hard Road: The Woody Guthrie Story*. New York: McGraw-Hill, 1970.

RECORDING SESSIONS

This section includes radio shows and recorded concerts as well as studio recording sessions.

Library of Congress Sessions

All titles in this section were recorded in Washington, D.C., in March 1940 by Alan and Elizabeth Lomax. An alphabetized listing of these titles can be found in Country Directory 1 *(November 1960): 6–7. Titles not marked by an asterisk (*) were issued on* Woody Guthrie: Library of Congress Recordings, Elektra Records EKL-271/272 *(3–12" LPs), 1964, notes by Alan Lomax, Robert Shelton, and Woody Guthrie, produced and edited by Jac Holzman; reissued by Rounder Records CD 1041/2/3 (compact disc) and C-1041 Part 1 and Part 2 (cassette), 1988 (notes are edited to fit format). The editor (Holzman) deleted portions from most of Woody's recorded monologues and dialogues.*

Autobiography of Woodrow Wilson (Woody) Guthrie   3407-3423

21 MARCH 1940. *Department of Interior, Radio Broadcasting Division, interviewed by Alan Lomax:*

Monologue: Boyhood of Woody Guthrie	3407 & 3408
"The Train" ("Lost Train Blues"), harmonica/guitar	3407-A
"Railroad Blues," harmonica	3407-B
"Rye Whiskey," vocal/guitar	3408-A, B1
"Old Joe Clark," vocal/guitar	3408-B2
"Beaumont Rag," harmonica/guitar	3408-B3
Dialogue on the "Green Valley Waltz"	3408-B4
*"Green Valley Waltz," harmonica/guitar	3409-A
Monologue on the Youth of Woody Guthrie	3409-A, B1
"Greenback Dollar," vocal/guitar/harmonica	3409-B1
"Boll Weevil Song," vocal/guitar/harmonica	3409-B2

Also issued in part on The Ballad Hunter, Part VI,
Library of Congress, Music Division, AAFS L51
originally issued on 16" disc (33⅓ rpm) recorded
in New York, Radio Recording Division, NBC.

*"Midnight Special" and dialogue vocal/guitar/harmonica	3410-A1
Dialogue on Dust Storms	3410-A2, B1
"So Long, It's Been Good to Know You," vocal/guitar	3410-B2
Dialogue on the Dust Bowl	3410-B3
Dialogue on the Dust Bowl, continued	3411-A1
"Talking Dust Bowl Blues"	3411-A2, B1
Dialogue on Experiences in California	3411-B2
"Do-Re-Mi," vocal/guitar/harmonica	3411-B3

22 MARCH 1940. *Department of Interior, Radio Broadcasting Division, interviewed by Alan Lomax:*

"Hard Times," vocal/guitar	3412-A1
*"Bring Back to Me My Blue Eyed Boy"	3412-A2
*Dialogue on Love Songs	3412-A3
Dialogue on Outlaws	3412-B1
*"Billy the Kid," vocal/guitar (fragment)	3412-B2
"Pretty Boy Floyd," vocal/guitar	3412-B4

"Pretty Boy Floyd," continued	3413-A
Dialogue about Jesse James	3413-B1
*"Jesse James," vocal/guitar	3413-B1
"They Laid Jesus Christ in His Grave," vocal/guitar	3413-B2
"They Laid Jesus Christ in His Grave," continued	3414-A1
"I'm a Jolly Banker," ("Jolly Banker," "Banker's Lament"), vocal/guitar	3414-A2
Dialogue on Bankers	3414-A2, A3
"I Ain't Got No Home in This World Anymore" ("I Ain't Got No Home"), vocal/guitar/harmonica	3414-A3, B1
"Dirty Overhauls (overalls)," vocal/guitar	3414-B2,
"Dirty Overhauls," continued	3415-A1
*"Mary Fagen" and dialogue	3415-A2, B1
"Chain Around My Leg" and dialogue, vocal/guitar	3415-B2
Dialogue on the Blues	3416-A1

> Also issued on *The Ballad Hunter, Part II*,
> Library of Congress, Music Division, AAFS L49
> originally issued on 16" disc (33⅓ rpm) recorded
> in New York, Radio Recording Division, NBC.

*"The Bluest Blues" (900 Miles?) and dialogue vocal/guitar	3416-A2
"Worried Man Blues," vocal/guitar	3416-B1
Church House Blues—"Lonesome Valley," vocal/guitar	3416-B2
Dialogue on Walking Railroad Ties	3416-B2
Monologue: Railroads and Men Out of Work	3417-A
"Railroad Line Blues" ("Walkin' Down That Railroad Line"), vocal/guitar	3417-B1
*"Goin' Down the Frisco Line," with dialogue vocal/guitar	3417-B2
"I'm Goin' Down the Road Feelin' Bad," vocal/guitar	3418-A1
*"Seven Cent Cotton," vocal/guitar (fragment)	3418-A2
*"Wagon Yard Blues," vocal/guitar (fragment)	3418-A3
"Dust Bowl Refugees," vocal/guitar	3418-B1
Dialogue about Man going to California for Contract Work	3418-B2,
Dialogue about Man going to Calif., continued	3419-A
"Great Dust Storm" ("Dust Storm Disaster") and dialogue vocal/guitar	3419-B1
"I'm Sittin' on the Foggy Mountain Top" ("Foggy Mountain Top") vocal/guitar	3419-B2

27 MARCH 1940. *Department of Interior, Radio Broadcasting Division, interviewed by Elizabeth Lomax:*

Story of Oil Booms and Dust Storms	3420-A1
"Dust Pneumonia Blues," vocal/guitar	3420-A2
*"Dust Bowl Blues," vocal/guitar	3420-B1
Dialogue about California	3420-B1
"California Blues," vocal/guitar	3420-B2

Dialogue about Jimmie Rodgers, "California Blues,"
    and California   3421-A
*"Do-Re-Mi," vocal/guitar   3421-B1
Living Conditions in California   3421-B1
*"Dust Bowl Refugees" and dialogue, vocal/guitar   3422-A
Dialogue about Okies in California, Pride in
    Oklahoma, and Will Rogers   3422-B1
"Highway 66" ("Will Rogers Highway"), vocal/guitar   3423-A1
"New Years Flood," vocal/guitar   3423-A2

4 JANUARY 1941. *Songs by Woody Guthrie with guitar, recorded in the Phonoduplica-
tion Studio by Alan Lomax and John Langenegger (16" disc; 4491):*

"Stewball," vocal/guitar   4491-A1
"Stagolee," vocal/guitar   4491-A2
"One Dime Blues," vocal/guitar   4491-A3
"Whoopee Ti Yi Yo, Git Along Little Dogies," vocal/guitar 4491-B1
    Issued in part on *The Ballad Hunter, Part III,*
    Library of Congress, Music Division, AAFS L50
    originally issued on 16" disc (33⅓ rpm) recorded
    in New York, Radio Recording Division, NBC.
"Trail to Mexico" (fragment), vocal/guitar   4491-B2
    Issued in part on *The Ballad Hunter, Part III,*
    Library of Congress, Music Division, AAFS L50,
    originally issued on 16" disc (33⅓ rpm) recorded
    in New York, Radio Recording Division, NBC.
"The Gypsy Davy," vocal/guitar   4491-B3
    Issued on *Anglo-American Ballads,* edited by
    Alan Lomax, Library of Congress, Music Divi-
    sion, AAFS 1 (10" discs) and on AFS L1 (LP),
    notes say recorded in Washington, D.C., 1940
    (should be 1941), by Alan Lomax. LC 14, AAFS
    2A, matrix A4357
"There Is a House in This Old Town" ("Hard,
    Ain't It Hard"), vocal/guitar   4491-B4

American School of the Air

2 APRIL 1940. *CBS Radio, this folk music series, written and narrated by Alan Lomax,
was inaugurated in October 1939. The folksong topics varied: "Lumberjack Songs,"
"Trail Songs," "Nonsense Songs," "Railroad Songs," "Blues," and so forth. Woody
Guthrie was introduced to the national radio audience during the segment "Farm
Songs" (aired 2 April 1940).*

"Boll Weevil," Alan Lomax, lead vocal/guitar; Woody   Library of Congress
    Guthrie, harmonica; Golden Gate Quartet,   4507A4
    vocals/chorus
"It's Hard on We Poor Farmers," Alan Lomax, lead   Library of Congress
    vocal/guitar; Woody Guthrie, harmonica; Golden   4507A3
    Gate Quartet, vocals/chorus

"Train Blues," Woody Guthrie, harmonica solo	Library of Congress 4508A1
"So Long, It's Been Good to Know You," Woody Guthrie, vocal/guitar; Alan Lomax, vocal	Library of Congress 4508A2
"Talking Dust Storm," Woody Guthrie, vocal/guitar	Library of Congress 4508A3

RCA Victor Sessions

26 APRIL 1940. New York. Woody recorded eleven songs that day, but with "Tom Joad" recorded in two parts, he actually recorded "twelve" songs. Of the twelve takes only one title, "Talkin' Dust Bowl Blues," was recorded twice (the second take was issued); the others required one recording only. On typescripts of "Dust Can't Kill Me" and "Dust Pneumonia Blues" Woody stated: "Recorded Friday, 3 May 1940, Studio #3," and according to the RCA log, Woody was correct; those two songs were recorded on that date with one take for each song. Of the thirteen titles ("Tom Joad" required two bands on the issued records), two, "Dust Bowl Blues" and "Pretty Boy Floyd," were not issued when the two albums, 78 rpm, 10" discs, were released: Dust Bowl Ballads, Vol. 1, Victor Records P-27 and Dust Bowl Ballads, Vol. 2, Victor Records P-28, notes by Woody Guthrie. They were included in the 1964 reissue Dust Bowl Ballads, RCA Victor LPV-502 Vintage Series (12" LP), 1964, notes by Peter J. Welding, produced by Frank Driggs, also reissued in England RCA Victor (Decca Record) RD-7642; reissued as Woody Guthrie: A Legendary Performer, RCA CPL1-2099(e), 1977, notes by Guy Logsdon; reissued as Dust Bowl Ballads, Rounder Records, 1040 (LP, cassette, and compact disc).

Woody Guthrie vocal: "The Great Dust Storm"

("Dust Storm Disaster"), guitar	(26622-A) BS-050145-1
"Talkin' Dust Bowl Blues," guitar	(26619-A) BS-050146-2
"Dust Pneumonia Blues," guitar	(26623-B) BS-050147-1
"Dusty Old Dust" ("So Long, It's Been Good to Know You"), guitar	(26622-B) BS-050148-1
"Dust Bowl Blues," guitar	LPV-502 BS-050149-1
"Blowin' Down This Road" ("I Ain't Going to be Treated This Way"), guitar/harmonica	(26619-B) BS-050150-1
"Tom Joad, Part 1," guitar/harmonica	(26621-A) BS-050151-1
"Tom Joad, Part 2," guitar/harmonica	(26621-B) BS-050152-1
"Do Re Mi," guitar	(26620-A) BS-050153-1
"Dust Bowl Refugee," guitar/harmonica	(26623-A) BS-050154-1
"I Ain't Got No Home in This World Anymore," guitar/harmonica	(26624-A) BS-050155-1
"Vigilante Man," guitar/harmonica	(26624-B) BS-050156-1
"Dust Cain't Kill Me," guitar/harmonica	(26620-B) BS-050600-1
"Pretty Boy Floyd," guitar	LPV-502 BS-050601-1

Moses Asch with Woody's encouragement (but not with RCA's license) took copies of the RCA Victor records and issued them as Talking Dust Bowl, Folkways Records FP 11 (10" LP), notes by John Asch and Woody Guthrie, 1950, using only eight cuts with titles as follows: "So Long, It's Been Good to Know You," "Dust Storm Disaster," "Talking Dust Bowl Blues," "Dust Can't Kill Me," "Blowing Down This Road Feeling

Bad," "Dust Bowl Refugee," "Tom Joad parts 1 & 2;" reissued as FA 2011; reissued
with additional songs as issued on the original RCA albums as Dust Bowl Ballads,
Folkways Records FH 5212 (12" LP), with additional cover notes by Millard Lampell,
1964; reissued as a part of 38 Favorite American Folk Songs, Disc/Folkways Records
FF1. The placement of songs on the disc varies on each reissued album. In 1947 on the
Disc label, Asch released Woody Guthrie's Ballads from the Dust Bowl Disc Album
610, but these were different songs from those listed above.

Lead Belly Radio Show (narrated by Woody Guthrie)

19 JUNE 1940. New York City. Little is known about this radio show other than what
the above title indicates. Arnold S. Caplin (Biograph Records) obtained a copy of the
show, but it contained no information other than the date and city. Joe Hickerson, Library of Congress, obtained a copy that appears to be the master 16" disc; it contains
information indicating that it was an audition for NBC, probably an audition disc for
a radio show (apparently never aired). Caplin issued the recording along with seven
other cuts under the title, Early Lead Belly: 1935–1940: Narrated by Woody Guthrie,
Biograph Records BLP-12013, 1969, notes by Chris Albertson; reissued Biograph
Records BCD 113 (compact disc). Side 1 is the radio show recorded 19 June 1940,
narrated by Woody Guthrie (he introduces each song). While no Guthrie songs are included, it is important, for his comments and conversation with Lead Belly reveal that
he was far more sophisticated than he usually portrayed himself.

Back Where I Come From

19 AUGUST 1940. New York City, program 10 in the CBS Radio Forecast series. This
series was an attempt to "try out new radio ideas;" each program was an introduction
to a proposed new radio series. Back Where I Come From was about notions on which
everybody has an opinion. Literary critic Clifton Fadiman was the host of this show
written by Alan Lomax and Nicholas Ray; featured performers were Woody Guthrie,
The Golden Gate Quartet, Len Doyle, Burl Ives, Josh White, and Willie Johnson. The
first topic was "weather," and each performer stated "Back where I come from, we always say . . ." and completed the sentence with a local belief or saying. The cast sang
"Erie Canal," but Woody's voice cannot be heard as a distinctive voice if, indeed, he
was singing with the others. He was introduced as having sung in every bar between
Oklahoma City and Los Angeles, and he responded that he changed trains (subway)
three times getting to the show: "It was so crowded that every time I changed trains, I
come out with a different pair of shoes on. . . . This weather talk reminds me of Texas
. . . last winter the Santee Fee train blowed the whistle and the steam froze right there
in the air and the next summer it thawed out and scared half the cattle out of the Pan-
handle." The dialogue progressed to the discussion of storms; Woody said, "Storms
hurt people, drive people out of their homes and take their living away from them, and
that very thing is happening right today back in the 'Dust Bowl' where I come from.
. . . Well, I come from Okemah, Oklahoma, out in that country ain't nothing in the
world to stop that north wind but a barbed wire fence, and that ain't much." He starts
singing:

"So Long, It's Been Good to Know You," Woody Guthrie, vocal/guitar (first verse)
and entire cast joins in singing the chorus; the cast acts out the other verses with Burl
Ives playing "Paw." Woody sings the verse about the preacher calling, and then the

cast and Woody use dialogue to move Woody onto the highway traveling west. Following a folk sermon by Willie Johnson and The Golden Gate Quartet, Woody and the entire cast close the musical portion of the show with the chorus of "So Long."

The entire show was issued on Folk Music Radio *by Radiola, Release 133, CMR-1133 (cassette) side B, ca. late 1970s.*

Cavalcade of America, Program 199

6 NOVEMBER 1940. *Wild Bill Hickock. On a TRO Richmond Music ms. ca. 1944, Woody typed "Cavalcade of America (DuPont): Show based on a ballad I wrote on the life of Wild Bill Hickock." I have not located a copy of this show, but the program log for this series indicates that program 199 was about Hickock: "The story of the fighting frontier marshal during a violent and colorful era in the growth of America." It starred Kenneth Delmar.*

Woody's ballad was titled "Wild Bill Hickock's Ruff Time," and a variant typed 20 June 1951 is twenty-five verses long. It is probable that the original was the same length.

18 NOVEMBER 1940. *New York City. Information about this show is limited, but it was aired as a WABC Radio Show featuring Woody Guthrie, Burl Ives, Josh White, and Lead Belly, written by Alan Lomax and Nicholas Ray, unidentified narrator. The theme is "outlaws," and the show opens and ends with the cast singing and humming "Buffalo Gals." Woody sings one verse of the traditional "Jesse James" and narrates why some men go bad; Ives sings "Brennan On the Moor;" Josh White introduces the song "Ella Speed" as sung by Lead Belly; Woody talks about small banks folding during the Great Depression and says that the bankers took most of the money but Pretty Boy Floyd was always blamed. He then sings his composition, "Pretty Boy Floyd"; a copy of the show is in the Smithsonian/Folkways Archives ACT 380.*

"Bower and Guthrie"

CA. LATE 1940. *Woody Guthrie and Pete Seeger recording in a New York City apartment on a borrowed home disc recorder late one night. Woody plays harmonica/mandolin, and Pete plays banjo/guitar (an excellent recording). Woody's voice has no pretensions. Donated by Mike Seeger to the Archive of Folk Song, Library of Congress. Includes:*
   "Train Whistles"
   "Ida Red"
   "Arkansas Traveler"
   "Things about Coming My Way"
   "900 Miles"

Bonneville Power Administration: The Columbia River Songs

MAY 1941. *Portland, Oregon. Woody Guthrie often stated that he wrote twenty-six songs, one per day, during his short-term employment by the Bonneville Power Authority (BPA) and recorded a few in a basement studio of the BPA in Portland. The songs were to be used in the BPA movie,* The Columbia; *only three were used. Bill Murlin, audiovisual specialist for the BPA, was authorized to locate and compile infor-*

mation about the BPA for their semicentennial celebration in 1987. The master acetates recorded by Woody had disappeared, but as Murlin publicized his project, former BPA employees gave him copies they had made in the 1940s from the original discs (see: Woody Guthrie, Roll on Columbia: The Columbia River Songs, Portland, Ore.: BPA, 1987; reissued under the same title in 1991 by the Sing Out Corporation). He received six discs containing fourteen recordings, or twelve songs (two songs were duplicated). Eleven of the twelve songs were included on Woody Guthrie: Columbia River Collection, Rounder Records C 1036 (cassette and CD), 1987. The six discs with the names of the donors are housed in the National Archives, Washington, D.C., items 305.01 to 305.06.

Disc 1 (305.01): 10" Claire Recordings, 33⅓ rpm
"Pastures of Plenty," as used in the movie *The Columbia*; not used on Rounder C/CD 1036
"The Biggest Thing That Man Has Ever Done," as used in the movie *The Columbia*; this cut is not on Rounder C/CD 1036
"Roll Columbia, Roll," vocal/guitar, opening theme for the movie *The Columbia*; included on *Hard Travelin'*, Arloco Records ARL-284 and Rounder C/CD 1036

Disc 2 (305.02): 10" acetate, 78 rpm
"Washington Talkin' Blues," vocal/guitar, Rounder C/CD 1036
"The Biggest Thing That Man Has Ever Done," vocal/guitar, Rounder C/CD 1036

Disc 3 (305.03): 12" acetate, 78 rpm
"Ramblin' Blues" ("Portland Town"), vocal/guitar, Rounder C/CD 1036
"It Takes a Married Man to Sing a Worried Song" ("Worried Song" and "Worried Blues"), vocal/guitar, Rounder C/CD 1036
"Song of the Grand Coulee Dam" ("Way Up in That Northwest"), vocal/guitar, Rounder C/CD 1036

Disc 4 (305.04): 12" acetate, 78 rpm
"Roll On, Columbia," vocal/guitar, Rounder C/CD 1036
"The Grand Coulee Dam," vocal/guitar, Rounder C/CD 1036

Disc 5 (305.05): 12" Duodisc acetate, 78 rpm
"Jackhammer Blues," vocal/guitar, Rounder C/CD 1036
"The Grand Coulee Dam," vocal/guitar; this cut not used on Rounder C/CD 1036

Disc 6 (305.06), 12" Duodisc acetate, 78 rpm
"Columbia Waters" ("Good Morning, Captain"), vocal/guitar/harmonica, Rounder C/CD 1036
"Talkin' Columbia Blues," vocal/guitar, Rounder C/CD 1036

Other Unissued Recordings in the Library of Congress

JANUARY 1942. *"Home Disc Recordings" made by members of the Almanac Singers in New York City, accessioned by the Library of Congress in February 1942; two 10" and four 12" glass-base records (M 173 A 8; 6100–6105). Only those with Woody or written by him are listed in this section.*

"Round and Round Hitler's Grave," Almanac Singers,
   lead singer Pete Seeger, Sis Cunningham, accordion;
   Lee Hayes; and others (Woody, guitar)   6100-B
"Hulaballobalay," Almanac Singers, unidentified male
   lead; Pete Seeger, banjo; Sis Cunningham, accordion   6101-A
"Taking It Easy," Almanac Singers, lead singer Woody
   Guthrie; Pete Seeger, banjo; Sis Cunningham,
   accordion; and others   6101-B
"Biggest Thing That Man Has Ever Done," sung by
   Woody Guthrie, guitar   6102-B
"High Cost of Living," Almanac Singers, lead singer
   Pete Seeger, banjo; Woody Guthrie, guitar;
   unidentified male and female voices   6103-A
"Sinking of the Reuben James," Almanac Singers, lead
   singer Bess Lomax Hawes; Woody Guthrie, guitar;
   Pete Seeger, banjo; Sis Cunningham, accordion;
   unidentified male voice   6103-B
"Goin' Down the Road Feelin' Bad," Woody Guthrie,
   vocal/harmonica; Pete Seeger, banjo   6105-A

AUGUST 1941. *Asheville, North Carolina, Folk Festival.*

"Pretty Boy Floyd"   4793-A1

Keynote Recordings

CA. JUNE 1941. *New York City. These Keynote recordings "Babe O' Mine," "Boomtown Bill," and "Keep That Oil A-Rollin'" have been reissued on* Songs for Political
Action, *Bear Family Records BCD 15720, discs 3 and 4.*

"Song for Bridges," Almanac Singers (K 304 A), Woody
   Guthrie, vocal, guitar; Lee Hays, vocal; Millard
   Lampell, vocal; Pete Seeger, banjo/vocal   QB 1548
"Babe O' Mine," Woody Guthrie (K 304 B), Woody
   Guthrie, guitar/vocal/harmonica; Pete Seeger, banjo   QB 1549

CA. JUNE 1942. *New York City, Woody Guthrie, mandolin/harmonica/vocal; Pete
Seeger, banjo/vocal; Baldwin "Butch" Hawes, guitar/vocal; Arthur Stern, vocal; (mandolin may be Bess Lomax Hawes)*

"Boomtown Bill," Almanac Singers (5000-A), Seeger,
   lead vocal   X-5000
"Keep That Oil A-Rollin,'" Almanac Singers (5000-B),
   Guthrie, lead vocal   X-5001

General Records

7 JULY 1941. *Recorded at Reeves Sound Studio, New York City, by Alan Lomax.
Woody Guthrie, John "Peter" Hawes, Lee Hays, and Pete Seeger were the singers and*

instrumentalists in this session; two albums, 78 rpm, three 10" discs in each album, were issued: Deep Sea Chanties and Whaling Ballads *General Album G-20, and* Sod Buster Ballads, *General Album G-21. With the exception of "The State of Arkansas" and "House of the Rising Sun" each song had a chorus that was sung by all four men, and it is probable that John "Peter" Hawes played the guitar, when one was used, instead of Woody Guthrie. All of the following General session songs have been reissued on* Songs for Political Action, *Bear Family Records BCD 15720, disc 3, 1996, and on* The Almanac Singers: Their Complete General Recordings, *MCA Records MCAD 11499, 1996.*

"Blow Ye Winds, Heigh Ho," Pete Seeger, lead vocal/
banjo; Peter Hawes, guitar   (5015-A) R-4160

"Away Rio," Peter Hawes, lead vocal; Woody Guthrie,
harmonica; Pete Seeger, banjo   (5017-A) R-4161

"Blow the Man Down," Woody Guthrie, lead vocal;
Pete Seeger, banjo/recorder; Peter Hawes, guitar   (5016-A) R-4162

"The Golden Vanity," Pete Seeger, lead vocal/banjo;
Woody Guthrie, harmonica; Peter Hawes, guitar   (5016-B) R-4174

"The Coast of High Barbary," Pete Seeger, lead vocal/
banjo   (5017-B) R-4175

"Haul Away, Joe," Peter Hawes, lead vocal; Pete
Seeger, banjo/recorder   (5015-B) R-4176
Issued on *Deep Sea Chanties and Whaling Bal-
lads,* General Album G-20, reissued on
Commodore Album CR-11, and reissued on *The
Soil and the Sea,* Mainstream Records 56005
(LP); released in Japan (1992) King KICP 2223
(compact disc).

"House of the Rising Sun," Woody Guthrie, lead vocal/
harmonica (no chorus); Pete Seeger, banjo; Peter
Hawes, guitar   (5020-B) R-4163

"Ground Hog," Pete Seeger, lead vocal/banjo; Peter
Hawes, guitar   (5018-B) R-4164

"State of Arkansas," Lee Hays, vocal (no chorus); Pete
Seeger, banjo   (5019-A) R-4165

"I Ride An Old Paint," Woody Guthrie, lead vocal/
guitar; Pete Seeger, banjo   (5020-A) R-4169

"Hard, Ain't It Hard," Woody Guthrie, lead vocal/
harmonica; Pete Seeger, banjo; Peter Hawes, guitar   (5019-B) R-4170

"The Dodger Song," Lee Hayes, lead vocal; Pete Seeger,
banjo; Woody Guthrie, harmonica; Peter Hawes,
guitar   (5018-A) R-4171
Issued on *Sod Buster Ballads,* General Album G-
21, reissued on Commodore Album CR-10, and
reissued on *The Soil and the Sea,* Mainstream
Records 56005 (LP); released in Japan (1992)
King KICP 2223 (compact disc).

"The Weaver's Song," the group sings together   R-4168
Unissued in U.S.

"Greenland Fishing," Pete Seeger sings the lead   R-4172
  Unissued in U.S. Issued on *The Soil and the Sea,*
  King KICP 2223, Japan (compact disc), 1992;
  Woody does not sing the lead.

Labor for Victory

29 AUGUST 1942. *Office of War Information (OWI); the CIO (Congress of Industrial Workers) in cooperation with NBC Red network, OWI # E12556; NBC 16" SF transcription; Library of Congress, tape LWO 5554, group 15, reel 4B, item 2 of 3, acetate discs. This fifteen-minute show was broadcast from 10:15 P.M. to 10:30 P.M. as propaganda to encourage farm and city laborers "to learn to work together to defeat fascism." Woody Guthrie sang a verse with mandolin accompaniment of his "Farmer Labor Train," and an unidentified female (possibly Bess Lomax Hawes) sang the chorus with him. As the train traveled through regions of this country (starting in the South), dialogue about workers and possible problems in the region was shared and resolved by encouraging rural and city workers to work together, and Woody would sing a verse as the train moved to another region.*

"Farmer-Labor Train," Woody Guthrie, vocal/mandolin

Outpost Concert Series, Music of the People No.2

CA. 1942. *Office of War Information, Overseas Branch; Woody sings the opening song and the Almanac Singers and Burl Ives sing the other songs; a copy is in the Asch/Folkways Collection.*

"Foggy Mountain Top," Woody Guthrie, vocal/guitar

Ballad Gazette

CA. 1943 OR 1944. *The show is about ships and the sea; the announcer starts this show with "The Ballad Gazette, with your editor and chief, Woody Guthrie." Following Woody's first verse of "This Land Is Your Land," the announcer introduces him as "a man who knows Americans as they really are." This is a live broadcast; Woody moves from one song to another with a few guitar chords and no dialog; copy in the Asch/Folkways Collection.*

"What Did the Deep Sea Say?"
"Blow Ye Winds in the Morning"
"Trouble on the Water" (fragment that sounds as if he made it up as he was singing)
"Blow the Man Down"
"Sinking of the Normandy"
"Reuben James"

Another Ballad Gazette *was found in the Asch/Folkways Collection by Jeff Place; it contained the information 28 January 1945, WNEW Radio Program. When Woody is introduced, he establishes a musical key and sings each song in that key. This program is about trains.*

"This Land Is Your Land"
"Bound for Glory"
"900 Miles"
"Casey Jones" (different from the standard version; similar to that of Furry Lewis)
"New River Train"
"Muleskinner Blues"
"Cannonball Blues"
"Good Morning, Mr. Railroad Man"
"Waiting for a Train"
"I've Been Working on the Railroad"
"Union Hammer (Railroad Hammer)"
"900 Miles" and "This Land Is Your Land"

The Martins and the Coys: A Contemporary Folk Tale

CA. LATE MARCH 1944. *Recorded in the Decca Studios, New York City, written by Elizabeth Lomax, arranged by Alan Lomax, and directed by Roy Lockwood. This radio show was an Alan Lomax concept for patriotic entertainment, but no American network was interested. He sold the idea to the British Broadcasting Corporation; they funded the production, but it had to be recorded in New York City; it was broadcast 26 June 1944. The liner notes stated: "Contemporary Songs by Woody Guthrie and the Almanacs." The "Soloists" were Burl Ives, guitar; Woody Guthrie, guitar; Pete Seeger, banjo and mandolin; and Lily May Pearson, guitar and bass. The cast included Burl Ives as the Narrator; Will Geer as Uncle Ben Martin; Geoffrey Bryant as Ben Martin; Jimmy Dobson as Oaty Martin; Katherine Raht as Dellie Coy; Helen Claire as Sary Coy; and Woody Guthrie as Alec Coy. Other cast members, group singers, and musicians were John Mitchell, Carson Robison, Carl Emory, Robert Haag, Donald Bain, Tom Glazer, Gilbert "Cisco" Houston, Margaret Johnson, Bella Allen, Rosalie Allen, and Sonny Terry. The notes also indicated that they were presenting "Contemporary American Life"; this contemporary life was set in the Smoky Mountains with the feuding Martin and Coy families facing the problems of World War II. A Romeo and Juliet (Ben Martin and Sary Coy) conflict was resolved when the two families were brought together by a common interest in fighting fascism. There were approximately fourteen songs performed; the first two listed here were written and performed by Woody Guthrie.*

"You Better Get Ready," Woody Guthrie, vocal/guitar; Sonny Terry, harmonica; group singers on the chorus
"You Fascists Bound to Lose," Woody Guthrie, lead vocal/guitar; Pete Seeger, banjo; Sonny Terry, harmonica; group singers on the chorus
"Bound for the Mountain," Burl Ives, vocal; Pete Seeger, banjo
"Run, Boys, Run" (adaptation of "Run, Nigger, Run"), Arthur Smith, fiddle; Pete Seeger, banjo; group singing
"Black Is the Color of My True Love's Hair," Burl Ives, vocal/guitar
"On Top Of Old Smoky," Lily May Pearson, vocal/guitar; Pete Seeger, mandolin
"Gonna Take Everybody (All Work Together)," female harmony, group singing; Pete Seeger, banjo
"When We March into Berlin" (adaptation of "When the Saints Go Marching In"), group singing; Sonny Terry, harmonica
"How Many Biscuits Can You Eat," female harmony/guitar/banjo

"Smoky Mountain Gals (Buffalo Gals) Won't You Come Out Tonight," group
    singing/guitar; Arthur Smith, fiddle; Pete Seeger, banjo
"Turtle Dove," Burl Ives, vocal/guitar; Lily May Pearson, vocal
Fiddle tune/square dance calls, Arthur Smith, fiddle
"Round and Round Hitler's Grave," Pete Seeger, Burl Ives, and Lily May Pearson
    each sing a verse; cast sings the chorus; Pete Seeger, banjo; guitar not identified
"The Martins and the Coys," Pete Seeger, vocal/banjo with the cast singing

British Broadcasting Corporation Recordings

7 JULY 1944. *Woody was a Merchant Marine, "washing dishes on a Liberty ship," the
troop ship* Sea Porpoise *which carried troops to the Normandy beach in early July
1944. After the troops were sent ashore, the ship hit a mine but made its way back to
England; Woody was routed through London toward Glasgow, Scotland, toward the
United States. On a song manuscript dated "July 13th, 1944" Woody wrote, "this
train is carrying me outside from London now; on up towards Belfast, and Glasgow."
While in London, he went to the offices of the BBC where he introduced himself as a
member of* The Martins and the Coys *and was given the opportunity to sing on the*
Children's Hour. *After an autobiographical statement, he was recorded singing with
his guitar accompaniment two railroad songs:*

"Wabash Cannonball"
"900 Miles" (this is the minor-key melody that Cisco made popular)

Also recorded by the BBC ca. 1944:

"Stagalee"
"Pretty Boy Floyd"

Cavalcade of America, Program #415

25 DECEMBER 1944. *America for Christmas, NBC Radio broadcast about an itinerant
USO camp show troupe, performed for homesick GIs on a small Pacific island; music
by Woody Guthrie and Earl Robinson, script by Peter Lyon, starring Walter Huston,
Earl Robinson, and the Spokesmen Quartette (statement in the introduction: "songs
from all over the land we love"). Woody Guthrie is not featured as a singer, but spoken
credits were "indebted to Woody Guthrie for use of songs arranged by Earl Robinson."
Of the approximately eleven songs used in the show, those written by Woody were:*

"Roll on Columbia," the chorus only, sung by the group
"Hard Traveling," Earl Robinson, vocal, one verse only
"Pastures of Plenty," Earl Robinson, vocal, two verses only
"Grand Coulee Dam (Biggest Thing Man Has Ever Done)," Earl Robinson with
    group singing

The show ends with the cast singing "Roll on Columbia."

Asch, Disc, and Folkways

*Moses Asch issued records on a variety of labels: Asch, Asch-Stinson, Asch-Signa-
ture-Stinson, Disc, Folkways, and Verve/Folkways. Unfortunately, he kept limited in-*

formation about recording sessions. Jim Kweskin visited Asch and copied as much of the session information as he could find and Asch would supply; his list was published under "Exploratory Research of Woodie [sic] Guthrie's Asch-Folkways Recordings" in Record Research, *issue 161–62 (February–March 1979), 13, and issue 163–64 (May–June), 13. Jeff Place and I have compared Kweskin's printed discography to the Asch ledger in the Folkways Archives, Center for Folklife Programs and Cultural Studies, Smithsonian Institution, and made a few corrections. The combined efforts follow with emphasis on Jim Kweskin's contributions; this is what he wrote:*

> I went to see Moe Asch of Folkways records awhile back to see if he could help me put together a Woody Guthrie discography. I was hoping that maybe he kept records and matrix charts or something. Well all he had was a very old, handwritten ledger with scribblings and notes and lists of his sessions in the forties with everyone from Lead Belly to Mary Lou Williams. I did the best I could to decipher and extract all that I could about Woody. This list is the result of that work. (*Record Research*, issue 161–62, p.13)

[11] MARCH 1944. Kweskin believed that this was a session with Woody; however, Woody did not participate in this session. He was aboard the William Floyd, and did not return to New York until later in the month. Asch listed this session as the Union Boys, a collective name for the individuals recording material that might be used in a union album [Songs for Victory: Music for Political Action, Asch 346] as well as antifascist collections. There was no Union Boys group or organization; I have not included the songs in this discography.

Asch entered shortened titles for the songs recorded during the following sessions. After listening to the surviving masters and transferring them to DAT and compact disc formats, Jeff Place supplied the better-known titles with alternate titles in parentheses. The list is basically what Kweskin used in his article, but it is more complete and includes some corrections.

Title	Matrix No.
16 April 1944	
"Hard Ain't It Hard"	LM-1
"More Pretty Gals Than One"	LM-2
19 April 1944 (Woody Guthrie and Cisco Houston)	
"Golden Vanity"	MA1
"When the Yanks Go Marching In"	MA2
"So Long, It's Been Good to Know You"	MA3
"Dollar Down Dollar A Week"	MA4
"Hen Cackle"	MA5
"I Ain't Got Nobody"	MA6
"Ida Red"	MA7
"Columbus Stockade"	MA8
"Whistle Blowing"	MA9
"John Henry"	MA10
"Hammer Ring" ("Union Hammer")	MA11
"Muleskinner Blues" ("New Road Line")	MA12
"What Are We Waiting On" ("Bloody Fight")	MA13

MA 60–MA 65 were listed by Kweskin, but they were actually recordings by Josh White and Lead Belly and have been deleted from this discography.

"Whistle Blowing"	MA66
"Billy the Kid"	MA67
"Stagger Lee" ("Stackerlee")	MA68

20 April 1944

"Down Yonder"	674
"Guitar Blues"	675
"Harmonica Breakdown"	676
"Fox Chase"	677
"Train"	678
"Lost John"	679
"Pretty Baby"	680
"Old Dog a Bone"	681
"Turkey in the Straw"	682

"Fox Chase," "Train," and "Lost John" were probably Sonny Terry, but Woody was capable of playing the tunes on the harmonica.

20 April 1944

"Give Me That Old Time Religion"	687
"Glory" ("Walk and Talk with Jesus")	688
"Hard Time Blues"	689
"Rubber Dolly"	690
"Bus Blues"	691
"Devilish Mary"	692
"Cripple Creek"	693
"Sandy Land"	694

24 April 1944

"Old Dan Tucker"	695
"Bile Dem Cabbage Down"	696
"Old Joe Clark"	697
"Buffalo Gals" ("Bottle in Hand")	698
"Rain Crow Bill"	699
"Skip to My Lou"	700
"Lonesome Train"	701
"Lonesome Train"	702
"Blues"	703
"Harmonica Breakdown"	704
"Harmonica Rag"	705
"Harmonica Rag #2"	706
"Crawdad Hole"	707
"Bury Me Beneath the Willow"	708
"I Ride an Old Paint" ("Ride Around Little Dogies")	709
"Blue Eyes"	710
"Going Down the Road Feeling Bad" ("Lonesome Road Blues")	711
"Old Dog a Bone"	712
"Having Fun"	713
"Blues"	714

Kweskin listed 715 and 716, but they are Lead Belly recordings and have been deleted from this discography.

25 April 1944

"Talking Fishing Blues" ("Fishing Blues")	MA75
"Talking Sailor" ("Talking Merchant Marine")	MA76
"Union Burial Ground"	MA77
"Jesse James"	MA78
"Ranger's Command"	MA79
"Sinking of the Rueben James"	MA80
"Put My Little Shoes Away"	MA81
"Picture from Life's Other Side"	MA82
"Will You Miss Me"	MA83
"Bed on the Floor"	MA84
"900 Miles" ("Lonesome Fiddle")	MA85
"Sourwood Mountain"	MA86
"Hoecake Baking"	MA87
"Ezekiel Saw the Wheel"	MA88
"Little Darling"	MA89
"Lonesome Day"	MA90
"Cumberland Gap"	MA91
"Fiddling Piece"	MA92
"Carry Me Back to Old Virginny"	MA93
"Stepstone"	MA94
"House of the Rising Sun"	MA96
"Brown's Ferry Blues"	MA98
"What Would You Give in Exchange for Your Soul?"	MA99
"When That Ship Went Down"	MA91-1
"Dust Bowl"	MA100
"Guitar Rag"	MA101
"I Ain't Got Nobody"	MA102
"Going Down the Road Feeling Bad" ("Ain't Gonna Be Treated This Way" and "Lonesome Road Blues")	MA103
"Polly Wolly Doodle"	MA104
"Guitar Rag"	1230
"Blowin' Down This Old Dusty Road"	1231

Kweskin listed MA95, MA97, 1232, and 1233, but they are Sonny Terry and others and have been deleted from this discography.

25 April 1944

There is no date in Moe Asch's ledger for this session but from the sequence of master numbers it would appear to be shortly after this date.

"Hey Lolly Lolly"	MA105
"Budded Roses"	MA106
"House of the Rising Sun"	MA107
"I Don't Feel at Home in the Bowery"	MA108
"Hobo's Lullaby"	MA109
"Frog Went A-courtin'" ("Mouse Went a Courting")	MA110
"Bad Reputation"	MA111

"Snow Deer"	MA112
"Ladies Auxiliary"	MA113
"This Land Is My Land"	MA114
"Hang Knot" ("Slip Knot")	MA115
"Breakdown"	MA116
"Go Tell Aunt Rhody"	MA117
"Union Going to Roll"	MA118
"Who Broke the Lock on the Hen House Door?"	MA119
"What Did the Deep Sea Say?"	MA120
"Strawberry Roan" (probably Cisco Houston)	MA121-1
"When the Yanks Go Marching In"	MA122-1
"Bed on the Floor"	MA123-1
"We Shall Be Free"	MA124-1
"Right Now"	MA125-1
"Jackhammer John"	MA126-1
Woody	MA127-1
Woody	MA128-1
"Keep Your Skillet Good and Greasy"	MA129-1
"Home" (?)	MA130-1
"Lost You"	MA131
"Slip Knot" ("Hang Knot")	MA134
"Jesus Christ"	MA135
"Hobo Bill"	MA136
"Little Black Train"	MA137
"Cannon Ball"	MA138
"Gypsy Davy"	MA139
"Bile Them Cabbage Down"	MA140

Kweskin listed MA132 and MA133, but they are Sonny Terry and others and have been deleted from this discography.

8 May 1944

Woody (title not found)	MA1240

1 March 1945

"Get Along, Little Dogies"	860
"Waltz"	861
"Waltz"	862
"Union Breakdown"	863
"Cackling Hen"	864
"Chisholm Trail"	865
"Bed on Your Floor"	866
"Rye Whiskey"	867

23 March 1945

"Old Joe Clark"	868
"Longway to France"	869
"Woody Blues"	870
"Down Yonder"	871
"Gal I Left Behind"	872

24 May 1945

"Mean Talking Blues"	900
"1913 Massacre"	901
"Ludlow Massacre"	902
"Buffalo Skinners"	903
"Harriet Tubman"	904
"Harriet Tubman"	905

Moe Asch says that Woody's children's songs were all recorded in February or March 1947; Sacco and Vanzetti was recorded 26 January–31 January 1947. Kweskin thinks the Midnight Special album with Woody, Lead Belly, and Cisco was also recorded in 1947. Possibly 25 February 1947 or 2 March 1947 or both.

There are many recordings not included in the Kweskin article, but the dates of the sessions are unknown. Jeff Place has compiled a list of the "Surviving Recordings in the Smithsonian Folklife Archive made by Woody Guthrie for Moses Asch"; its length makes it impossible to include in this discography.

Hootenanny

10 MARCH 1947. CBS Radio, broadcast featuring Woody Guthrie, Pete Seeger, Sonny Terry, Eddie Smith, Brownie McGee, Hally Wood, Sidney Bechet, Pops Foster, Cisco Houston, and the Coleman Brothers with John Henry Faulk as host, written and produced by Alan Lomax. A mixture of nine songs including folk, blues, gospel, and jazz simulated, as Faulk stated, "forty-eight states doing a musical jamboree." "Raise a Ruckus Tonight" was the theme song with Woody adding a square-dance verse when they ended it as the opening song. The following songs feature Woody:

"Raise a Ruckus Tonight," Pete Seeger, banjo/vocal; Sonny Terry, harmonica; Woody Guthrie and entire cast, vocals

"Hard, Ain't It Hard," Woody Guthrie, vocal/guitar; Cisco Houston, vocal harmony/guitar; Pete Seeger, banjo/vocal harmony; Sonny Terry, harmonica; Pops Foster, bass fiddle; Eddie Smith, fiddle

Woody finishes his song and says, "Here before you, you see an Oklahomeean [sic], nothin' up my sleeves and nothin' in my pocket, nothin' in my pocketbook, nothin' but just a purty good little piece of advice—don't cost nothin' to listen to it—goes like this."

"Talkin' Blues," Woody Guthrie, vocal/guitar

"John Henry," verses sung and/or performed by members in the cast to show how one song can be performed in many different musical styles; Woody is heard singing with Pete Seeger

The entire show was issued on Folk Music Radio by Radiola, Release 133 CMR-1133 (cassette) side A, ca. late 1970s.

Woody Guthrie Concert

14 APRIL 1951. St. John's College, Annapolis, Maryland, recorded by J. W. Mavor Jr., on a wire recorder using a hand-held mike while sitting on the front row. Forty to fifty

people in attendance including Mike and Peggy Seeger and Glenn Yarbrough with comments made from the stage by Woody's wife, Marjorie Guthrie. This tape was donated to the Library of Congress, Archive of Folk Culture, by James Mavor Jr.; it is an interesting tape even though the sound quality is poor, made a few months before his illness was diagnosed.

Woody is showing his sickness, although he sounds as if he is intoxicated (both conditions were probable); the concert is Woody, vocals/guitar. Woody talks about the Bonneville Power songs and then sings "Grand Coulee Dam," "Jesus Christ" (has to hold notes while he tries to remember the words), "Goodby, Centralia, Goodby," "Gypsy Davy" (forgets the words), and "So Long" (starts, stops, changes key; sings a verse while Marjorie leads audience in singing; changes key and sings the first verse and others of the original version and the audience sings the chorus)

Richmond Recordings

MARCH 1951. *Woody was hospitalized as the doctors were diagnosing his illness, and "Howie" Richmond, his music publisher and owner of Ludlow Music, TRO Richmond, and other music publishing firms, took a tape recorder and tapes to Woody. While hospitalized and later at home, he recorded more than two hundred songs for Richmond; none of the songs has been issued, and many reflect his illness.*

Decca Recordings

7 JANUARY 1952. *Woody recorded two songs for Decca; they were never issued, but "This Land" was included on* Songs for Political Action, *Bear Family Records BCD 15720, disc 10, 1996.*
"Kissin' On"   matrix 82077
"This Land Is Your Land"   matrix 82078

Guthrie, Elliott, and Terry Session

18 JANUARY 1954. *Woody, Jack Elliott, and Sonny Terry were enjoying a day of drinking when they decided to record some of their favorite songs. They went to the Asch Studio and attempted to perform; Woody was sick and with the others was inebriated. Eventually Asch turned off the recording machine; there are no songs worthy of issuing.*

78 RPM RECORDS

Almanac Singers, The

Deep Sea Chanties and Whaling Ballads, General Album G-20, 7 July 1941, reissued on Commodore Album CR-11, and reissued on *The Soil and the Sea,* Mainstream Records 56005 (LP); released in Japan (1992) King KICP 2223 (CD); Woody Guthrie, John "Peter" Hawes, Lee Hays, and Pete Seeger (Woody sings during the chorus unless otherwise noted); the label number is followed by the matrix number in parentheses.

"Blow Ye Winds, Heigh Ho," Pete Seeger, lead vocal/
    banjo; Peter Hawes, guitar   5015-A (R-4160)

"Haul Away, Joe," Peter Hawes, lead vocal; Pete Seeger,
   banjo/recorder   5015-B (R-4176)
"Blow the Man Down," Woody Guthrie, lead vocal;
   Pete Seeger, banjo/recorder; Peter Hawes, guitar   5016-A (R-4162)
"The Golden Vanity," Pete Seeger, lead vocal/banjo;
   Woody Guthrie, harmonica; Peter Hawes, guitar   5016-B (R-4174)
"Away Rio," Peter Hawes, lead vocal; Woody Guthrie,
   harmonica; Pete Seeger, banjo   5017-A (R-4161)
"The Coast of High Barbary," Pete Seeger, lead vocal/
   banjo   5017-B (R-4175)

Sod Buster Ballads, General Album G-21, 7 July 1941, reissued on Commodore Album CR-10, and reissued on *The Soil and the Sea,* Mainstream Records 56005 (LP); released in Japan (1992) King KICP 2223 (CD); Woody Guthrie, John "Peter" Hawes, Lee Hays, and Pete Seeger:

"The Dodger Song," Lee Hayes, lead vocal; Pete Seeger,
   banjo; Woody Guthrie, harmonica; Peter Hawes,
   guitar   5018-A (R-4171)
"Ground Hog," Pete Seeger, lead vocal/banjo; Peter
   Hawes, guitar   5018-B (R-4164)
"State of Arkansas," Lee Hays, vocal (no chorus, WG
   not on this cut); Pete Seeger, banjo   5019-A (R-4165)
"Hard, Ain't It Hard," Woody Guthrie, lead vocal/
   harmonica; Pete Seeger, banjo; Peter Hawes, guitar   5019-B 0(R-4170)
"I Ride An Old Paint," Woody Guthrie, lead vocal/
   guitar; Pete Seeger, banjo   5020-A (R-4169)
"House of the Rising Sun," Woody Guthrie, lead
   vocal/harmonica (no chorus); Pete Seeger, banjo;
   Peter Hawes, guitar   5020-B (R-4163)

Blues, Asch Records 550, anthology includes Josh White, Jack Dupree, Sonny Terry, Nora Lee King, Mary Lou Williams, Woody Guthrie; also issued by Stinson Records, Album 550.

"Lonesome Train," Sonny Terry, vocal/harmonica;
   Woody Guthrie, guitar   550-3A (MA-1210)
"Ain't Gonna Be Treated This Way," Woody Guthrie,
   vocal/guitar; Cisco Houston, vocal harmony/guitar   550-3B (MA-1231)

Folk Music of the United States: Anglo-American Ballads, Library of Congress, Division of Music, Album 1, AAFS 1, edited by Alan Lomax from the Archive of American Folk Song, 1942.

"The Gypsy Davy," Woody Guthrie, recorded in
   Washington, D. C., 1941, by Alan Lomax   LC14 AAFS 2A
                                              (4491-B3)

Folksay: American Ballads and Dances, Vol. 1, Asch Records 432, anthology includes Woody Guthrie, Baldwin "Butch" Hawes, Cisco Houston, Lead Belly, Bess Lomax,

Pete Seeger, Alex Stewart, Sonny Terry, and Josh White. Notes by Woody Guthrie; label copy submitted 11 August 1944 (marked as Album 332); also issued by Stinson Records, Album 432

"Mule Skinner Blues," Woody Guthrie, vocal/guitar;
    Cisco Houston, Pete Seeger, banjo   432-1A (MA 12)
"900 Miles," Woody Guthrie, fiddle; Baldwin Hawes,
    guitar; Bess Lomax, mandolin (the label includes
    Cisco Houston, but he did not participate in this cut)   432-1B (MA 85)
"Glory," Woody Guthrie, vocal/mandolin; Sonny Terry,
    harmonica; Alek Stewart, guitar; Cisco Houston,
    vocal harmony   432-2A (688)
"Poor Lazarus," Woody Guthrie, vocal/guitar   432-2B (MA 56)
"Biggest Thing," Woody Guthrie, vocal/guitar   432-3B (MA 15)
"Who's Gonna Shoe Your Pretty Little Feet," Woody
    Guthrie, vocal/guitar; Cisco Houston, vocal harmony
    ("Take Me Back Babe," Woody Guthrie with
    Cisco Houston, was listed in the catalogue as 332-B,
    but not included in the album; however "Take Me
    Back Babe" may have been their title for "Who's
    Gonna Shoe")   432-4B (MA 27)
"Gambling Man," Woody Guthrie with Cisco
    Houston (332-A) was also listed in the catalogue,
    but "Cindy" by Pete Seeger (432-4A) was the song
    actually included.

Guthrie, Woody

Ballads From the Dust Bowl, Disc 610, Woody Guthrie, vocals/guitar and harmonica; notes by Woody Guthrie (ca. 1947):

"Pastures of Plenty"   5010 A (D 199)
"Hard Travelling"   5010 B (D 200)

"Rambling Blues"   5011 A (D 201)
"When the Curfew Blows"   5011 B (D 203)

"Talking Columbia Blues"   5012 A (D 202)
"My New Found Land"   5012 B (D 204)

Dust Bowl Ballads, Vol. 1, Victor Records P-27, Woody Guthrie, vocals/guitar and harmonica; notes by Woody Guthrie, 1940 (26 April 1940):

"Talkin' Dust Bowl Blues"   P 27-1 (26619-A)
"Blowin' Down This Road"   P 27-2 (26619-B)

"Do Re Mi"   P 27-3 (26620-A)
"Dust Cain't Kill Me"   P 27-4 (26620-B)

"Tom Joad, Part 1"   P 27-5 (26621-A)
"Tom Joad, Part 2"   P 27-6 (26621-B)

Dust Bowl Ballads, Vol. 2, Victor Records P-28, Woody Guthrie, vocals/guitar and harmonica; notes by Woody Guthrie, 1940 (26 April 1940):

"The Great Dust Storm"	P 28-1 (26622-A)
"Dusty Old Dust"	P 28-2 (26622-B)
"Dust Bowl Refugee"	P 28-3 (26623-A)
"Dust Pneumonia Blues"	P 28-4 (26623-B)
"I Ain't Got No Home in This World Anymore"	P 28-5 (26624-A)
"Vigilante Man"	P 28-6 (26624-B)

[*The Passion of Sacco and Vanzetti,* by Woody Guthrie, three *12"* records as Disc Album 40 announced in the 1947 catalog, but the album was not released until later on LP.]

Songs to Grow On: Nursery Days, Disc 605, Woody Guthrie, vocals/guitar; prepared under the supervision of Beatrice Landeck, booklet with notes and lyrics, 1946.

"Wake Up"	5050A (D301)
"Clean-o"	5050B (D302)
"Dance Around"	5051A (D304)
"Put Your Finger in the Air"	5051B (D303)
"Don't Push Me"	5052A (D305)
"Jig Along Home"	5052B (D306)

Songs to Grow On, Nursery Days, Vol. 1, Folkways Records F5 and FOL 105, yellow label, also issued as F 105, blue label, vocal/guitar ("Composed, sung, and played by Woody Guthrie"), 1951.

"Wake Up"	F5-1A-1
"Car Song"	F5-1A-2 and Fol-5-1A
"Clean-o"	F5-1B-1
"Dance Around"	F5-1B-2 and Fol-5-1B
"Don't Push Me Down"	F5-2A-1
"My Dolly"	F5-2A-2 and Fol-5-2A
"Put Your Finger in the Air"	F5-2B-1
"Come See"	F5-2B-2 and Fol-5-2B
"Race You Down the Mountain"	F5-3A-1
"Pick It Up"	F5-3A-2 and Fol-5-3A
"Merry Go 'Round"	F5-3B-1
"Sleepy Eyes"	F5-3B-2 and Fol-5-3B

Songs to Grow On, Nursery Days, Vol. 1, Folkways Records 809, 1950. This is a *12"* 78 rpm with three songs on each side, yellow label.

"Put Your Finger"	809 A1
"Come See"	809 A2
"Race You Down the Mountain"	809 A3 SF 1228

"Pick It Up"	809 B1
"Merry Go Round"	809 B2
"Sleepy Eyes"	809 B3 SF 1229

Songs to Grow On: Work Songs for Nursery Days, Disc 602, Woody Guthrie, vocal/ guitar; prepared under the supervision of Beatrice Landek, booklet with notes and lyrics, 1947.

"Build a House"	5073A (D596)
"Pretty and Shinyo"	5073B (D593)
"Needle Song"	5074A (D592)
"Pick It Up"	5074B (D597)
"My Little Seed"	5075A (D594)
"All Work Together"	5075B (D595)

Struggle: Asch American Documentary No. 1, Asch Records No. 360. Woody Guthrie, vocal/guitar; booklet with notes and lyrics, 1946; also issued by Stinson Records Album 360.

"Buffalo Skinners"	360-1A (903)
"Pretty Boy Floyd"	360-1B (MA-57)
"Ludlow Massacre"	360-2A (902)
"1913 Massacre"	360-2B (901)
"Lost John," with Sonny Terry & Cisco Houston	360-3A (679)]
"Union Burying Ground"	360-3B (MA-77)

Woody Guthrie, Asch Records 347, Woody Guthrie, vocal/guitar (I have not seen this album; my information is from Moe Asch's catalogs, but some of the song titles vary in the catalogs; one has the listing marked through with the number 530 written in); label copy submitted 11 August 1944 listing first six titles; this was also issued by Stinson Records as Album 347, Vol.1; in their price list they have Vol. 2 listed under the same number (I have not seen the album).

"Talking Sailor"	347-1A
"Coulee Dam"	347-1B
"Ranger's Command"	347-2A
"Gypsy Davy"	347-2B
"Jesus Christ"	347-3A (MA 135)
"New York Town"	347-3B (MA 21)

["Pretty Boy" listed but not issued]
["Stacker Lee" listed but not issued]

10" Single Records

Keynote Records (ca.1941)

"Song for Bridges," Almanac Singers	K 304 A (QB 1548)
"Babe O' Mine," Woody Guthrie	K 304 B (QB 1549)

Keynote Records (ca. 1942)

"Boomtown Bill," Almanac Singers	5000-A (X-5000)
"Keep That Oil A-Rollin'," Almanac Singers	5000-B (X-5001)

Asch-Stinson Records (ca. 1 May 1946)

"Chicken Sneeze"	Asch 625A
"Those Brown Eyes"	625B
"At My Window"	Asch 626A
"Bed on the Floor"	626B
"Railroad Whistle"	Asch 627A
"Lolly Lo"	627B
"Poor Boy"	Asch 628A
"John Henry"	628B

Folk Tunes (another label title that also states "recorded by Asch Studios"; printed on green labels)

"Hard Ain't It Hard," Woody Guthrie, lead vocal/ mandolin; Cisco Houston, harmony vocal/guitar	Asch S 150 A (LM 1)
"More Pretty Gals," Woody Guthrie, lead vocal/ mandolin; Cisco Houston, harmony vocal/guitar	Asch S 150 B (LM 2)

CUB Records (Folkways Records), *Songs to Grow On* (activity-"to-do") series. I haven't found a copy of No. 8.

4. SIDE 1
   "Grow, Grow, Grow," vocal/drum   4A (C215)
   SIDE 2
   "Swimmy Swim," vocal/guitar/harmonica   4B (C216)
8. SIDE.1
   "Wake Up"
   SIDE 2
   "Clean-o"
9. SIDE 1
   "Put Your Finger in the Air," guitar/vocal   9A (C228)
   SIDE 2
   "Don't You Push Me Down," guitar/vocal 9B (C229)
10. SIDE 1
   "I'll Spell You a Word (ABC-Numbers)"   10B (C225)
   SIDE 2
   "Train Song (Train Sounds)"   10A (C224)

Lead Belly

Midnight Special, Disc 726, with Woody Guthrie and Cisco Houston; story about Lead Belly by Woody Guthrie

"Midnight Special," Lead Belly, lead vocal/guitar;
  Woody Guthrie, mandolin/harmony vocal; Cisco
  Houston, harmony vocal   6043A (D 674)
"Yellow Gal," Lead Belly, guitar/lead vocal; Woody
  Guthrie, harmony vocal; Cisco Houston,
  harmony vocal   6044B
"Alabama Bound," Lead Belly, lead vocal/guitar;
  Woody Guthrie, harmony vocal/mandolin; Cisco
  Houston/harmony vocal   6045A (D 669)
"Stew Ball," Lead Belly, lead vocal/guitar; Woody
  Guthrie, mandolin/harmony vocal; Cisco Houston,
  harmony vocal   6045B (D 672)

Take This Hammer, Folkways Records FOL 4

"Green Corn," accompaniment by Woody Guthrie and
  Cisco Houston   804 A (F 1211)

Songs For Victory: Music For Political Action, Asch Records 346, The Union Boys
with Tom Glazer, Woody Guthrie, Cisco Houston, Brownie McGhee, Sonny Terry,
Josh White; no notes in my copy, n.d. (The Union Boys was a name Moe Asch arbi-
trarily gave to these singers; there was not an organized group of singers using that
title, and there was only one Woody Guthrie recording in this album.)

"Sally Don't You Grieve," Woody Guthrie and
  Cisco Houston   346-3A (MA 34)

LONG PLAY, CASSETTE, AND COMPACT DISC

*There are numerous foreign reissues of Woody's songs and albums; for this discogra-
phy I decided to list only domestic issues and recent foreign issues available in the
United States. Recordings issued in Woody Guthrie's name are listed at the end of this
section.*

Almanac Singers: Their Complete General Recordings, The. MCA Records MCAD
11499 (CD), 1996; booklet written by Mary Katherine Aldin; see "General Records,"
in the Recording Sessions section, and *The Soil and the Sea* in this section.

   Track 1. "Blow Ye Winds, Heigh Ho," Pete Seeger, lead vocal/banjo; Peter
      Hawes, guitar
   Track 2. "Away Rio," Peter Hawes, lead vocal; Woody Guthrie, harmonica; Pete
      Seeger, banjo
   Track 3. "Blow the Man Down," Woody Guthrie, lead vocal; Pete Seeger,
      banjo/recorder; Peter Hawes, guitar
   Track 4. "House of the Rising Sun," Woody Guthrie, lead vocal/harmonica; Pete
      Seeger, banjo; Peter Hawes, guitar
   Track 5. "Ground Hog," Pete Seeger, lead vocal/banjo; Peter Hawes, guitar
   Track 6. "State of Arkansas," Lee Hays, vocal; Pete Seeger, banjo
   Track 7. "The Weaver's Song," the group sings together

Track 8. "I Ride An Old Paint," Woody Guthrie, lead vocal/guitar; Pete Seeger, banjo

Track 9. "Hard, Ain't It Hard," Woody Guthrie, lead vocal/harmonica; Pete Seeger, banjo; Peter Hawes, guitar

Track 10. "The Dodger Song," Lee Hayes, lead vocal; Pete Seeger, banjo; Woody Guthrie, harmonica; Peter Hawes, guitar

Track 11. "Greenland Fishing," Pete Seeger, lead vocal/banjo

Track 12. "The Golden Vanity," Pete Seeger, lead vocal/banjo; Woody Guthrie, harmonica; Peter Hawes, guitar

Track 13. "The Coast of High Barbary," Pete Seeger, lead vocal/banjo

Track 14. "Haul Away, Joe," Peter Hawes, lead vocal; Pete Seeger, banjo/recorder

American Folksay: Ballads and Dances, Vol. 1. Stinson Records SLP 5 (10" LP), n.d. Woody Guthrie, Baldwin Hawes, Cisco Houston, Lead Belly, Bess Lomax, Pete Seeger, Alex Stewart, Sonny Terry, and Josh White; notes by Kenneth Goldstein.

SIDE 1

Band 3. "Mule Skinner Blues," Woody Guthrie, Cisco Houston, and Pete Seeger

Band 4. "Who's Gonna Shoe Your Pretty Little Feet," Woody Guthrie and Cisco Houston

SIDE 2

Band 1. "Glory," Woody Guthrie, Sonny Terry, Alex Stewart, and Cisco Houston

Band 2. "Poor Lazarus," Woody Guthrie

Band 3. "It Was Sad When That Great Ship Went Down," Woody Guthrie, Sonny Terry, and Cisco Houston

Band 4. "900 Miles," Woody Guthrie, Cisco Houston, Bess Lomax, and Butch Hawes

American Folksay: Ballads and Dances, Vol. 2. Stinson Records SLP 6 (10" LP), n.d. Woody Guthrie, Cisco Houston, Sonny Terry, Lead Belly, Bob Carey, Roger Sprung, and Eric Darling; notes by Kenneth Goldstein.

SIDE 1

Band 2. "Alabama Bound," Woody Guthrie, Cisco Houston, and Lead Belly

Band 4. "Devilish Mary," Woody Guthrie and Cisco Houston

SIDE 2

Band 1. "Midnight Special," Woody Guthrie, Cisco Houston, and Lead Belly

Band 3. "Crawdad Song," Woody Guthrie, Cisco Houston, and Sonny Terry

American Folksay, Vol. 3. Stinson Records LP 9 (10" LP), n.d. Woody Guthrie, Cisco Houston, Lead Belly, Pete Seeger, Sonny Terry, and Josh White.

SIDE 1

Band 3. "Hard Traveling," Woody Guthrie, vocal, guitar, harmonica

Band 4. "Bile Dem Cabbage Down," Woody Guthrie, lead vocal/fiddle; Cisco Houston, vocal harmony/guitar; Sonny Terry, harmonica

SIDE 2

Band 2. "Lost John," Woody Guthrie, vocal/guitar; Sonny Terry, harmonica
"Railroad Whistle (900 Miles)" Woody Guthrie, vocal/mandolin; Cisco Houston, guitar; Sonny Terry, harmonica

American Folksay, Vol. 4. Stinson Records LP 11 (10" LP), n.d. Woody Guthrie, Cisco Houston, Lead Belly, Pete Seeger, Sonny Terry, and Josh White.

SIDE 1
> Band 2. "Sowing on the Mountain" Woody Guthrie, vocal harmony/guitar; Cisco Houston, lead vocal
> Band 4. "Cripple Creek," Woody Guthrie, vocal/guitar; Cisco Houston, vocal/guitar; Sonny Terry, harmonica

SIDE 2
> Band 1. "Stewball," Lead Belly, guitar/lead vocal; Woody Guthrie, vocal harmony/mandolin; Cisco Houston, vocal harmony

American Folksay, Vol. 5. Stinson Records LP 12 (10" LP), n.d. Woody Guthrie, Cisco Houston, Hally Wood, Pete Seeger, Lead Belly, Frank Warner, and Sonny Terry.

SIDE 1
> Band 4. "Go Tell Aunt Rhody," Woody Guthrie, lead vocal/mandolin; Cisco Houston, vocal harmony/guitar; Sonny Terry, harmonica

SIDE 2
> Band 4. "House of the Rising Sun," Woody Guthrie, vocal/guitar

American Folksay, Vol. 6. Stinson Records LP 13 (10" LP), n.d. Pete Seeger, Tom Glazer, Woody Guthrie, Cisco Houston, Frank Warner, Lead Belly, Ernie Liberman, Gary Davis, and Sonny Terry.

SIDE 2
> Band 3. "Froggy Went A-Courting," Woody Guthrie, vocal/mandolin; Cisco Houston, guitar; Sonny Terry, harmonica

The American Folksay *series as issued by Stinson was reissued on cassette and in 1995 was reissued on compact disc. The songs are the same as on the LP, but in a different sequence.*

American Folksay: Ballads and Dances, Vols. 1 and 2, Stinson Records CA 5, n.d.; *American Folksay, Vols. 3 and 4,* Stinson Records CA 9, n.d.; *American Folksay: Ballads and Dances, Vols. 5 and 6,* Stinson Records CA 12, n.d.; *American Folksay: Ballads and Dances, Vols. 1–4,* Collectables Records Corp., COL-CD-5600, 1995; *American Folksay: Ballads and Dances, Vols. 5–6* and *Chain Gang,* Collectables Records Corp. COL-CD-5600, 1995.

American History in Ballad and Song. Folkways Records FH 5801, 1960. Woody Guthrie, vocal/guitar

SIDE 5
> Band 3. "Dust Storm Disaster"

SIDE 6
> Band 1. "The Flood and the Storm"

American Roots Collection. Smithsonian Folkways Recordings SF CD 40062, 1996, a sampler of available recordings.

Track 15. "This Land Is Your Land," from *Folkways: The Original Vision*, SF 40001

Track 16. "Two Good Men," from *Woody Guthrie: Ballads of Sacco & Vanzetti*, SF 40060

Asch Recordings, 1939–1945, Vol. 2. Asch Records AA 3/4, 1967 (two LP album).

3A SIDE 1
Band 6. "House of the Rising Sun," Woody Guthrie
SIDE 2
Band 7. "Cowboy Waltz," Woody Guthrie, fiddle
4B SIDE 2
Band 4. "900 Miles," Woody Guthrie, fiddle; others unidentified, probably Bess Lomax Hawes, mandolin, and Butch Hawes, guitar
SIDE 2
Band 5. "Railroad Blues (900 Miles)." In his notes Moe Asch identified the following, Woody Guthrie, harmonica; Sonny Terry, harmonica; Cisco Houston, guitar, but I believe it is Woody playing the guitar and only Sonny on harmonica.

Cowboy Songs on Folkways. Smithsonian/Folkways Recordings CD SF 40043, C-SF 40043, 1991; compiled and annotated by Guy Logsdon.

Track 4. "Whoopie-ti-yi-yo, Get Along Little Dogies," Woody Guthrie, vocal/mandolin; Cisco Houston, vocal harmony/guitar
Track 11. "Buffalo Skinners," Woody Guthrie, vocal/guitar
Track 18. "Jesse James (Lead Belly's Version)," Woody Guthrie, vocal/guitar
Track 24. "Philadelphia Lawyer," Woody Guthrie, vocal; Cisco Houston, vocal harmony/guitar

Early Lead Belly: 1935–1940. Narrated by Woody Guthrie, Biograph Records BLP-12013 and BCD 113 (CD); notes by Chris Albertson, 1969.

SIDE 1
This is the radio show recorded 19 June 1940 in New York City that is narrated by Woody Guthrie. While no Guthrie songs are included, it is important, for it reveals that Guthrie was far more sophisticated than he usually portrayed himself.

Fish That's a Song, A. Smithsonian/Folkways Recordings SF 45037 (cassette), 1990; compiled by Andrew Connors and Lori Elaine Taylor.

SIDE 1
Band 3. "Build My House," Woody Guthrie, vocal/guitar/harmonica
Band 9. "Talkin' Fishing Blues," Woody Guthrie, vocal/guitar

Folk: Life, Times, and Music Series, The. Friedman/Fairfax Publishers A24894, 1994 (book and compact disc; CD manufactured by Sony Music); book by Anna Hunt Graves, *Folk* (New York: Friedman/Fairfax Publishers, 1994), 72 pp.

Track 3. "Do-Re-Mi," Woody Guthrie, vocal/guitar

Folk Box, The. Elektra Records EKL 9001 (12" LP); in cooperation with Folkways Records, compiled and annotated by Robert Shelton, 1964.

SIDE 2
  Band 8. "Oregon Trail," Woody Guthrie, vocal/guitar/harmonica
SIDE 7
  Band 10. "This Land Is Your Land," Woody Guthrie, vocal/guitar
SIDE 8
  Band 3. "Talking Dust Bowl," Woody Guthrie, vocal/guitar

Folk Hits Around the Campfire. K-TEL 3455-2 (CD), 1995.

  Track 2. "This Land Is Your Land," Woody Guthrie, vocal/guitar

Folk Music Radio. Radiola CMR 1133 (cassette), n.d. Woody Guthrie and others; no notes.

SIDE A
  Hootenanny, 10 March 1947, CBS radio broadcast, written and produced by Alan Lomax, New York City; Pete Seeger, Woody Guthrie, Cisco Houston, Brownie McGhee, Sonny Terry, Hally Wood, Coleman Brothers, Eddie Smith (fiddle), Sidney Bechet, and John Henry Faulk, announcer.
  "Raise a Ruckus Tonight," Pete Seeger and entire cast, Woody Guthrie calls a square-dance verse
  "Hard Ain't It Hard," Woody Guthrie with Cisco Houston, Sonny Terry, and Pete Seeger
  "Talking Blues," Woody Guthrie (some lyrics different from standard verses), Pete Seeger ends the song with "Raise a Ruckus Tonight"
  "John Henry," entire cast with Woody Guthrie making comments and singing harmony during Pete Seeger's verses
SIDE B
  Back Where I Come From, 19 August 1940, program 10 in CBS Radio's *Forecast* series, written by Alan Lomax and Nicholas Ray, New York City. Clifton Fadiman, narrator; Woody Guthrie, Golden Gate Quartet, Len Doyle, Burl Ives, Willy Johnson, and Josh White
  Woody Guthrie talks about weather (humor)
  "So Long, It's Been Good to Know You," Woody Guthrie and cast, the song is woven into a story with singing and storytelling

Folk Song America: A 20th Century Revival. Smithsonian Collection of Recordings RD 046 (CD), A4 21489 (cassette), A 21490; compiled and notes by Norm Cohen.

  Vol. 1, track 14. "So Long, It's Been Good to Know You," Woody Guthrie, vocal/guitar

Folkways: The Original Vision. Smithsonian Folkways SF 40001 (12" LP, cassette, CD), 1988. Woody Guthrie and Lead Belly; notes by Alan Lomax and Anthony Seeger. Woody Guthrie (vocal/guitar) unless otherwise noted. Song sequence is the same on the cassette and compact disc.

SIDE A
   Band 2. "Pretty Boy Floyd"
   Band 3. "Do Re Mi"
   Band 4. "I Ain't Got No Home"
   Band 5. "Jesus Christ"
   Band 8. Will Geer reading Guthrie
   Band 9. "Hard Travelling"
SIDE B
   Band 1. "Philadelphia Lawyer"
   Band 2. "Hobo's Lullaby"
   Band 6. "Vigilante Man"
   Band 7. "This Land Is Your Land"
   Band 8. "Woody's Rag (Hard Work)"
   Band 10. with Lead Belly, Cisco Houston, and Sonny Terry, "We Shall Be Free"

Folkways: A Vision Revisited. Tradition 2200 (cassette), n.d. (ca.1992) and Legacy International CD-300 (CD), "The Original Performances of Lead Belly / Woody Guthrie/ Pete Seeger." Woody Guthrie, vocal/guitar, unless otherwise noted (cassette).

SIDE 1
   "Pretty Boy Floyd"
   "Little Black Train"
SIDE 2
   "Gypsy Davy"
   "More Pretty Girls Than One"
   "Hey Lolly Lolly"

Compact disc Legacy International CD 300, n.d. (ca. 1992).
   Track 2. "House of the Rising Sun"
   Track 5. "Little Black Train"
   Track 8. "Pretty Boy Floyd"
   Track 11. "Gypsy Davy"
   Track 14. "More Pretty Girls Than One"
   Track 17. "Hey Lolly Lolly"

Good Morning Blues: Early Lead Belly, 1935–1940. Narrated by Woody Guthrie; Biograph BLP 12013 (12" LP), n.d. See *Early Lead Belly, 1935–1940.*

Greatest Songs of Woody Guthrie, The. Vanguard VSD 35/36, Woody Guthrie and others, no notes; Sides 1 and 2 on VSD-35 reissued on VMS 73105 (same song sequence), notes by Nancy Toff; cassette Vanguard 35/36-4 and CD 35/36-2.

VSD-35 SIDE 1
   Band 1. "This Land Is Your Land," Woody Guthrie
   Band 2. "Do Re Mi," Cisco Houston
   Band 3. "So Long—It's Been Good to Know Yuh," The Weavers
   Band 4. "Pastures of Plenty," Odetta
   Band 5. "Roll On Columbia," Country Joe McDonald
   Band 6. "Hard, Ain't It Hard," Woody Guthrie and Cisco Houston
   Band 7. "Deportee (Plane Wreck at Los Gatos)," Cisco Houston

VSD-35 SIDE 2

Band 1. "A Group of Children's Songs"
    (a) "Pick It Up," The Babysitters
    (b) "(Take Me) Riding in My Car," Woody Guthrie
    (c) "Why, Oh Why," The Babysitters
    (d) "Ship in the Sky," Cisco Houston
    (e) "Grassey Grass Grass," Woody Guthrie
Band 2. "Old Lone Wolf," Cisco Houston
Band 3. "Woody's Rag and 900 Miles," The Weavers
Band 4. "900 Miles," Cisco Houston
Band 5. "Jackhammer John," The Weavers
Band 6. "Tom Joad," Country Joe McDonald

VSD-36, SIDE 1

Band 1. "I Ain't Got No Home," Cisco Houston
Band 2. "The Sinking of the Reuben James," The Weavers
Band 3. "Dirty Overhalls," Woody Guthrie
Band 4. "The Great Historical Bum," Odetta
Band 5. "Talking Fishing Blues," Jack Elliott
Band 6. "Ladies Auxiliary," Cisco Houston
Band 7. "Blowing Down That Old Dusty Road," Country Joe McDonald
Band 8. "Buffalo Skinners," Jim Kweskin
Band 9. "Curly Headed Baby," Cisco Houston

VSD-36, SIDE 2

Band 1. "1913 Massacre," Jack Elliott
Band 2. "Jesus Christ," Cisco Houston
Band 3. "Rambling Round Your City," Odetta
Band 4. "When the Curfew Blows," Country Joe McDonald
Band 5. "Pretty Boy Floyd," Joan Baez
Band 6. "Hard Travellin'," Woody Guthrie
Band 7. "This Land Is Your Land," The Weavers

Houston, Cisco. *The Folkways Years, 1944–1961.* Smithsonian/Folkways Recordings SF 40059, compact disc and cassette; compiled and annotated by Guy Logsdon, 1994.

    Track 5. "There's a Better World a-Comin'," with Woody Guthrie
    Track 17. "What Did the Deep Blue Sea Say," with Woody Guthrie

Lead Belly: Complete Recorded Works, 1939–1947, Vol., 4 May to October 1944. Document Records DOCD-5310, 1994, compact disc.

    Track 3. "We Shall be Free," with Woody Guthrie, Cisco Houston, and Sonny Terry

Lead Belly: Complete Recorded Works, 1939–1947, Vol. 5, 27 October 1944 to October 1946. Document Records DOCD-5311, 1994, compact disc. Lead Belly, vocal/guitar; Woody Guthrie, vocal harmony (mandolin on 21, 24, 26, 27, 28); Cisco Houston, vocal harmony/guitar.

    Track 21. "Alabama Bound"
    Track 22. "Ham and Eggs"
    Track 23. "Yellow Gal"

Track 24. "Stew Ball"
Track 25. "Gray Goose"
Track 26. "Midnight Special"
Track 27. "Green Corn"
Track 28. "Fiddler's Dram"

Lead Belly Memorial, Vols. 3 and 4: The Stinson Collectors Series, Collectables Records
COL-CD-5604, 1995, compact disc.

Track 3. "Ham and Eggs," with Woody Guthrie and Cisco Houston

Lead Belly Sings and Plays. Stinson Records SLPS 91, Collector's Series, 1962; reissued on *Lead Belly: Party Songs and Sings and Plays: The Stinson Collectors Series,*
Collectables Records COL-CD-5609, 1995, compact disc.

SIDE 1
Band 1. "Alabama Bound," with Woody Guthrie and Cisco Houston
Band 2. "Yellow Gal," with Woody Guthrie and Cisco Houston
Band 3. "Midnight Special," with Woody Guthrie and Cisco Houston
SIDE 2
Band 5. "Stewball," with Woody Guthrie and Cisco Houston

Collectables Records Col-CD-5609
Track 13. "Alabama Bound"
Track 15. "Stewball"
Track 17. "Yellow Gal"
Track 18. "Midnight Special"

Lead Belly Sings Folk Songs. Folkways Records FA 2488, 1962; reissued as Folkways
Records FT 1006 (mono) and FTS 31006 (stereo) and as *Lead Belly: Keep Your Hands
off Her,* Verve/Folkways FV-9021. With Woody Guthrie, Cisco Houston, Sonny Terry,
and Brownie McGhee; reissued Smithsonian/Folkways SF 40010 (LP), C SF 40010
(cassette), CD SF 40010 (CD), 1989. Foreign reissues: Transatlantic Records XTRA
1064 (England). Notes from Woody Guthrie, *American Folksong,* Oak Publications,
1947, 1961. Lead Belly (vocal/guitar).

SIDE 1
Band 2. "Stewball," with Cisco Houston and Woody Guthrie
Band 6. "Outskirts of Town," with Sonny Terry and Woody Guthrie
Band 7. "We Shall Be Free," with Cisco Houston, Woody Guthrie, and Sonny
    Terry
SIDE 2
Band 3. "Alabama Bound," with Cisco Houston and Woody Guthrie
Band 7. "Fiddler's Dram," with Cisco Houston and Woody Guthrie

Lead Belly Sings Midnight Special and Other Folk Songs. Folkways Records FTS
31046, 1976, notes by Frederic Ramsey Jr.

SIDE 1
Band 1. "Midnight Special," with Woody Guthrie and Cisco Houston

Band 7. "Ham and Eggs," with Woody Guthrie and Cisco Houston

Life Treasury of American Folk Music, The (produced as a supplement to the book by the same title). [Life Records] L1001, n.d.

SIDE 2
"Billy the Kid," Woody Guthrie
"Hard Work," Woody Guthrie

Lonesome Valley: A Collection of American Folk Music. Folkways Records FA 2010 (10" LP), 1950. Woody Guthrie, Bess Lomax, Pete Seeger, Butch Hawes, Cisco Houston, Tom Glazer, and Lee Hays; no notes, lyrics only.

SIDE 2
Band 4. "Cowboy Waltz," instrumental; Woody Guthrie, fiddle and group
Band 5. "Sowing on the Mountain," Woody Guthrie and Cisco Houston

Music Never Stopped, The: Roots of the Grateful Dead. Shanachie 6014, 1995, compact disc.

Track 16. "Goin' Down This Road Feelin' Bad," Woody Guthrie, vocal/mandolin; Cisco Houston, vocal harmony/guitar; Sonny Terry, harmonica

Real Music Box, The: 25 Years of Rounder Records, 25 Years of Folk Music on Rounder Records. Rounder Records CD AN 25, 9 compact disc set.

PART 1
Disc 1, track 1. "Do-Re-Mi"

Sing Out! 10th Anniversary Issue. Sing Out magazine, SO-1 (7" micro-groove 33⅓ rpm), 1961.

SIDE 2
Band 4. "Ladies Auxiliary"
Band 5. "Clean-o"

Smithsonian Collection of Classic Country Music. Selected and annotated by Bill Malone. The Smithsonian Collection of Recordings, Division of Performing Arts, R025 P8 15640, 1981.

SIDE 6
Band 5. "Do Re Mi," Woody Guthrie

Smithsonian Folkways American Roots Collection. See American Roots Collection.

Soil and The Sea, The. Mainstream Records "Commodore Classics" 56005 (12" LP), n.d. Woody, Guthrie, Pete Seeger, Lee Hays, and Peter Hawes; notes by Peter Spargo. Originally issued as *Deep Sea Chanties and Whaling Ballads,* General Album G-20 and *Sod Buster Ballads,* General Album G-21 (see Recording Session—General Records); the following feature Woody as the lead/solo singer.

SIDE I
> Band 3. "Blow the Man Down"
> Band 4. "Hard, Ain't It Hard"

SIDE 2
> Band 5. "I Ride an Old Paint"
> Band 6. "House of the Rising Sun"

Songs for Political Action. Compiled and with a book by Ronald D. Cohen and Dave Samuelson, Bear Family Records BCD 15720, 10 discs, 1996.

DISC 3
> Track 14. "Song for Bridges," with the Almanac Singers
> Track 15. "Babe O' Mine"
> Track 18. "Blow the Man Down"
> Track 26. "Hard, Ain't It Hard"
> Track 27. "I Ride an Old Paint"
> Track 28. "House of the Rising Sun"

DISC 4
> Track 8. "Keep That Oil A-Rollin'" (Woody sings the lead)

DISC 5
> Track 19. "Farmer-Labor Train"
> Track 20. "So Long, It's Been Good to Know You"
> Track 21. "Talking Sailor"
> Track 22. "Sally, Don't You Grieve"

DISC 10
> Track 30. "I've Got to Know"
> Track 31. "This Land Is Your Land" (Decca session, 1952 variant)

Songs of the Lincoln Brigade and International Brigades. Stinson SLP 52 (includes the 78 rpm album issued by Asch Records as *Six Songs for Democracy*), 1962.

SIDE 2
> Band 6. "Jarama Valley," Woody Guthrie, guitar/vocal

Songs of the Lincoln Brigade and International Brigades and Southern Mountain Hoedown: Stinson Collector's Series. Collectables Records COL-CD-5606, 1995.

> Track 12. "Jarama Valley," Woody Guthrie, vocal/guitar
> Track 13. "Ida Red," Woody Guthrie, vocal/manolin; Cisco Houston, vocal/guitar
> Track 14. "Fiddle Breakdown," Woody Guthrie, fiddle; Cisco Houston, guitar
> Track 15. "Old Dan Tucker," Woody Guthrie, vocal/mandolin; Cisco Houston, vocal/guitar; Sonny Terry, harmonica
> Track 16. "Hoe Cakes Fritter," Woody Guthrie, vocal/mandolin; Cisco Houston, vocal/guitar; Sonny Terry, harmonica
> Track 17. "Cripple Creek," Woody Guthrie, vocal/guitar; Cisco Houston, vocal/guitar
> Track 18. "Sally Gooden," Woody Guthrie, vocal/fiddle; Cisco Houston, guitar; Sonny Terry, harmonica
> Track 19. "Salty Dog Breakdown," Woody Guthrie, vocal/mandolin; Cisco Houston/guitar
> Track 20. "Buffalo Gals," Woody Guthrie, vocal/mandolin; Cisco Houston, vocal/guitar; Sonny Terry, harmonica

Track 21. "(Old) Joe Clark," Woody Guthrie, vocal/mandolin; Cisco Houston, vocal/guitar; Sonny Terry, harmonica

Track 22. "Froggy Went A-Courting," Woody Guthrie, vocal/mandolin; Cisco Houston, guitar; Sonny Terry, harmonica

Songs of the Spanish Civil War, Vol. 2. Folkways Records FH 5437, 1962. Woody Guthrie (vocal/guitar).

SIDE 1

Band 1. "Jarama"

That's Why We're Marching: World War II and the American Folk Song Movement, featuring Woody Guthrie and Other Artists. Smithsonian/Folkways 40021 (cassette and CD), 1996; compiled by Jeff Place and Guy Logsdon; annotated by Guy Logsdon and Jeff Place; featuring Woody Guthrie, The Almanac Singers, Lead Belly, Tom Glazer, Cisco Houston, Pete Seeger, Josh White, and others.

Track 2. "Talking Sailor," Woody Guthrie

Track 7. "What Are We Waiting On," Woody Guthrie

Track 9. "Sinking of the Reuben James," Woody Guthrie

Track 13. "So Long, It's Been Good to Know You," Woody Guthrie

Track 16. "Sally, Don't You Grieve," Woody Guthrie and Cisco Houston

Track 18. "When the Yanks Go Marching In," Woody Guthrie, Cisco Houston, and Sonny Terry

Track 21. "Miss Pavlichencko" Woody Guthrie

38 Favorite American Folk Songs. Disc/FolkwaysRecords FF1 (three 12" LPs). Contains Woody Guthrie, *Dust Bowl Ballads* FH 5212; Lead Belly FA 2014; and Pete Seeger FA 2043. See *Dust Bowl Ballads* FH 5212 for sequence of songs.

This Land Is My Land. Folkways Records FP 27 (10" LP), 1951; reissued as *Vol. 3, Songs to Grow On: American Work Songs* Folkways Records FC 7027, 1961; anthology with Sam Eskin, Bill Bonyon, "Mac" McClintock, Pete Seeger, Cisco Houston, Lead Belly, and Woody Guthrie. Woody Guthrie (vocal/guitar).

SIDE 1

Band 1. "This Is My Land (This Land Is Your Land)"

Band 6. "Columbia River" (irrigation song)

Troubadours of the Folk Era, Vol. 1. Rhino Records R2 70262 (cassette and CD), 1992.

Track 1. "This Land Is My Land," Woody Guthrie

Woody Guthrie: Hard Travelin'. Arloco Records ARL-284, "Sound Track from the Film."

SIDE 2

Band 7. "This Land Is Your Land" (dubbed), Woody Guthrie and Arlo Guthrie

World of Popular Music: Folk and Country. Follett Publishing Company XL 12, 1975. Woody Guthrie, vocal/guitar.

SIDE 5
> Band 7. "Grand Coulee Dam"
> Band 8. "Talking Columbia"
> Band 9. "Pastures of Plenty"
> Band 10. "This Land Is Your Land"

Albums Issued in Woody Guthrie's Name

Ballads of Sacco and Vanzetti. Folkways Records FH 5485 (12" LP), 1960. Composed and sung by Woody Guthrie (1946–47); commissioned by Moses Asch (1945); "Sacco's Letter To His Son," sung by Pete Seeger; accompanying booklet edited by Moses Asch and Irwin Silber, published by Oak Publication, New York, 1960; reissued by Smithsonian/Folkways SF 40060 (cassette and CD), 1996, with additional notes by Anthony Seeger and a letter by Woody Guthrie to Judge Thayer. Woody Guthrie, vocal/guitar.

SIDE 1
> Band 1. "I Just Want to Sing Your Name"
> Band 2. "Red Wine"
> Band 3. "You Souls of Boston"
> Band 4. "Suassos Lane"
> Band 5. "The Flood and the Storm"
> Band 6. "Vanzetti's Rock"
> Band 7. "Root Hog and Die"

SIDE 2
> Band 1. "Old Judge Thayer"
> Band 2. "We Welcome to Heaven"
> Band 3. "Vanzetti's Letter (parts 1 and 2)"
> Band 4. "Two Good Men"
> Band 5. "Sacco's Letter to His Son" (Pete Seeger)

Cassette and CD sequence
> Track 1. "The Flood and the Storm"
> Track 2. "Two Good Men"
> Track 3. "I Just Want to Sing Your Name"
> Track 4. "Red Wine"
> Track 5. "Suassos Lane"
> Track 6. "You Souls of Boston"
> Track 7. "Old Judge Thayer"
> Track 8. "Vanzetti's Rock"
> Track 9. "Vanzetti's Letter"
> Track 10. "Root Hog and Die"
> Track 11. "We Welcome to Heaven"
> Track 12. "Sacco's Letter to His Son" (Pete Seeger)

Bed on the Floor. Verve/Folkways FV/FVS 9007 (12" LP), n.d. Woody Guthrie, Cisco Houston, Sonny Terry; notes anon. Woody Guthrie, vocal/guitar, unless otherwise noted. Reissued as *Woody Guthrie: Poor Boy,* Folkways Records FT 1010/FTS 31010, notes by Woody Guthrie.

SIDE 1
Band 1. "Baltimore to Washington"
Band 2. "Little Black Train"
Band 3. "Who's Going to Shoe Your Pretty Feet," with Cisco Houston
Band 4. "Slip Knot"
Band 5. "Poor Boy"
Band 6. "Mean-Talking Blues"
Band 7. "Stepstone," with Cisco Houston and Sonny Terry
SIDE 2
Band 1. "Bed on the Floor," with Cisco Houston
Band 2. "Little Darling," with Cisco Houston and Sonny Terry
Band 3. "Miner's Song"
Band 4. "Train Blues," instrumental
Band 5. "Danville Girl #2," with Cisco Houston
Band 6. "Ride an Old Paint," with Cisco Houston

Bonneville Dam and Other Columbia River Songs. Verve/Folkways FV 9036 (12" LP), ca. 1967. Notes by Moses Asch; reissued as *This Land Is Your Land,* Folkways Records FT 1001. Woody Guthrie (vocal/guitar).

SIDE 1
Band 1. "Talking Columbia"
Band 2. "Pastures of Plenty"
Band 3. "New Found Land"
Band 4. "Oregon Trail"
Band 5. "End of My Line"
SIDE 2
Band 1. "This Land Is Your Land"
Band 2. "The Grand Coulee Dam"
Band 3. "Ramblin' Round"
Band 4. "Goin' Down the Road"

Bound For Glory: The Songs and Story of Woody Guthrie. Folkways Records FP 78/1 (12" LP), 1956. Sung by Woody Guthrie, narrated by Will Geer, edited by Millard Lampell. Woody Guthrie, vocal/guitar.

SIDE 1
Band 1. "Stagolee"
Band 2. Children's Songs
    (a) "Little Sack of Sugar"
    (b) "My Daddy (Ship in the Sky)"
    (c) "Swimmy Swim Swim"
Band 3. "Vigilante Man"
Band 4. "Do Re Mi"
Band 5. "Pastures of Plenty"
Band 6. "Grand Coulee Dam"
SIDE 2
Band 1. "This Land Is Your Land"
Band 2. "Talkin Fishing Blues"
Band 3. "Reuben James (The Sinking of)"

Band 4. "Jesus Christ"
Band 5. "There's a Better World A-Coming"

Chain Gang, Vol. 1. Stinson Records SLP 7 (10" LP) n.d.; reissued on Stinson CA 7 (cassette). Woody Guthrie, Sonny Terry, and Alek Stewart; notes by Ken Goldstein; no notes with cassette.

SIDE 1
Band 1. "Chain Gang Blues"
Band 2. "Cornbread, Meat and Molasses"
Band 3. "Stackolee"
SIDE 2
Band 1. "Long John"
Band 2. "Rock Me Mama"
Band 3. "Chain Gang Special"

Chain Gang, Vol. 2. Stinson Records SLP 8 (10" LP) n.d.; reissued on Stinson CA 7 (cassette). Woody Guthrie, Sonny Terry, and Alek Stewart; notes by Ken Goldstein; no notes with cassette.

SIDE 1
Band 1. "Red River"
Band 2. "Ham 'n Eggs"
Band 3. "Betty and Dupree"
SIDE 2
Band 1. "Pick a Bale of Cotton"
Band 2. "It Takes a Chain Gang Man"
Band 3. "Lost John"

Both albums were reissued as Woody Guthrie: Chain Gang, *Stinson CA 7 (cassette), and as* Sonny Terry: Chain Gang Blues, *Golden Classics, Collectables Records, 1990 (CD); some of the songs were reissued as a part of* American Folksay: Ballads and Dances, Vols 5–6 *and* Chain Gang, *Collectables Records, COL-CD-5600, 1995; the song sequence varies on each issue.*

Cisco Houston. Archive of Folk Music/Everest Records Production FM-105 (mono) and FS-205 (stereo), (12" LP), n.d. This record was released as a tribute to Cisco Houston, but Woody Guthrie sings the lead, while Cisco Houston sings harmony; it is a Woody Guthrie album. The selections are from Stinson Records releases featuring Woody Guthrie. The songs on Side 2 were released on the compact disc *Alan Lomax and Cisco Houston,* Magnum America TKCD 013, 1996. Woody Guthrie, vocal/guitar and mandolin.

SIDE 1
Band 1. "Take a Whiff on Me," with Cisco Houston
Band 2. "Bad Lee Brown"
Band 3. "The Golden Vanity," with Cisco Houston
Band 4. "Cumberland Gap," with Cisco Houston and Sonny Terry
Band 5. "Sourwood Mountain," with Cisco Houston and Sonny Terry
Band 6. "Old Time Religion," with Cisco Houston and Sonny Terry

SIDE 2

    Band 1. "Columbus Stockade," mandolin with Cisco Houston

    Band 2. "Johnny Hard"

    Band 3. "Foggy Mountain Top," mandolin, with Cisco Houston

    Band 4. "Buy [*sic*(Bury)]Me Beneath the Willow," mandolin, with Cisco Houston
       and Sonny Terry)

    Band 5. "Skip to my Lou," mandolin, with Cisco Houston and Sonny Terry)

    Band 6. "Ezekill [*sic* (Ezekiel)] Saw (the) Wheel," mandolin with Cisco Houston
       and Sonny Terry)

Columbia River Collection. See *Woody Guthrie: Columbia River Collection.*

Cowboy Songs. Stinson SLP 32 (10" LP and 12" [1963] LP); reissued as Stinson CA 32 (cassette), n.d.; also, reissued on *Woody Guthrie: Cowboy Songs/Southern Mountain Hoedowns,* Stinson CD 32 (CD). Woody Guthrie and Cisco Houston; notes by Kenneth S. Goldstein; no notes with cassette or compact disc. Woody Guthrie, vocal/guitar, and Cisco Houston, vocal/guitar.

SIDE 1

    Band 1. "Chisholm Trail"

    Band 2. "Billy the Kid"

    Band 3. "Whoopie Ti Yi Yo"

    Band 4. "Philadelphia Lawyer"

SIDE 2

    Band 1. "Ride Around Little Dogies"

    Band 2. "Gambling Man"

    Band 3. "Red River Valley"

    Band 4. "Jessie [*sic*] James"

Dust Bowl Ballads. RCA Victor LPV-502 Vintage Series (12" LP); originally issued in 1940), 1964, with two previously unissued songs, notes by Peter J. Welding, produced by Frank Driggs; reissued as *Woody Guthrie: A Legendary Performer,* RCA CPL1-2099(e), 1977, and Rounder Records 1040 (LP, cassette, and CD), 1988 Woody Guthrie, vocal/guitar.

SIDE 1

    Band 1. "The Great Dust Storm"

    Band 2. "I Ain't Got No Home in This World Anymore"

    Band 3. "Talkin' Dust Bowl Blues"

    Band 4. "Vigilante Man"

    Band 5. "Dust Cain't Kill Me"

    Band 6. "Pretty Boy Floyd" (previously unissued)

    Band 7. "Dust Pneumonia Blues"

SIDE 2

    Band 1. "Blowin' Down This Road"

    Band 2. "Tom Joad, Part 1"

    Band 3. "Tom Joad, Part 2"

    Band 4. "Dust Bowl Refugee"

    Band 5. "Do Re Mi"

    Band 6. "Dust Bowl Blues" (previously unissued)

Band 7. "Dusty Old Dust"

Dust Bowl Ballads Sung by Woody Guthrie. Folkways Records FH 5212 (12" LP), 1964, Woody Guthrie; notes by John Asch and Woody Guthrie (contains all of *Talking Dust Bowl,* Folkways FA 2011, 1950); reissued as a part of *38 Favorite American Folk Songs* Disc/Folkways Records FF1. Woody Guthrie, vocal/guitar.

SIDE 1
    Band 1. "Talkin' Dust Bowl Blues"
    Band 2. "Blowin' Down This Road"
    Band 3. "Do Re Mi"
    Band 4. "Dust Cain't Kill Me"
    Band 5. "Tom Joad (Part 1 and Part 2)"
SIDE 2
    Band 1. "The Great Dust Storm"
    Band 2. "Dusty Old Dust"
    Band 3. "Dust Bowl Refugee"
    Band 4. "Dust Pneumonia Blues"
    Band 5. "I Ain't Got No Home in This World Anymore"
    Band 6. "Vigilante Man"

Early Masters: Woody Guthrie. Tradition TCD 1017 (CD), 1996 (original 12" LP issue Stinson SLP 44), notes by Thane Tierney; for song sequence, see: *Woody Guthrie and Cisco Houston, Vol 1,* Stinson Records SLP 44 (12" LP) and the first twelve songs on *Woody Guthrie: The Early Years,* Legacy International CD 345 (CD).

Hard Travelin'. Disc D-110 (12" LP), 1964; Woody Guthrie, Cisco Houston, Lead Belly, Sonny Terry, and Pete Seeger.

SIDE 1
    Band 1. "Springfield Mountain"
    Band 2. "Hey, Little Water Boy (Muleskinner Blues)"
    Band 3. "Chisholm Trail"
    Band 4. "Rubber Dolly"
    Band 5. "Lindberg [*sic*]"
    Band 6. "Hard Travelin'"
SIDE 2
    Band 1. "Jiggy Bum Bum"
    Band 2. "Put My Little Shoes Away"
    Band 3. "I Ain't Got Nobody"
    Band 4. "Yeller Gal"
    Band 5. "Philadelphia Lawyer"
    Band 6. "Ida Red"

Immortal Woody Guthrie. Olympic Records 7101 (12" LP), 1973; Woody Guthrie, Cisco Houston, and Sonny Terry; notes, anon.; distributed by Everest Records. Reissued as *Immortal Woody Guthrie, Golden Classics, Part Two,* Collectables Records COL 5098 (cassette) and COL-CD 5098 (CD), 1990. Woody Guthrie, vocal/guitar, unless otherwise noted. Song sequence is the same on cassette COL 5098 and compact disc COL-CD-5098.

SIDE 1
    Band 1. "Brown Eyes," with Cisco Houston
    Band 2. "Jack Hammer Blues," with Cisco Houston and Sonny Terry
    Band 3. "John Henry," with Cisco Houston
    Band 4. "House of the Rising Sun"

SIDE 2
    Band 1. "Little Black Train"
    Band 2. "Who's Going to Shoe Your Pretty Feet," with Cisco Houston
    Band 3. "Bed on the Floor," with Cisco Houston
    Band 4. "Danville Girl, No.2," with Cisco Houston
    Band 5. "Ride Old Paint," with Cisco Houston

Immortal Woody Guthrie, Golden Classics, Part Two. Collectables Records, 1990.

In Memoriam. See *The Legendary Woody Guthrie: In Memoriam.*

Legendary Woody Guthrie, The: In Memoriam. Tradition/Everest Records 2058, ca. 1968. Reissued as *Woody Guthrie,* Archive of Folk Music/Everest Records FS 204 and reissued (songs and sequence same on Woody Guthrie) as *Worried Man Blues, Golden Classics, Part One,* Collectables Records COL 5095 (cassette) and COL-CD 5095 (CD), 1990. [On *Woody Guthrie* FS-204 the liner notes are spelled Woodie and "Gypsy Davy" is listed as "Gypsy Baby."] The songs are the same as on Stinson SLP 44. Woody Guthrie, vocal/guitar, unless otherwise noted.

SIDE 1
    Band 1. "Hey Lolly Lolly"
    Band 2. "Buffalo Skinners"
    Band 3. "John Henry"
    Band 4. "Gypsy Davy"
    Band 5. "Worried Man Blues"
    Band 6. "More Pretty Girls Than One"

SIDE 2
    Band 1. "Ain't Gonna Be Treated This Way"
    Band 2. "Rangers Command"
    Band 3. "Poor Boy"
    Band 4. "Lonesome Day"
    Band 5. "Pretty Boy Floyd"
    Band 6. "Hard, Ain't It Hard"

Long Ways to Travel: The Unreleased Folkways Masters, 1944–1949. Smithsonian/Folkways Recordings SF 40046 (cassette and CD), 1994; compiled by Jeff Place and Guy Logsdon; annotated by Guy Logsdon.

    Track 1. "Hard Travelin'"
    Track 2. "Talking Centralia"
    Track 3. "Farmer-Labor Train"
    Track 4. "Harriet Tubman's Ballad"
    Track 5. "Warden in the Sky"
    Track 6. "Train Narration"
    Track 7. "Seattle to Chicago"

Track 8. "Rain Crow Bill"
Track 9. "Along in the Sun and the Rain"
Track 10. "Budded Roses"
Track 11. "Train Ride Medley (part 1)"
Track 12. "Girl I Left Behind Me"
Track 13. "Wiggledy Giggledy"
Track 14. "Kissin' On"
Track 15. "Rocky Mountain Slim and Desert Rat Shorty"
Track 16. "Train Ride Medley (part 2)"
Track 17. "Long Ways to Travel"

Nursery Days. Smithsonian/Folkways Recordings SF 45036 (cassette and CD), 1992.

Track 1. "Wake Up"
Track 2. "Clean-o"
Track 3. "Dance Around"
Track 4. "Riding in My Car (Car Song)"
Track 5. "Don't You Push Me Down"
Track 6. "My Dolly"
Track 7. "Put Your Finger in the Air"
Track 8. "Come See"
Track 9. "Race You Down the Mountain"
Track 10. "Howdido"
Track 11. "Merry-go-round"
Track 12. "Sleep Eye"
Track 13. "My Yellow Crayon"
Track 14. "Roll On"
Track 15. "Jiggy Jiggy Bum"
Track 16. "Bubble Gum"

Original Recordings Made By Woody Guthrie: 1940–1946. Warner Bros. Records BS2999 (12" LP), 1977; notes by Moses Asch. Woody Guthrie, vocal/guitar.

SIDE 1
Band 1. "Gypsy Davey"
Band 2. "Jesus Christ"
Band 3. "Pastures of Plenty"
Band 4. "Columbus Georgia Stockade"
Band 5. "So Long (Dusty Old Dust)"
SIDE 2
Band 1. "Howdido"
Band 2. "Pretty Boy Floyd"
Band 3. "Hard Travellin'"
Band 4. "Better World"
Band 5. "This Land Is Your Land"

Songs To Grow On, Vol. 1, Nursery Days. Folkways Records FC 7005 (10" LP), n.d. Woody Guthrie; introduction by Beatrice Landeck. Woody Guthrie, vocal/guitar.

SIDE 1
Band 1. "Wake Up"

Band 2. "Clean-o"
Band 3. "Dance Around"
Band 4. "Car Song"
Band 5. "Don't You Push Me"
Band 6. "My Dolly""
SIDE 2
Band 1. "Put Your Finger (in the Air)"
Band 2. "Come See"
Band 3. "Race You Down the Mountain"
Band 4. "How Doo Do"
Band 5. "Merry Go Round"
Band 6. "Sleepy Eyes"

Songs to Grow On for Mother and Child, Vol. O. Folkways Records FC 7015 (10"
LP), 1950, 1953. Composed and sung by Woody Guthrie; introduction by Beatrice
Landeck. Woody Guthrie, vocal.

SIDE 1
Band 1. "Grassy-y, Grass, Grass," with drum
Band 2. "Swim-y, Swim, Swim," with guitar
Band 3. "Little Sack of Sugar," with guitar
Band 4. "Rattle My Rattle," with rattle
Band 5. "I Want My Milk," with guitar
Band 6. "Grow, Grow, Grow," with drum
SIDE 2
Band 1. "1,2,3,4,5,6,7,8," with guitar
Band 2. "1 Day, 2 Days, 3 Days Old," with guitar
Band 3. "Wash-y, Wash Wash," with rattle
Band 4. "I'll Eat You, I'll Drink You," with drum
Band 5. "Make a Bubble," with guitar
Band 6. "Who's My Pretty Baby," with tamborine
Band 7. "Write a Word," with guitar, (also titled "I'll Spell You a Word" on the
    12" LP reissue).

Songs to Grow on for Mother and Child. Smithsonian/Folkways Recordings SF 45035,
1991 (cassette and CD); notes by Woody Guthrie.

Track 1. "Grassy Grass Grass (Grow, Grow, Grow)"
Track 2. "Swimmy Swim"
Track 3. "Little Sugar (Little Saka Sugar)"
Track 4. "Rattle My Rattle"
Track 5. "I Want My Milk (I Want It Now)"
Track 6. "1, 2, 3, 4, 5, 6, 7, 8"
Track 7. "One Day Old"
Track 8. "Wash-y Wash Wash (Warshy Little Tootsy)"
Track 9. "I'll Eat You, I'll Drink You"
Track 10. "Make a Blobble"
Track 11. "Who's My Pretty Little Baby (Hey Pretty Baby)"
Track 12. "I'll Write and I'll Draw"
Track 13. "Why, Oh Why"

Track 14. "Pick It Up"
Track 15. "Pretty and Shiny-o"
Track 16. "Needle Song"
Track 17. "Bling-Blang"
Track 18. "Goodnight Little Arlo (Goodnight Little Darlin')"

Southern Mountain Hoedowns. Stinson Records SLPS 54 (12" LP), 1962, notes anon.; reissued on Stinson CA 54 (cassette), also on *Woody Guthrie: Cowboy Songs/Southern Mountain Hoedowns* Stinson CD 32 (CD); also issued with *Songs of the Lincoln Brigade and International Brigades and Southern Mountain Hoedown* Collectables Records COL-CD-5606, 1995. Woody Guthrie, vocal/guitar; Cisco Houston, vocal/guitar; Sonny Terry, harmonica; and Alec Stewart, guitar?

SIDE I
    Band 1. "Ida Red"
    Band 2. "Fiddle Breakdown"
    Band 3. "Old Dan Tucker"
    Band 4. "Hoe Cakes Fritter"
    Band 5. "Cripple Creek"
SIDE 2
    Band 1. "Sally Gooden"
    Band 2. "Salty Dog Breakdown"
    Band 3. "Buffalo Gals"
    Band 4. "(Old) Joe Clark"
    Band 5. "Froggy Went A-Courting"

Struggle. Folkways Records FA 2485 (12" LP), 1976. Woody Guthrie, Cisco Houston, and Sonny Terry; notes by Moses Asch. Six songs (all on Side 2) originally were issued as *Struggle: Documentary #1,* Asch Records. Reissued by Smithsonian/Folkways CD SF 40025 (CD), 1990; notes by Anthony Seeger. Woody Guthrie, vocal/guitar, unless otherwise noted. Song sequence is the same on Smithsonian/Folkways cassette and compact disc reissues.

SIDE I
    Band 1. "Struggle Blues," with Cisco Houston, harmonica solo/guitar
    Band 2. "A Dollar Down and a Dollar a Week," with Cisco Houston
    Band 3. "Get Along Little Doggies," with Cisco Houston
    Band 4. "Hang Knot"
    Band 5. "Waiting at the Gate"
    Band 6. "The Dying Miner"
SIDE 2
    Band 1. "Union Burying Ground"
    Band 2. "Lost John"
    Band 3. "Buffalo Skinners"
    Band 4. "Pretty Boy Floyd"
    Band 5. "Ludlow Massacre"
    Band 6. "1913 Massacre"

Talking Dust Bowl. Folkways Records FP 11 (10" LP), 1950; reissued as FA 2011; reissued with additional songs as *Dust Bowl Ballads,* Folkways Records FH 5212 (liner notes are the same). The placement of songs on the disc varies on the reissued albums. Woody Guthrie, vocal/guitar.

SIDE 1
Band 1. "Dust Storm Disaster"
Band 2. "So Long It's Been Good to Know You"
Band 3. "Talking Dust Blues"
Band 4. "Dust Can't Kill"
SIDE 2
Band 1. "Blowing Down This Road Feeling Bad"
Band 2. "Dust Bowl Refugee"
Band 3. "Tom Joad, Part 1"
Band 4. "Tom Joad, Part 2"

This Land Is Your Land. Folkways Records FT 1001 Mono, FTS 31001 Stereo (12" LP), 1967; reissue of *Bonneville Dam and Other Columbia River Songs*, Verve/Folkways FV-9036, 1966. Woody Guthrie; notes by Moses Asch. Woody Guthrie, vocal/guitar.

SIDE 1
Band 1. "Talking Columbia"
Band 2. "Pastures of Plenty"
Band 3. "New Found Land"
Band 4. "Oregon Trail"
Band 5. "End of My Line"
SIDE 2
Band 1. "This Land Is Your Land"
Band 2. "The Grand Coulee Dam"
Band 3. "Ramblin' Round"
Band 4. "Goin' Down the Road"

This Land Is Your Land: An All-American Children's Folk Classic. Rounder Records 8050 (CD and cassette), 1997; Woody Guthrie, vocals/guitar; Arlo Guthrie, vocals/guitar/piano/harmonica; James Hutchinson, bass guitar; Russ Kunkel, drums; Bob Jones, National steel guitar; Emil Richards, Native American percussion; Sid Page, violin; Steve Conn, accordion; Danny Wilson, mandolin; Frank Fuchs, guitar; Tom Burton, vocals/spoons; Sam Riney, clarinet/saxophone; Eric Weissberg, banjo/jaw harp/mandolin; Doug Noewine, soprano sax; Vincent Tividad, flute (Arlo's voice and the different instruments heard in Woody's vocals are obviously dubbed).

Track 2. "Riding in My Car," Woody Guthrie, vocal/guitar; Eric Weissberg, jaw harp/banjo; James Hutchinson, bass guitar (dubbed over), and possibly others
Track 5. "This Land Is Your Land," Woody Guthrie, vocal/guitar; Arlo Guthrie, vocal/harmonica; James Hutchinson, bass guitar; Bob Jones, National steel guitar
Track 8. "Grassey Grass Grass," Woody Guthrie, vocal; Emil Richards, Native American percussion; Vincent Tividad, flute

Why, Oh, Why? and other nonsense and activity songs for very early childhood. Folkways Records FC 7016 and FC 7016C (cassette), 1985; notes "Very Early Songs for

Mother and Child" by Stackabones, and Mommy, and Woody Guthrie; compiled by Moses Asch and edited by Sam Charters. Woody Guthrie, vocal/guitar.

SIDE I
Band 1. "Why, Oh Why?"
Band 2. "Pick It Up"
Band 3. "Pretty and Shiny-o"
Band 4. "Needle Sing"
Band 5. "Build My House"
Band 6. "Goodnight Little Darling"

SIDE 2
Band 1. "My Yellow Crayon"
Band 2. "Roll On"
Band 3. "Jiggy Jiggy Bum"
Band 4. "Bubble Gum"
Band 5. "Goodnight Little Darling" (reprise)

Woody Guthrie. Archive of Folk Music (Everest Records) FM-104, FS-204 (12" LP), n.d., notes, anon.; back of slipcase "Woodie [*sic*] Guthrie"; for songs, see *Legendary Woody Guthrie, The: In Memoriam.*

Woody Guthrie. Stinson Records SLP 44 (10" LP), CA 44 (cassette), n.d., notes by Kenneth S. Goldstein. Woody Guthrie, vocal/guitar; and Cisco Houston, vocal/guitar.

SIDE I
Band 1. "Gypsy Davy"
Band 2. "More Pretty Girls Than One"
Band 3. "Pretty Boy Floyd"
Band 4. "Poor Boy"

SIDE 2
Band 1. "John Henry"
Band 2. "Ranger's Command"
Band 3. "Ain't Gonna Be Treated This Way"
Band 4. "Buffalo Skinners"

Woody Guthrie. TKO Records (United Audio Entertainment, import) UAE30242, 1996. Members Edition, picture disc CD. (From previously issued Stinson material only in a different sequence. The insert has so many mistakes that "*sic*" would have to follow each entry; therefore, I have made corrections.)

Track 1. "John Henry"
Track 2. "Long John"
Track 3. "Hey Lolly"
Track 4. "Buffalo Skinners"
Track 5. "Gypsy Davy"
Track 6. "Worried Man Blues"
Track 7. "More Pretty Girls Than One"
Track 8. "Ain't Gonna Be Treated This Way"
Track 9. "Rangers Command"
Track 10. "Poor Boy"

Track 11. "Lonesome Day"
Track 12. "Pretty Boy Floyd"
Track 13. "Hard, Ain't It Hard"
Track 14. "Stackolee"
Track 15. "Cumberland Gap"
Track 16. "Old Time Religion"
Track 17. "Sourwood Mountain"
Track 18. "Lost John"
Track 19. "Columbus Stockade"
Track 20. "Bury Me Beneath the Willow"
Track 21. "Chain Gang Special"
Track 22. "Ezekiel Saw the Wheel"

Woody Guthrie, Vol. 1. Joker SM 3960 (12" LP), 1982, [Italy]; the songs are the same as heard on *Immortal Woody Guthrie,* but the producers changed the sequence.

SIDE 1
Band 1. "Little Black Train"
Band 2. "Who's Going to Shoe Your Pretty Feet"
Band 3. "Bed on the Floor"
Band 4. "Jack Hammer Blues"
Band 5. "John Henry"
SIDE 2
Band 1. "Brown Eyes"
Band 2. "The House of the Rising Sun"
Band 3. "Danville Girl, No. 2"
Band 4. "Ride Old Paint"

Woody Guthrie and Cisco Houston, Vol 1. Stinson Records SLP 44 (12" LP) and CA 44 (cassette), n.d., notes anon. Woody Guthrie, vocal/guitar; and Cisco Houston, vocal/guitar.

SIDE 1
Band 1. "Gypsy Davy"
Band 2. "More Pretty Gals Than One"
Band 3. "Pretty Boy Floyd"
Band 4. "Buffalo Skinners"
Band 5. "Hey Lolly Lolly"
Band 6. "Lonesome Day"
SIDE 2
Band 1. "John Henry"
Band 2. "Ranger's Command"
Band 3. "Ain't Gonna Be Treated This Way"
Band 4. "Poor Boy"
Band 5. "Hard, Ain't It Hard"
Band 6. "Worried Man Blues"

Woody Guthrie and Cisco Houston: More Songs, Vol. 2. Stinson Records SLP 53 (10" LP and 12" LP), 1963. Woody Guthrie and Cisco Houston; notes anon. On the back of slipcase it states, "Volume 1." Woody Guthrie (vocal/guitar) and Cisco Houston (vocal/guitar).

SIDE 1

Band 1. "Take a Whiff on Me"
Band 2. "Bad Lee Brown"
Band 3. "The Golden Vanity"
Band 4. "Cumberland Gap"

SIDE 2

Band 1. "Columbus Stockade"
Band 2. "Johnny Hard"
Band 3. "Foggy Mountain Top"
Band 4. "Bury Me Beneath the Willow"

Woody Guthrie and Cisco Houston, Vol. 1 and 2: The Stinson Collectors Series. Collectables Records COL-CD-5605, 1995 (this is a reissue of songs issued by Stinson Records on SLP 44 and SLP 53, and the song sequence is the same as on the long-play recordings).

Track 1. "Gypsy Davy," Woody Guthrie, vocal/guitar

Track 2. "More Pretty Gals Than One," Woody Guthrie, vocal/mandolin; Cisco Houston, vocal/guitar

Track 3. "Pretty Boy Floyd," Woody Guthrie, vocal/guitar

Track 4. "Buffalo Skinners," Woody Guthrie, vocal/guitar

Track 5. "Hey Lolly Lolly," Woody Guthrie, vocal/mandolin; Cisco Houston, vocal/guitar; Sonny Terry, harmonica

Track 6. "Lonesome Day," Woody Guthrie, vocal/mandolin; Cisco Houston, vocal/guitar; Sonny Terry, harmonica

Track 7. "John Henry," Woody Guthrie, vocal/guitar; Cisco Houston, vocal/guitar

Track 8. "Ranger's Command," Woody Guthrie, vocal/guitar

Track 9. "Ain't Gonna Be Treated This Way," Woody Guthrie, vocal/guitar; Cisco Houston, vocal/guitar

Track 10. "Poor Boy," Woody Guthrie, vocal/guitar; Cisco Houston, vocal/guitar [?]

Track 11. "Hard, Ain't It Hard," Woody Guthrie, vocal/mandolin; Cisco Houston, vocal/guitar

Track 12. "Worried Man Blues," Woody Guthrie, vocal/guitar; Cisco Houston, vocal

Track 13. "Take a Whiff on Me," Woody Guthrie, vocal/guitar; Cisco Houston, vocal

Track 14. "Skip to My Lou," Woody Guthrie, vocal/mandolin; Cisco Houston, guitar; Sonny Terry, harmonica

Track 15. "Ezekial Saw the Wheel," Woody Guthrie, vocal/guitar; Cisco Houston, vocal; Sonny Terry, harmonica

Track 16. "Johnny Hard," Woody Guthrie, vocal/guitar

Track 17. "Columbus Stockade," Woody Guthrie, vocal/mandolin (?); Cisco Houston, vocal/guitar

Track 18. "Foggy Mountain Top," Woody Guthrie, vocal/mandolin; Cisco Houston, vocal/guitar

Track 19. "Sourwood Mountain," Woody Guthrie, vocal/mandolin; Cisco Houston, vocal/guitar; Sonny Terry, harmonica

Track 20. "Bad Lee Brown (Cocaine Blues)," Woody Guthrie, vocal/guitar

Track 21. "Cumberland Gap," Woody Guthrie, vocal/mandolin; Cisco Houston, vocal/guitar; Sonny Terry, harmonica

Track 22. "The Golden Vanity," Woody Guthrie, vocal/guitar; "Peter" Hawes, vocal harmony?

Track 23. "Old Time Religion," Woody Guthrie, vocal/mandolin; Cisco Houston, vocal/guitar; Sonny Terry, harmonica; Brownie McGhee, background response [?]

Track 24. "Bury Me Beneath the Willow," Woody Guthrie, vocal/mandolin; Cisco Houston, vocal/guitar; Sonny Terry, harmonica

Woody Guthrie: The Asch Recordings, Vol. 1, This Land Is Your Land. Smithsonian/Folkways Recordings (CD) 40100, 1997. Compiled by Jeff Place and Guy Logsdon, and annotated by Guy Logsdon and Jeff Place.

Track 1. "This Land Is Your Land," Woody Guthrie, vocal/guitar

Track 2. "Car Song," Woody Guthrie, vocal/guitar

Track 3. "Ramblin' Round," Woody Guthrie, vocal/guitar/harmonica

Track 4. "Talking Fishing Blues," Woody Guthrie, vocal/guitar

Track 5. "Philadelphia Lawyer," Woody Guthrie, lead vocal/guitar; Cisco Houston, harmony vocal

Track 6. "Lindbergh," Woody Guthrie, vocal/guitar

Track 7. "Hobo's Lullaby," Woody Guthrie, vocal/guitar

Track 8. "Pastures of Plenty," Woody Guthrie, vocal/guitar/harmonica

Track 9. "Grand Coulee Dam," Woody Guthrie, vocal/guitar

Track 10. "End of the Line," Woody Guthrie, vocal/guitar; Sonny Terry, harmonica

Track 11. "New York Town," Woody Guthrie, lead vocal/guitar; Cisco Houston, harmony vocal

Track 12. "Gypsy Davy," Woody Guthrie, vocal/guitar

Track 13. "Jesus Christ," Woody Guthrie, vocal/guitar

Track 14. "This Land Is Your Land," Woody Guthrie, vocal/guitar

Track 15. "Do-Re-Mi," Woody Guthrie, vocal/guitar

Track 16. "Jarama Valley," Woody Guthrie, vocal/guitar

Track 17. "The Biggest Thing Man Has Ever Done," Woody Guthrie, vocal/guitar

Track 18. "Picture from Life's Other Side," Woody Guthrie, lead vocal/mandolin; Cisco Houston, harmony vocal/guitar; Bess Lomax Hawes, harmony vocal

Track 19. "Jesse James," Woody Guthrie, vocal/guitar

Track 20. "Talking Hard Work," Woody Guthrie, vocal/guitar

Track 21. "When That Great Ship Went Down," Woody Guthrie, lead vocal/mandolin; Cisco Houston, harmony vocal/guitar; Sonny Terry, harmonica

Track 22. "Hard, Ain't It Hard," Woody Guthrie, lead vocal/mandolin; Cisco Houston, harmony vocal/guitar

Track 23. "Going Down the Road Feeling Bad," Woody Guthrie, lead vocal/mandolin; Cisco Houston, harmony vocal/guitar; Sonny Terry, harmonica

Track 24. "I Ain't Got Nobody," Woody Guthrie, vocal/lead guitar; Cisco Houston, rhythm guitar

Track 25. "Sinking of the Reuben James," Woody Guthrie, vocal/guitar

Track 26. "Why, Oh Why?" Woody Guthrie, vocal/guitar/harmonica

Track 27. "This Land Is Your Land," Woody Guthrie, vocal/guitar; Cisco Houston, vocal

Woody Guthrie: The Asch Recordings, Vol. 2, Muleskinner Blues. Smithsonian/Folkways Recordings (CD) 40101, 1997. Compiled by Jeff Place and Guy Logsdon, and annotated by Guy Logsdon and Jeff Place.

Track 1. "Muleskinner Blues," Woody Guthrie, lead vocal/guitar; Cisco Houston, harmony vocal; Pete Seeger, banjo

Track 2. "Wreck of the Old 97," Woody Guthrie, vocal; Cisco Houston, guitar

Track 3. "Sally Goodin'," Woody Guthrie, vocal/fiddle; Cisco Houston/guitar; Sonny Terry, harmonica

Track 4. "Little Black Train," Woody Guthrie, vocal/guitar

Track 5. "Who's Gonna Shoe Your Pretty Little Feet," Woody Guthrie, lead vocal/guitar; Cisco Houston, harmony vocal

Track 6. "Baltimore to Washington," Woody Guthrie, vocal/harmony/guitar; Cisco Houston, vocal/harmony/guitar

Track 7. "Rubber Dolly," Woody Guthrie, lead vocal/mandolin; Cisco Houston, harmony vocal/guitar; Sonny Terry, harmonica

Track 8. "21 Years," Woody Guthrie, lead vocal/mandolin; Cisco Houston, harmony vocal/guitar

Track 9. "Sowing on the Mountain," Woody Guthrie, harmony vocal (bass line); Cisco Houston, lead vocal/guitar

Track 10. "Bed on the Floor," Woody Guthrie, lead vocal/mandolin; Cisco Houston, harmony vocal/guitar

Track 11. "Take a Whiff on Me," Woody Guthrie, lead vocal/guitar; Cisco Houston, harmony vocal/guitar

Track 12. "Stepstone," Woody Guthrie, lead vocal/mandolin; Cisco Houston, harmony vocal/guitar; Sonny Terry, harmonica; Bess Lomax Hawes, harmony vocal

Track 13. "Put My Little Shoes Away," Woody Guthrie, lead vocal/mandolin; Cisco Houston, harmony vocal/guitar; Sonny Terry, harmonica

Track 14. "Hen Cackle," Woody Guthrie, fiddle; Cisco Houston, vocal/guitar

Track 15. "Poor Boy," Woody Guthrie, vocal/guitar

Track 16. "Stackolee," Woody Guthrie, vocal/guitar

Track 17. "Johnny Hart," Woody Guthrie, vocal/guitar

Track 18. "Worried Man Blues," Woody Guthrie, lead vocal/guitar; Cisco Houston, harmony vocal/guitar

Track 19. "Danville Girl," Woody Guthrie, lead vocal/guitar; Cisco Houston, harmony vocal/guitar

Track 20. "Gambling Man," Woody Guthrie, lead vocal/mandolin; Cisco Houston, harmony vocal/guitar

Track 21. "Rye Straw," Woody Guthrie, fiddle; Cisco Houston, guitar; Bess Lomax Hawes, mandolin

Track 22. "Crawdad Song," Woody Guthrie, lead vocal/mandolin; Cisco Houston, harmony vocal/guitar; Sonny Terry, harmonica

Track 23. "Ida Red," Woody Guthrie, lead vocal/mandolin; Cisco Houston, harmony vocal/guitar; Bess Lomax Hawes, harmony vocal

Track 24. "Keep My Skillet Good and Greasy," Woody Guthrie, lead vocal/mandolin; Cisco Houston, harmony vocal/guitar; Sonny Terry, harmonica

Track 25. "Train 45," Woody Guthrie, vocal; Bess Lomax Hawes, mandolin; Butch Hawes, guitar

Woody Guthrie: Columbia River Collection. Rounder Records LP (record), CS (cassette), CD (compact disc) 1036, 1987. Notes by Bill Murlin; reissued in England by Topic Records 12T448. Issued as a part of the fiftieth anniversary of the Bonneville Power Administration; refer to Woody Guthrie's book *Roll On Columbia: The Columbia River Songs,* edited by Bill Murlin, Portland, Ore.: Bonneville Power Administration, 1987, reissued by Sing Out, 1991. Woody Guthrie (vocals/guitar).

SIDE 1
- Band 1. "Oregon Trail"
- Band 2. "Roll on Columbia"
- Band 3. "New Found Land"
- Band 4. "Talking Columbia"
- Band 5. "Roll Columbia, Roll"
- Band 6. "Columbia's Water"
- Band 7. "Ramblin' Blues"
- Band 8. "It Takes a Married Man to Sing a Worried Song"
- Band 9. "Hard Travelin'"

SIDE 2
- Band 1. "The Biggest Thing That Man Has Ever Done"
- Band 2. "Jackhammer Blues"
- Band 3. "Song of the Grand Coulee"
- Band 4. "Grand Coulee Dam"
- Band 5. "Washington Talkin' Blues"
- Band 6. "Ramblin' Round"
- Band 7. "Pastures of Plenty"
- Band 8. "End of My Line"

Woody Guthrie: The Early Years. Tradition/Everest Records 2088 (12" LP), n.d., notes anon. Woody Guthrie, vocal/guitar, unless otherwise noted.

SIDE 1
- Band 1. "Stackolee," with Sonny Terry
- Band 2. "Cumberland Gap," with Cisco Houston and Sonny Terry
- Band 3. "Old Time Religion," with Cisco Houston and Sonny Terry
- Band 4. "Sourwood Mountain"
- Band 5. "Long John"

SIDE 2
- Band 1. "Lost John," with Sonny Terry
- Band 2. "Columbus Stockade," with Cisco Houston
- Band 3. "Bury Me Beneath the Willow," with Cisco Houston and Sonny Terry
- Band 4. "Chain Gang Special," with Sonny Terry
- Band 5. "Ezekial Saw the Wheel," with Cisco Houston and Sonny Terry

Woody Guthrie: The Early Years. With guest artists Cisco Houston and Sonny Terry. Legacy International CD 345 (CD); reissued without the last two cuts in Austria, GEMA CM 8018, 1993.

- Track 1. "Hey, Lolly Lolly"
- Track 2. "Buffalo Skinners"
- Track 3. "John Henry"
- Track 4. "Gypsy Davy"
- Track 5. "Worried Man Blues"
- Track 6. "More Pretty Girls Than One"
- Track 7. "Ain't Gonna Be Treated That Way"
- Track 8. "Rangers Command"
- Track 9. "Poor Boy"
- Track 10. "Lonesome Day"

Track 11. "Pretty Boy Floyd"
Track 12. "Hard, Ain't It Hard"
Track 13. "Stackolee"
Track 14. "Cumberland Gap"
Track 15. "Old Time Religion"
Track 16. "Sourwood Mountain"
Track 17. "Long John"
Track 18. "Lost John"
Track 19. "Columbus Stockade"
Track 20. "Bury Me Beneath the Willow"
Track 21. "Chain Gang Special"
Track 22. "Ezekiel Saw the Wheel"

Woody Guthrie/Folk Hero. Magnum America TKCD 005, 1996; notes by Patrick Humphries. The songs are from Stinson Records releases and have been issued under numerous collection titles by Stinson, Tradition/Everest, Collectibles, and many other company labels.

Track 1. "John Henry"
Track 2. "Worried Man Blues"
Track 3. "Pretty Boy Floyd"
Track 4. "Lost John"
Track 5. "Bury Me Beneath the Willow"
Track 6. "Ezekiel Saw the Wheel"
Track 7. "Lonesome Day"
Track 8. "Buffalo Skinners"
Track 9. "Gypsy Davy"
Track 10. "Cumberland Gap"
Track 11. "Poor Boy"
Track 12. "Chain Gang Special"
Track 13. "Columbus Stockade"
Track 14. "Hard, Ain't It Hard"
Track 15. "More Pretty Girls Than One"
Track 16. "Long John"

Woody Guthrie—A Legendary Performer (Dust Bowl Ballads). RCA Records CPL 1-2099(e) (12" LP), 1977; reissue of RCA Victor LPV-502; illustrated booklet by Guy Logsdon. Reissued by Rounder Records (LP, cassette, CD) 1040, 1988; notes edited to fit format. Woody Guthrie, vocal/guitar. Song sequence is the same on Rounder cassette and compact disc.

SIDE 1
Band 1. "The Great Dust Storm"
Band 2. "I Ain't Got No Home in This World Anymore"
Band 3. "Talkin' Dust Bowl Blues"
Band 4. "Vigilante Man"
Band 5. "Dust Cain't Kill Me"
Band 6. "Pretty Boy Floyd" previously unreleased
Band 7. "Dust Pneumonia Blues"
SIDE 2
Band 1. "Blowin' Down This Road"

Band 2. "Tom Joad, Part 1"
Band 3. "Tom Joad, Part 2"
Band 4. "Dust Bowl Refugee"
Band 5. "Do Re Mi"
Band 6. "Dust Bowl Blues" previously unreleased
Band 7. "Dusty Old Dust"

Woody Guthrie: Library of Congress Recordings. Elektra Records EKL-271/272 (three 12" LPs), 1964. Woody Guthrie recorded by Alan Lomax, March 1940; notes by Alan Lomax, Robert Shelton, and Woody Guthrie; produced and edited by Jac Holzman; reissued by Rounder Records CD 1041/2/3 (CD) and C-1041 Part 1 and Part 2 (cassette), 1988; notes are edited to fit format. Woody Guthrie (vocals/guitar/harmonica).

SIDE 1
"Lost Train Blues"
"Railroad Blues"
"Rye Whiskey"
"Old Joe Clark"
"Beaumont Rag"
SIDE 2
"Greenback Dollar"
"Boll Weevil Song"
"So Long, It's Been Good to Know You"
"Talking Dust Bowl"
"Do Re Mi"
SIDE 3
"Hard Times"
"Pretty Boy Floyd"
"They Laid Jesus Christ in His Grave"
"Jolly Banker"
"I Ain't Got no Home"
SIDE 4
"Dirty Overalls"
"Chain Around My Leg"
"Worried Man Blues"
"Lonesome Valley"
"Walkin' Down That Railroad Line"
SIDE 5
"Goin' Down That Road Feeling Bad"
"Dust Storm Disaster"
"Foggy Mountain Top"
"Dust Pneumonia Blues"
SIDE 6
"California Blues"
"Dust Bowl Refugees"
"Will Rogers Highway"
"Los Angeles New Year's Flood"

Woody Guthrie: One of a Kind. Pair Records PCD-2-1294 (CD), 1991.

Track 1. "Worried Man Blues (A Worried Man)"
Track 2. "More Pretty Girls Than One"
Track 3. "John Henry"
Track 4. "Ain't Gonna Be Treated This Way"
Track 5. "Hard, Ain't It Hard"
Track 6. "Pretty Boy Floyd"
Track 7. "Black Jack Davis [*sic*]"
Track 8. "Buffalo Skinners"
Track 9. "Rangers Command"
Track 10. "Cumberland Gap"
Track 11. "Ezekial Saw the Wheel"
Track 12. "Sourwood Mountain"
Track 13. "Stack-o-Lee"
Track 14. "Lost John"
Track 15. "Chain Gang Special"
Track 16. "Hey, Lolly Lolly"
Track 17. "Bury Me Beneath the Willow"
Track 18. "Columbus Stockade Blues"

Woody Guthrie: Poor Boy. Folkways Records FT 1010 Mono, FTS 31010 Stereo (12″ LP), 1968; notes from *Born To Win* by Woody Guthrie. Formerly released as *Bed On The Floor*, Verve/Folkways FV/FVS 9007. Woody Guthrie, vocal/guitar, unless otherwise noted.

SIDE 1
Band 1. "Baltimore to Washington"
Band 2. "Little Black Train"
Band 3. "Who's Going to Shoe Your Pretty Feet," with Cisco Houston
Band 4. "Slip Knot"
Band 5. "Poor Boy"
Band 6. "Mean Talking Blues"
Band 7. "Stepstone," with Cisco Houston and Sonny Terry
SIDE 2
Band 1. "Bed on the Floor," with Cisco Houston
Band 2. "Little Darling," with Cisco Houston and Sonny Terry
Band 3. "Miner's Song"
Band 4. "Train Blues," instrumental
Band 5. "Danville Girl #2," with Cisco Houston
Band 6. "Ride an Old Paint," with Cisco Houston

Woody Guthrie Sings Folk Songs, Vol. 1. Folkways Records FA 2483 (12″ LP), 1962. Woody Guthrie, Lead Belly, Cisco Houston, Sonny Terry, and Bess Hawes; notes by Pete Seeger. Reissued by Smithsonian/Folkways CD SF 40007 (CD), C SF 40007 (cassette), 1989, original notes by Pete Seeger. Woody Guthrie, vocal/guitar, unless otherwise noted.

SIDE 1
Band 1. "Hard Traveling," with Sonny Terry and Cisco Houston
Band 2. "What Did the Deep Sea Say?" with Cisco Houston
Band 3. "House of the Rising Sun"

Band 4. "Nine Hundred Miles," instrumental; Woody Guthrie, fiddle; and Cisco
   Houston, guitar
Band 5. "John Henry," with Cisco Houston
Band 6. "Oregon Trail"
Band 7. "We Shall Be Free," with Leadbelly, Cisco Houston, and Sonny Terry
SIDE 2
Band 1. "Dirty Overalls" with Cisco Houston
Band 2. "Jack Hammer Blues" with Cisco Houston and Sonny Terry
Band 3. "Springfield Mountain" with Sonny Terry, Cisco Houston, and Bess
   Hawes
Band 4. "Brown Eyes," with Cisco Houston
Band 5. "Boll Weevil Blues," with Sonny Terry and Cisco Houston
Band 6. "Guitar Blues," instrumental, with Cisco Houston
Band 7. "Will You Miss Me?" with Cisco Houston and Bess Hawes

Woody Guthrie Sings Folk Songs, Vol. 2. Folkways Records FA 2484 (12" LP), 1964.
Woody Guthrie, Cisco Houston, and Sonny Terry; notes by Pete Seeger. Woody
Guthrie, vocal/guitar, unless otherwise noted.

SIDE 1
Band 1. "Keep My Skillet Good and Greasy"
Band 2. "Talking Hard Luck Blues"
Band 3. "Whoopee Ti Yi Yo, Get Along Little Dogies"
Band 4. "A Picture From Life's Other Side," with Cisco Houston
Band 5. "Hen Cackle"
Band 6. "Danville Girl"
Band 7. "Put My Little Shoes Away"
SIDE 2
Band 1. "Sally Goodin'"
Band 2. "Hard, Ain't It Hard"
Band 3. "Gamblin' Man"
Band 4. "The Wreck of the Old '97"
Band 5. "Take a Whiff on Me"
Band 6. "Make Me a Pallet on Your Floor"
Band 7. "Buffalo Gal"
Band 8. "Goin' Down This Road Feelin' Bad"

Woody's 20 Grow Big Songs. Featuring the voice of Woody Guthrie, with the voices of
his children and grandchildren (Arlo Guthrie, Joady Guthrie, Nora Guthrie Rotante,
Abraham Guthrie, Cathyaliza Guthrie, Annie Guthrie, Anna Rotante, Sarah Lee
Guthrie, Damon Guthrie). Rising Son Records RSR 0004 (cassette and CD), 1992;
Warner Bros. Records 45020-2 (CD), 45021 and 45022 (cassettes), 1992.

SIDE 1
Track 1. "Wake Up"
Track 2. "Cleano"
Track 3. "Mailman"
Track 4. "Put Your Finger in the Air"
Track 5. "Dance Around"
Track 6. "Don't You Push Me Down"

Track 7. "Merry Go Round"
Track 8. "Jig Along Home"
Track 9. "Howdy Doo"
Track 10. "All Work Together"
SIDE 2
Track 1. "Bling Blang"
Track 2. "Needle Song"
Track 3. "Pick It Up"
Track 4. "Riding in My Car"
Track 5. "Race You Down the Mountain"
Track 6. "My Dolly"
Track 7. "Little Seed"
Track 8. "Little Bird"
Track 9. "Pretty and Shinyo"
Track 10. "Sleep Eye"

Worried Man Blues, Golden Classics, Part One. See Legendary Woody Guthrie, The: In Memoriam.

Worried Man Blues. Top Ten (Special Music Company) SCD-4824, 1991 (CD; different from Golden Classics, Part One).

Track 1. "Worried Man Blues (A Worried Man)"
Track 2. "John Henry"
Track 3. "Pretty Boy Floyd"
Track 4. "Black Jack Davie"
Track 5. "Cumberland Gap"
Track 6. "Ezekial Saw the Wheel"
Track 7. "Sourwood Mountain"
Track 8. "Stack-O-Lee"
Track 9. "Lost John"
Track 10. "Chain Gang Special"

RADIO SHOWS

See the following Radio Shows entered in Recording Sessions:

American School of the Air, 2 April 1940
Lead Belly Radio Show, no date, ca. 1940
Back Where I Come From, 19 August 1940
Cavalcade of America, 6 November 1940
Labor for Victory, 29 August 1942
Ballad Gazette, ca. 1943 or 1944
The Martins and the Coys: A Contemporary Folk Tale
British Broadcasting Corporation Recordings, 7 July 1944
Cavalcade of America, 25 December 1944
Hootenanny, 10 March 1947

In a ca. 1944 MS, TRO Richmond Music, Woody typed that he also had appeared on the following radio shows, but I have been unable to locate copies or logs of the programs:

Hobby Lobby
We the People
It's the Navy (songs)
Meet Your Neighbor (interview)
Pursuit of Happiness (two or three times)
OWI Broadcasts to *Fighting Fronts, Parade of the States,* several other OWI shows
"Old Chisholm Trail" (BBC)
WABF "Tomorrow's People" interview
The Author and The Critic (Upper New York somewhere)
Labor for Victory (two or three times; see entry above for one show)
"This Is War," Norman Corwin with the Almanac Singers
Pipe Smoking Time (U.S. Tobacco Co.) (for a while)
Other local stations over the country.

MOTION PICTURES, TELEVISION, AND VIDEOS

[1940] The Fight for Life
Directed and edited by Para Lorentz; produced by the United States Film Service for the Public Health Service and distributed by Columbia Pictures; a full-length black-and-white feature film. Woody made a cameo appearance in this film that was based on Dr. Paul de Kruif's book by the same title; the themes were the problems of childbirth among the unemployed and malnutrition. The basic setting was the Chicago Maternity Center, and even though Woody made reference to being employed as an actor, he is seen only as a man walking into a small café; his wife, Mary Jennings Guthrie, is also seen seated in the café. He plays no music and speaks no dialogue. His is a cameo appearance as an extra. The copy I viewed is in the National Archives, Washington, D.C. For complete information about this film, see Robert L. Snyder, *Pare Lorentz and the Documentary Film* (Norman: University of Oklahoma Press, 1968).

[1945] The Library of Congress
Office of War Information, Overseas Branch, American Scene Series 11. Woody is filmed (45-second clip) singing "Rangers Command."

[1947] To Hear Your Banjo Play
Directed and narrated by Alan Lomax, Brandon Films and Independent Films; features Woody Guthrie, Pete Seeger, Brownie McGhee, Sonny Terry, Texas Gladden, and Horton Barker.
    "John Henry," Woody Guthrie, vocal/guitar; Sonny Terry, vocal/harmonica; Brownie McGhee, vocal/guitar

[1941, 1949] The Columbia
Production information missing from my copy of the film, filmed and recorded ca. 1941, released in 1949. For more information and the lyrics sung by Woody Guthrie, see Woody Guthrie, *"Roll on Columbia": The Columbia River Songs,* edited by Bill Murlin, Portland, Ore.: Bonneville Power Administration, 1988 and *Woody Guthrie: Columbia River Collection,* Rounder Records LP (cassette, CD) 1036, 1987.
    "Pastures of Plenty," Woody Guthrie
    "Roll, Columbia," Woody Guthrie
    "The Biggest Thing That Man Has Ever Done," Woody Guthrie

[1965–66] A Tribute to Woody Guthrie
Pete Seeger in his Rainbow Quest series, produced and directed by Sholom Rubinstein, 1965–66, distributed by Central Sun Video, Reston, Virginia. Pete Seeger, vocals/banjo/twelve-string guitar, sings ten Woody songs, plus "John Henry." Woody Guthrie, Sonny Terry, and Brownie McGhee film clip from *To Hear Your Banjo Play*

[1972] VD Blues
Presented by Educational Broadcasting Corporation, 1972, with Dick Cavett, produced by Don Fouser and WNET/New York, directed by Sidney Smith, 1972. "A Child of VD" written by Woody Guthrie, 1949, and sung by Arlo Guthrie

[1976] Bound For Glory
Produced by Robert F. Blumofe and Harold Leventhal; directed by Hal Ashby; starring David Carradine, United Artists, 1976. Music by Woody Guthrie, adapted and conducted by Leonard Rosenman, and sung by Carradine and/or orchestral adaptations.

[1981] The Weavers: Wasn't That a Time
Jim Brown Productions, 1981; distributed by MGM/UA Home Video MB500218. "Woody's Rag" is performed by the Weavers.

[1984] Woody Guthrie: Hard Travelin'
Produced by Jim Brown, Harold Leventhal, and Ginger Turek; directed by Jim Brown, 1984 (see *Woody Guthrie: Hard Travelin'*, Arloco Records ARL-284, 1984). Hoyt Axton, Joan Baez, Judy Collins, Jack Elliott, Ronnie Gilbert, Arlo Guthrie, Rose Maddox, Bill Murlin, Holly Near, Pete Seeger, Sonny Terry, and Matt Jennings perform Woody Guthrie songs.
> "This Land Is Your Land," Woody Guthrie, voice over photographs
> "Oklahoma Hills," Arlo Guthrie and the Oklahoma Swing Band
> "Philadelphia Lawyer," Rose Maddox with Arlo Guthrie and the Oklahoma Swing Band
> "Hard Travelin'," Jack Elliott and Arlo Guthrie with Sonny Terry
> "Deportee (Plane Wreck at Los Gatos)," Hoyt Axton and Arlo Guthrie
> "Roll Columbia Roll (Grand Coulee Dam)," Bill Murlin and Arlo Guthrie
> "Union Maid" Pete Seeger and Arlo Guthrie
> "New York Town," Arlo Guthrie and Jack Elliott
> "Pastures of Plenty," Holly Near and Ronnie Gilbert with Jeff Langley (piano)
> "The Sinking of the Reuben James," Pete Seeger and Arlo Guthrie
> "Talking Sailor (Talking Merchant Marine)," Jack Elliott
> "Riding in My Car," Judy Collins and Arlo Guthrie
> "Lonesome Valley," Joan Baez
> "Hobo's Lullaby (G Reeves)," Arlo Guthrie and Pete Seeger
> "This Land Is Your Land," Arlo Guthrie, Pete Seeger, and each of the performers singing different lines

[1987] Woody Guthrie. Arena
British Broadcasting Company; Paul Lee, director; Anthony Wall and Nigel Finch, executive producers; 1987. The first five songs listed came from the album *Woody Guthrie: Library of Congress Recordings*.
> "Lost Train Blues"

"So Long, It's Been Good to Know You"
"I Ain't Got No Home"
"Talking Dust Bowl Blues"
"Jesus Christ"
"This Land Is Your Land," Matt Jennings, harmonica
"This Land Is Your Land," Pete Seeger
"Pastures of Plenty," Woody Guthrie, from the film *The Columbia*
"Hard Travelin'," Woody Guthrie
"Ranger's Command," Woody Guthrie, film clip from *The Library of Congress*
"John Henry," Woody Guthrie, Sonny Terry, and Brownie McGhee, film clip
"Pastures of Plenty," Pete Seeger
"Riding in My Car," Woody Guthrie, from BBC *Children's Hour* radio broadcast, 1947
"Hard Traveling," Pete Seeger, from BBC (television) *Tonight in Person*, 1964
"Pretty Boy Floyd," Jack Elliott
"This Land Is Your Land," Woody Guthrie

[1988] A Vision Shared: A Tribute to Woody Guthrie and Lead Belly
Directed by Jim Brown; produced by Jim Brown, Harold Leventhal, and The Ginger Group. CBS Music Video Enterprises VHS 49006, 1988. Arlo Guthrie, Bruce Springsteen, John Mellencamp, U2, Emmylou Harris, Pete Seeger, and Sweet Honey in the Rock perform Woody Guthrie songs; narrated by Robbie Robertson (songs by Lead Belly are included as well as Bob Dylan singing "Hey, Woody Guthrie")
"This Land Is Your Land," Woody Guthrie (voice over photographs)
"Do Re Mi," John Mellencamp
"Vigilante Man," Bruce Springsteen
"Deportee," Arlo Guthrie and Emmylou Harris
"I Ain't Got No Home," Bruce Springsteen
"Jesus Christ," U2
"Grand Coulee Dam," Arlo Guthrie
"Union Maid," Arlo Guthrie and Pete Seeger
"I've Got to Know," Sweet Honey in the Rock
"Put Your Finger in the Air," Pete Seeger
"Ramblin' Round," Woody Guthrie (voice over photographs)
"Hobo's Lullaby (G Reeves)," Emmylou Harris
"This Land Is Your Land," Woody Guthrie with Arlo Guthrie (voice dubbed), followed by Bruce Springsteen, Taj Mahal, Emmylou Harris, Little Richard, U2, and John Mellencamp, each singing a verse.

Contributors

MARY KATHERINE ALDIN has been involved in the preservation of American roots music since 1962. As a freelance independent reissue producer, she is responsible for the award-winning series of twenty-four live Newport Folk Festival CDs for Vanguard Records. In addition, she has produced and/or annotated more than one hundred reissues of American roots music on various labels. Her writing credits include fourteen years as contributing and associate editor of *Living Blues Magazine,* a 1990 Grammy Award nomination for her liner notes to *Muddy Waters: The Chess Box* (MCA), a 1991 NAIRD Award for her liner notes to *The Kentucky Colonels: Long Journey Home* (Vanguard); and a 1993 NAIRD Award for her liner notes to the Weavers' box set *Wasn't That a Time* (Vanguard). She contributed the concluding chapter to the Deems Taylor award-winning book *Nothing But the Blues* (Abbeville Press, 1993). She is also at work on a biography of Muddy Waters and another on the Reverend Gary Davis.

ROBERT CANTWELL is associate professor of American Studies at the University of North Carolina, Chapel Hill. He also served as a writer and scholar in the Office of Folklife Programs at the Smithsonian Institution from 1985 to 1989. He has taught English at Georgetown University (1988–89), the University of Iowa (1986–87), Kenyon College (1970–80) and Exeter University, U.K. (1979–80). He is the author of *Ethnomimesis: Folklife and the Representation of Culture* (University of North Carolina Press, 1993) and *Bluegrass Breakdown: The Making of the Old Southern Sound* (University of Illinois Press, 1984). His latest book, *When We Were Good: The Folk Revival* (Harvard University Press, 1996), focuses on the history of twentieth-century folk music and its ability to cross boundaries of race and class as well as geography.

RONALD D. COHEN is professor of history at Indiana University (Northwest) where he has taught since 1970. He is the author of *"Wasn't That a Time!": Firsthand Accounts of the Folk Music Revival* (Scarecrow Press, 1995) and is currently working on a book called *Rainbow Quest: Folk Music and American Society, 1940–1970.* Cohen has also coproduced, with Dave Samuelson, a ten-CD box set with book, *Songs For Political Action: Folk Music, Topical Songs and the American Left, 1926–1954* (Bear Family Records, 1996).

EMILY DAVIDSON manages academic and scholastic programs at the Rock and Roll Hall of Fame and Museum where she has worked since 1995. Her ongoing responsibilities include popular music curriculum development and directing the museum's American Music Masters conferences and the annual summer teacher institute. Recently, she has also created symposia on Janis Joplin and Elvis Presley. Prior to joining the museum, Davidson was assistant curator of education at the Cincinnati Art Museum.

Davidson holds a B.A. in English from Williams College and an M.A. in Art History from Case Western Reserve University.

ARLO GUTHRIE, the eldest son of Woody and Marjorie Guthrie, started making a name for himself on the folk scene in the late 1960s, gaining notoriety with his twenty-minute song/story/anthem "Alice's Restaurant Massacree." More than ten years ago, he started his own label, Rising Son, on which he reissued his own music and released the soundtrack to the PBS documentary *Woody Guthrie: Hard Travelin'*. Most recently, Guthrie has released an album titled *Mystic Journey*, and has written an award-winning children's book, *Mooses Come Walking*.

NORA GUTHRIE, Woody Guthrie's daughter, began her professional career as a modern dancer in New York City. A graduate of New York University School of the Arts in 1971, she choreographed and performed her works throughout the United States for many years. She now acts as director of the Woody Guthrie Archives and president of Woody Guthrie Productions, creating and developing new projects and outlets for her father's materials. A recent project was serving as cocurator for the major Woody Guthrie traveling exhibition organized by the Smithsonian Institution.

ELLEN G. LANDAU is a professor in the Case Western Reserve University/Cleveland Museum of Art Joint Program in Art History. She is a specialist in modern and contemporary art, particularly abstract expressionism. Her scholarly interests include popular culture of the 1940s and 1950s. Landau has been the guest curator for exhibitions in the United States, Germany, and Switzerland, and has written numerous articles and catalogue essays. She has written two books: *Jackson Pollack* (Abrams, 1989) and *Lee Krasner: A Catalogue Raisonné* (Abrams, 1995).

HAROLD LEVENTHAL, long-time personal manager of the Weavers, Pete Seeger, Judy Collins, and Arlo Guthrie, took care of Woody Guthrie's affairs beginning in 1953, when Woody was hospitalized with Huntington's disease. In 1972 Leventhal helped organize the Woody Guthrie Foundation with Woody's widow Marjorie Guthrie and in 1995, the Woody Guthrie Archives. Leventhal has been on the music scene for some fifty years as manager, film and theatrical producer, music publisher, and concert promoter. His early concert performers include Johnny Cash, Bob Dylan, Neil Young, Peter, Paul and Mary, and Joan Baez among many others. His film credits include *Bound For Glory, Hard Travelin'*, *Wasn't That a Time* and *A Vision Shared*.

GUY LOGSDON is an internationally recognized authority on Woody Guthrie as well as on cowboy music, poetry, and musicians. In 1990–91, he received a senior post-doctoral fellowship at the Smithsonian Institution to compile a biblio/discography of the songs of Woody Guthrie, and in 1993 the National Endowment for the Humanities awarded him a major independent scholar grant to continue the project. Logsdon, along with Jeff Place, has compiled and annotated numerous CD collections including: *Woody Guthrie: Long Ways to Travel, The Unreleased Folkways Masters, 1944–1949* (Smithsonian/Folkways, 1994); *That's Why We're Marching: World War II and the American Folk Song Movement* (Smithsonian/Folkways, 1996); and their latest collaboration, *Woody Guthrie: This Land Is Your Land, The Asch Recordings, Vol. 1* and *Woody Guthrie: Muleskinner Blues, The Asch Recordings, Vol. 2* (Smithsonian/Folkways Recordings, 1997). In addition, he worked on *Cisco Houston: The Folkways Years, 1944–1961* (Smithsonian/Folkways, 1994) and four cowboy/western collections for Bear Family Records. Logsdon is also the author of the award-wining

"The Whorehouse Bells Were Ringing" and Other Songs Cowboys Sing (University of Illinois Press, 1989) and, with Mary Rogers and William Jacobson, *Saddle Serenaders* (Gibbs Smith Publisher, 1994). Logsdon served as director of libraries and as professor of education and American folklife at the University of Tulsa before becoming a freelance writer/scholar, publisher, and entertainer.

DAVE MARSH, rock critic, historian, anticensorship activist, and "Louie Louie" expert, has written more than a dozen books about rock and popular music, as well as editing several others. He cofounded *Creem*, the legendary Motor City rock and roll magazine that helped launch heavy metal, glam, and punk, among other styles, and spent five years as an associate and contributing editor of *Rolling Stone*, where he was chief music critic, columnist, and feature writer. Marsh writes monthly record reviews for *Playboy*, and for the past decade has written and edited the monthly music and politics newsletter, *Rock and Rap Confidential*. He has lectured widely on music, politics, and censorship. He compiled *50 Ways to Fight Censorship* (Thunder's Mouth, 1990), and was coeditor with Don Henley of *Heaven Is Under Our Feet: A Book for Walden Woods* (Longmeadow, 1991), essays in honor of Walden Woods and Henry David Thoreau, written by everyone from Jimmy Buffet and Jimmy Carter to Janet Jackson and Jesse Jackson. Marsh also edited the first two editions of the *Rolling Stone Record Guide*, and *Pastures of Plenty,* the papers of Woody Guthrie.

CHARLES F. MCGOVERN is curator of twentieth-century popular culture at the National Museum of American History, Smithsonian Institution. He received his Ph.D from Harvard University in American civilization. He is author of the forthcoming *Sold American: Inventing the Consumer, 1890–1940* and has written for *American Quarterly* and the *Maryland Historical Review*. He is currently at work on an exhibition and research project, *Rock 'n' Soul: Social Crossroads*, that will trace the social history of popular music in America from the 1920s through the 1970s.

JEFF PLACE has been the head archivist for the Center for Folklife and Cultural Heritage at the Smithsonian since the center's beginning in 1988. He has worked with the Folkways Collection almost from its arrival at the Smithsonian in 1987 and has overseen the cataloging of the Moses Asch collection. He has a master's degree in library science from the University of Maryland and specializes in sound archives. He has been involved in the compilation of a number of compact discs for Smithsonian/Folkways including Woody Guthrie's *Long Ways to Travel: The Unreleased Folkways Masters,* which won him the 1994 Brenda McCallum Prize from the American Folklore Society. He has produced a number of archival CDs by such artists as Doc Watson, Clarence Ashley, Lead Belly, and Woody Guthrie. He has been a collector of traditional music for more than twenty-five years.

ROBERT SANTELLI joined the staff of the Rock and Roll Hall of Fame and Museum in January 1994 as a curatorial consultant and became director of education in July 1995. He is currently vice-president of education and public programs. Santelli has spent the past twenty years studying, writing about, and teaching American popular music history at Rutgers and Monmouth Universities in New Jersey. As a freelance music journalist, Santelli has contributed to a number of magazines including *Rolling Stone, CD Review, Downbeat,* and *New Jersey Monthly* as well as newspapers such as the *New York Times,* the *Plain Dealer* and *Asbury Park Press*. He has written numerous books on rock and roll and the blues including *The Big Book of Blues* (Penguin, 1994) and *The Best of the Blues* (Penguin, 1997). In addition, he recently edited *Bruce*

Springsteen's Songs (Avon, 1998). Santelli holds a B.A. in American History from Monmouth University and an M.A. in American Studies from the University of Southern California.

PETE SEEGER began his career in 1938, at the age of nineteen, assisting noted folk archivist and field recorder Alan Lomax on his song-collecting trips through the American South. He soon began to perform on banjo, guitar, and vocals. In 1940 he formed the Almanac Singers (which Woody Guthrie would join in 1941), which recorded union songs and peace anthems. After a short stint in the army during World War II, Seeger discovered commercial success with the Weavers. Formed in 1948, the group had a huge run of hits, including "So Long, It's Been Good to Know You" (written by Woody Guthrie), "Kisses Sweeter Than Wine," and "Goodnight Irene" (written by Lead Belly). As a songwriter, Seeger is responsible for such folk standards as "Where Have All the Flowers Gone?" and "If I Had a Hammer." During the 1950s, Seeger's outspoken socialist sympathies caused him to be blacklisted by the House Un-American Activities Committee; however, he continued to perform wherever he could and recorded for Folkways and Columbia records in the early 1960s. With his outspoken commitment to the antiwar movement, Seeger was rediscovered by a younger audience and inspired such musicians as Bob Dylan, the Byrds (who had a number-one hit with Seeger's "Turn! Turn! Turn!" in 1965), and Joni Mitchell. A gifted storyteller and music historian, Seeger has always brought to his audiences not just the songs but the stories behind them as well.

DAVID R. SHUMWAY is associate professor of literary and cultural studies in the English Department of Carnegie Mellon University. He is author of *Michel Foucault* (Twayne, 1989) and *Creating American Civilization: A Genealogy of American Literature as an Academic Discipline* (University of Minnesota Press, 1994), and coeditor with Richard Ohmann and others of *Making and Selling Culture* (Wesleyan University Press, 1996). He is a series editor of *Knowledge: Disciplinary and Beyond* (University Press of Virginia), and coeditor with Ellen Messer-Davidow and David J. Sylvan of its inaugural volume, *Knowledges: Historical and Critical Studies in Disciplinarity* (1993). His publications on music include "Rock & Roll as a Cultural Practice" (in *Present Tense: Rock & Roll and Culture*, Duke University Press, 1992), "Watching Elvis: The Male Rock Star as Object of the Gaze" (in *American Culture in the 50s*, University of Illinois Press, 1997), and "Rock 'n' Roll Soundtracks and the Production of Nostalgia" (*Cinema Journal*, 1998). Shumway is currently working on a book on the discourses of romantic love (film, fiction, songs, self-help, and so forth) in twentieth-century America, and on a book of readings of major rock and roll performers from Elvis to Springsteen.

CRAIG WERNER is professor of Afro-American studies at the University of Wisconsin at Madison, where he has taught cultural history courses since 1983. Before that, he taught at the Center for the Study of Southern Culture at the University of Mississippi. He has published five books on literature and one on music, *Playing the Changes: From Afro-Modernism to the Jazz Impulse* (University of Illinois Press, 1994). For more than a decade, he has taught a class on black music and American cultural history for which he earned an all-university award for teaching excellence. He has supplemented this course with seminars on music and politics in the 1960s, hip-hop and/as literature, and the "minstrel dynamic" in American culture. Werner's recent books include *A Change Is Gonna Come: Music, Race & the Soul of America* (Plume, 1999) and *Up Around the Bend: An Oral History of Creedence Clearwater Revival* (Avon, 1999).

Index

(Page references in **boldface** refer to illustrations.)

UNIVERSITY PRESS OF NEW ENGLAND publishes books under its own imprint and is the publisher for Brandeis University Press, Dartmouth College, Middlebury College Press, University of New Hampshire, Tufts University, and Wesleyan University Press.

LIBRARY OF CONGRESS CATALOGING-IN-PUBLICATION DATA

Hard travelin' : the life and legacy of Woody Guthrie / edited by
    Robert Santelli and Emily Davidson.
        p.   cm. — (American music masters)
    Includes bibliographical references, discography, and index.
    ISBN 0–8195–6366–8 (cl. : alk. paper). — ISBN 0–8195–6391–9 (pa. :
alk. paper)
        1. Guthrie, Woody, 1912–1967.   1. Santelli, Robert.
    II. Davidson, Emily.   III. Title: Hard travelin'   IV. Series.
    ML410.G978H.37   1999
    782.42162'13'0092—dc21
    [B]   99–21098